Weimar in

New Directions in German Studies

Series Editor:
IMKE MEYER

Weimar in Princeton

*Thomas Mann and the
Kahler Circle*

Stanley Corngold

BLOOMSBURY ACADEMIC
NEW YORK • LONDON • OXFORD • NEW DELHI • SYDNEY

BLOOMSBURY ACADEMIC
Bloomsbury Publishing Inc
1385 Broadway, New York, NY 10018, USA
50 Bedford Square, London, WC1B 3DP, UK
29 Earlsfort Terrace, Dublin 2, Ireland

BLOOMSBURY, BLOOMSBURY ACADEMIC and the Diana logo are trademarks of
Bloomsbury Publishing Plc

First published in the United States of America 2022

Volume Editors' Part of the Work © Stanley Corngold, 2022

For legal purposes the Acknowledgments on p. 173 constitute
an extension of this copyright page.

Cover design by Andrea F. Bucsi
Cover image courtesy of ETH-Bibliothek Zürich, Thomas-Mann-Archiv

Bloomsbury Publishing Inc does not have any control over, or responsibility for, any
third-party websites referred to or in this book. All internet addresses given in this book
were correct at the time of going to press. The author and publisher regret any
inconvenience caused if addresses have changed or sites have ceased
to exist, but can accept no responsibility for any such changes.

Library of Congress Cataloging-in-Publication Data

Names: Corngold, Stanley, author.
Title: Weimar in Princeton : Thomas Mann and the Kahler Circle / by Stanley Corngold.
Description: New York : Bloomsbury Academic, 2022. | Series: New directions in German
studies; 35 | Includes bibliographical references and index. | Summary: "An evocative
account of German émigrés in America in the wake of Nazism, centered around Thomas
Mann's early exile in Princeton and his encounters with a brilliant group of intellectuals,
including Albert Einstein, Hermann Broch, and Erich Kahler, which came to be known as the
Kahler Circle"-- Provided by publisher.
Identifiers: LCCN 2021040986 (print) | LCCN 2021040987 (ebook) |
ISBN 9781501386497 (hardback) | ISBN 9781501386480 (paperback) |
ISBN 9781501386503 (epub) | ISBN 9781501386510 (pdf) | ISBN 9781501386527 (ebook other)
Subjects: LCSH: Mann, Thomas, 1875–1955–Exile–United States. | Mann, Thomas, 1875–1955–
Homes and haunts–New Jersey–Princeton | Mann, Thomas, 1875-1955–Friends and associates.
| Mann, Thomas, 1875–1955–Political and social views. | Princeton (N.J.)–Intellectual life. |
Authors, German–20th century–Biography.
Classification: LCC PT2625.A44 Z544199 2022 (print) | LCC PT2625.A44 (ebook) |
DDC 833/.912 [B]—dc23/eng/20211019
LC record available at https://lccn.loc.gov/2021040986
LC ebook record available at https://lccn.loc.gov/2021040987

ISBN: HB: 978-1-5013-8649-7
         ePDF: 978-1-5013-8651-0
         eBook: 978-1-5013-8650-3
         PB: 978-1-5013-8648-0

Series: New Directions in German Studies

Typeset by RefineCatch Limited, Bungay, Suffolk
Printed and bound in the United States of America

To find out more about our authors and books visit www.bloomsbury.com
and sign up for our newsletters.

Contents

Preface

I began teaching German and Comparative Literature at Princeton University in 1966—in courses including Goethe's *Faust* and Thomas Mann's *Doctor Faustus*. Ever since then, I have been intrigued by Mann's presence in Princeton. He lived in Princeton and lectured at the university in the years 1938–41; and substantial traces of his presence remain, as in the stone tablet affixed to his residence at 65 Stockton Street, which reads "THOMAS MANN LIVED HERE 1938–1941."[1] The ceremony was conducted in 1964 by Professor Victor Lange, Chair of the Department of Germanic Languages and Literatures. "At its dedication," writes Alexander Leitch, the author of *A Princeton Companion*, "[Professor] Lange [. . .] expressed the hope that as 'a lasting reminder of Thomas Mann's presence in Princeton,'" this tablet "might 'strengthen the spirit of courageous humanism among us and reaffirm the vision of a community of free men to which his life and work bore such eloquent testimony.'"[2]

My interest in Mann's Princeton exile in the years 1938–41—and the circle of émigré intellectuals in which he figured—was revived some years ago by an invitation from the ETH Zurich to lecture on a "fundamental issue of the modern era that features in the work of Thomas Mann."[3]

---

[1]   Mann's Georgian villa has not enjoyed the good fortune of his later residence in Pacific Palisades, California. The Princeton house was bought and renovated by private persons with little interest in preserving the interior of the site as Thomas Mann's dwelling, whereas the house in California was bought by the German government (for $13 million!). Its original interior has been respected, and it now serves as a study center for younger German intellectuals.

[2]   "Mann, Thomas," in Alexander Leitch, *A Princeton Companion* (Princeton, NJ: Princeton University Press, 1978), 312–13.

[3]   The Thomas Mann Lectures are organized by the Thomas Mann Archives in conjunction with the Chair of Literary and Cultural Studies at ETH Zurich. My talk, "II. Thomas Mann Lecture," was titled "Thomas Mann im Lichte unserer Erfahrung. Zum amerikanischen Exil" (Thomas Mann in the light of our experience: on his American exile), November 21, 2018 (https://www.video.ethz.ch/campus/bibliothek/thomas_mann.html). The lecture, slightly revised, was published with the German title in the *Thomas Mann Jahrbuch* 32 (2019): 169–81.

One did not have to live in Princeton to know that during the first years of his exile in the United States, Mann was a highly articulate and visible spokesman for what he termed "The Coming Victory of Democracy"—this at a time when "democracy" was a fatally threatened ideal, even more gravely endangered than at this writing (spring 2021). If, by a happy chance, even as a casual reader of *The New York Times*, you saw the issue of December 14, 2017—to cite one occasion—you would have been reminded of Mann's importance as a spokesman for democratic ideals. In a piece titled "The Glory of Democracy," David Brooks registered the ongoing assault on the values of democracy in the United States and abroad. Seeking first principles, Brooks chose to "start with Thomas Mann's 'The Coming Victory of Democracy,'" in which Mann argues that

> democracy begins with one great truth [. . .] the infinite dignity of individual man and woman. [. . .] Democracy [. . .] is the only system built on respect for the infinite dignity of each individual man and woman, on each person's moral striving for freedom, justice, and truth. It would be a great error to think of and teach democracy as a procedural or political system, or as the principle of majority rule.

> It is [thus Mann] a "spiritual and moral possession." It is not just rules; it is a way of life. It encourages everybody to make the best of their capacities—holds that we have a moral responsibility to do so. It encourages the artist to seek beauty, the neighbor to seek community, the psychologist to seek perception, the scientist to seek truth.[4]

In Princeton Mann functioned as the artist: he came to Princeton to find the security to finish writing his novels *Lotte in Weimar* (*The Beloved Returns*) and *Joseph and His Brothers*. He functioned as the creative figure in a "community": the greater community of the country at large, to which he brought vigorous speeches on behalf of democratic ideals; and the community of Princeton University, which he enthralled as Lecturer in the Humanities. He was also the lodestar of a small community of German-speaking European exiles and American scholars at the university and the Institute for Advanced Studies, in which the historian Erich Kahler (1885–1970), the philosopher Hermann

---

4   David Brooks, "The Glory of Democracy," *The New York Times*, December 14, 2017, https://www.nytimes.com/2017/12/14/opinion/democracy-thomas-mann .html.

Broch (1886–1951), and Albert Einstein (1879–1955) each played his part. Among them, the values of art, friendship, perception, and science were represented and indeed realized to a degree that may not ever have been achieved before and after within a circle of four friends.

A year after Mann's departure from Princeton for California in spring 1941, Hermann Broch moved into the house of Erich and Lili Kahler at One Evelyn Place. With his hosts, he became the nucleus of what was to be termed the Kahler Circle—a group of scholars and writers who from 1939 to 1970 would meet for "cultural conversation."[5] "In hosting a cast of regulars and boarders on the several floors [of his house in Princeton]," writes Alexander Wolff, "Kahler re-created the Prague in which he had lived before the war."[6]

And so, Kahler is the neighbor par excellence, "seeking community"; Broch, the psychologist (of mass pathology) "seeking perception"; and Einstein, the scientist—let it be said—"seeking truth." In the next chapters, I want to describe something of the interactions within the nascent Kahler Circle during the two and a half years of Thomas Mann's stay in Princeton. A complete history of the Circle for its three decades would be a grand enterprise requiring an entire team of scholars, since exceptionally creative figures in many different fields are involved. This book means to make a beginning, when Thomas Mann was the center of this Circle.

A Conversation with a Critic

Critic: I understand your personal interest in this Circle, but is that reason enough to write an entire book about Thomas Mann and a few of his acquaintances in Princeton, New Jersey, in the years 1938–41? After all, Erich Kahler and Hermann Broch are no longer household names. True, Einstein remains a compelling figure, but putting Mann's proclaimed faith in democracy to one side, can such a chronicle be anything more than a slice of antiquarian history?

---

5   See "Kahler-Kreis" in Wikipedia, last edited January 29, 2021, at 18:26 (UTC). This entry is accurate if in one respect, perhaps unintentionally, misleading. It is true that "One Evelyn Place welcomed Jewish intellectual refugees from Europe," but it also welcomed Gentile artists and intellectuals from the United States, like the poet John Berryman and the poet Charles Greenleaf Bell, who gave the Circle its name. In listing the entry, much-maligned Wikipedia "establishes" this group event, lending it a stable identity and a (noteworthy) place in history. https://en.wikipedia.org/wiki/Kahler-Kreis.

6   Alexander Wolff, *Endpapers: A Family Story of Books, War, Escape, and Home* (New York: Atlantic Monthly Press, 2021), 185.

Author: Let some readers agree and turn away: this book is for the happy few who find the life of Thomas Mann, his circle of friends, and, above all, his great, uncanny life's work a matter of compelling interest. And since it is no longer feasible to write a book of any precision about the whole of his life and work, one must make a beginning—one hopes, a strong beginning.[7]

Is this book such a strong beginning—Mann in Princeton in the years 1938 to 1941?

Yes, Mann's life and work from 1938 to 1941 at his new home in Princeton is such a beginning. He is on the very knife-edge of his American exile and with it the importation of the genuine culture of Germany: "Where I am there is Germany," he declared on his arrival. "I carry my German culture in me."[8] After fleeing Germany and Switzerland, possibly fearing for his life, he settled in Princeton with the intention of living in America for the incalculable future. He chose Princeton, he wrote, for its park-like beauty; its university, where he was hired to lecture; and its closeness to New York, where he could meet dignitaries and address entire crowds with his deeply felt antifascist orations. What would be most remarkable about this place, despite its shortcomings as a provincial town, is the productivity it nourished in him and his acquaintances.

So, was Mann really productive in Princeton?

There he wrote the final, intricate chapters of his novel *Lotte in Weimar* (*The Beloved Returns*); composed almost all of a lengthy "Legend of India," *The Transposed Heads*; and began work on the fourth volume of his *Joseph* tetralogy, in fact completing Parts I and II. Over and beyond these works of fiction, there is his prolific composition of anti-Nazi books, speeches, and articles. One bibliography counts thirty-odd items written in this period, chiefly in Mann's effort to defend American democracy, which he often loved, from fascism, here and abroad. His efforts will concentrate our minds on our present historical predicament. In the following years, in 1947—after the House

---

[7]   It is no longer feasible. We do have the excellent biography in 2,253 tightly printed pages by Klaus Harpprecht, *Thomas Mann, Eine Biographie*. Harpprecht writes clearly and elegantly, as befits Willy Brandt's ghostwriter, but it has been observed that this biography does little in the way of treating Mann's *work*, which would have required another 1,000 pages. And in the intervening thirty years, let us say, a good deal of incisive, newborn secondary literature on the life and work cries out for attention.

[8]   Tobias Boes, *Thomas Mann's War: Literature, Politics, and the World Republic of Letters* (Ithaca, NY: Cornell University Press, 2019), 3.

Un-American Activities Committee had attacked the "Hollywood Ten"—Mann wrote spontaneously: "As an American citizen of German birth, I finally testify that I am painfully familiar with certain political trends. Spiritual intolerance, political inquisitions, and declining legal security, and all this in the name of an alleged 'state of emergency'. [. . .] That is how it started in Germany."[9] Treating even this limited timespan of Mann's life and oeuvre adequately will create a model of how one may live through tribulations and emerge, like the biblical Joseph, "with the fair proportions of a life intact."[10]

Well, that might be worth considering.
Yes! Mann's Princeton years, as my colleague the Mann-scholar Hans Rudolf Vaget observes, "mark a stunningly productive period [for Mann] as writer and public intellectual."[11] And so, I want to produce a sense of his works and days among his friends, commenting on the exchanges that I hope will be most interesting. There are unsuspected rewards along the way, some coincidences hitherto hardly noted, which make the matter all the more enticing.

For example?
One. Sitting in the audience of Mann's first Princeton lecture (on Goethe's *Faust*), which was enthusiastically received, was the Faustian Morris (Moe) Berg, Princeton '23—big-league baseball catcher, master linguist (Sanskrit, Japanese, German, et al.), and OSS spy. One might imagine that Berg was impressed enough to want to speak to Mann afterwards. But what topic might they have discussed? Perhaps it was premature for them to attend to the figure of the atomic physicist Werner Heisenberg, whom, six years later, in 1944, under certain circumstances—namely, on discovering that Heisenberg was directing a successful program in Germany to produce an atom bomb—Berg was ordered to kill on the spot.

What?!
Let me go on! What remains of extraordinary interest is the fact that Thomas Mann's beloved grandson Frido—who, as "Echo," figures importantly in the depiction of Adrian Leverkühn's demonic anguish in Mann's later novel *Doctor Faustus*—was to marry *Werner Heisenberg's daughter* Christine, born that very year, 1944. Little could either of these

[9]   Cited in Jeffrey Meyers, "Thomas Mann in America," *Michigan Quarterly*, 51:4 (Fall 2012), http://hdl.handle.net/2027/spo.act2080.0051.419.
[10] J.B. "St. Joseph," in *De La Salle Monthly* 3–4 (July 1870–71): 225.
[11] *Thomas Mann und Agnes Meyer: Briefwechsel 1937–1955*, ed. Hans Rudolf Vaget (Frankfurt am Main: S. Fischer Verlag, 1992), 38.

formidable humanists, on sharing the space of Alexander Hall in Princeton in 1938 with 1,000 auditors, anticipate that six years later Morris (Moe) Berg would be tasked with assassinating the father of Thomas Mann's grand-daughter-in-law in the year of her birth.

That's remarkable.

And in the matter of unsuspected linkages, there is the ongoing play between the novels and stories that occupied Mann in Princeton—chiefly, the masterpieces *Lotte in Weimar* and *Joseph the Provider*—and his political essays and speeches, relations that Mann held to be indispensable. One such text from *Lotte* was to acquire world-historical importance. In his closing charge against the Nazi criminals at the Nuremberg War Crimes Trials, Sir Hartley Shawcross, the chief British prosecutor, cited a page from *Lotte in Weimar*—a fictive jeremiad by Goethe hurled against his own country—*attributing the quote to Goethe himself* and thence arousing considerable consternation.[12]

I see that.

Good. And so, this book has several facets. Amiable reader! Feel free to read consecutively—or wherever you are taken by your intellectual predilection. And to you, dear critic—hypocrite, my double, my sister or my brother—*commençons!*

---

[12] I discuss this matter at length in chapter 4 of a related book, *The Mind in Exile: Thomas Mann in Princeton* (Princeton, NJ: Princeton University Press, 2022).

Abbreviations for Citations

B   *Thomas Mann: "On Myself" and Other Princeton Lectures: An Annotated Edition Based on Mann's Lecture Typescripts.* Edited by James N. Bade. Frankfurt am Main: Peter Lang, 1996.

BR.H   *Letters of Heinrich and Thomas Mann, 1900–1949.* Edited by Hans Wysling and translated by Don Reneau with additional translations by Richard and Clara Winston. Berkeley: University of California Press, 1998.

BR.HG   *Thomas Mann/Heinrich Mann: Briefwechsel 1900–1945.* Edited by Hans Wysling. Frankfurt am Main: Fischer Taschenbuch Verlag, 1995.

BR.K   *Thomas Mann/Erich Kahler: Briefwechsel 1931–1955.* Edited by Michael Assmann. Hamburg: Luchterhand Literaturverlag, 1993.

BR.M   *Thomas Mann und Agnes Meyer: Briefwechsel 1937–1955.* Edited by Hans Rudolf Vaget. Frankfurt am Main: S. Fischer Verlag, 1992.

C   *The City of Man, A Declaration on World Democracy, Issued by G. A. Borgese, Lewis Mumford, Thomas Mann, Erich Kahler, Hermann Broch, et al.* New York: The Viking Press, 1940.

D   *Thomas Mann: Diaries 1918–1939.* Selection and foreword by Hermann Kesten. Translated from the German by Richard and Clara Winston. New York: Harry N. Abrams, 1982.

EF   *An Exceptional Friendship: The Correspondence of Erich Kahler and Thomas Mann.* Translated by Richard Winston and Clara Winston. Ithaca, NY: Cornell University Press, 1975.

EM   *Essays.* Edited by Hermann Kurzke and Stephan Stachorski. 6 vols. Frankfurt am Main: S. Fischer Verlag, 1975–81.

GKFA   Thomas Mann. *Große kommentierte Frankfurter Ausgabe—Werke, Briefe, Tagebücher.* Edited by Heinrich Detering, Eckhard Heftrich, Hermann Kurzke, Terence J. Reed, Thomas Sprecher, Hans Rudolf Vaget, and Ruprecht Wimmer in collaboration with the Thomas-Mann-Archiv of the ETH, Zurich. 17 vols. Frankfurt am Main: S. Fischer Verlag, 2002–. Volume and page numbers are indicated in Arabic numerals.

GW   Thomas Mann. *Gesammelte Werke in dreizehn Bänden*. Edited by Peter de Mendelssohn. 13 vols. Frankfurt am Main: S. Fischer Verlag, 1974. Volume number is indicated in Roman numerals, followed by page numbers in Arabic numerals.

H   Klaus Harpprecht. *Thomas Mann, Eine Biographie*. Reinbek bei Hamburg: Rowohlt, 1995.

L   *The Letters of Thomas Mann, 1889–1955*. Selected and translated from the German by Richard Winston and Clara Winston. New York: Knopf, 1970.

LW   *Lotte in Weimar, Roman*. Edited by Werner Frizen. GKFA 9.1. Frankfurt am Main: S. Fischer Verlag, 2003.

LWA   *The Beloved Returns: Lotte in Weimar*. Translated by H. T. Lowe-Porter. New York: Knopf, 1940.

P   Franz Kafka. *Der Proceß*. Edited by Malcolm Pasley. S. Fischer Verlag, 1990.

T3   Thomas Mann. *Tagebücher 1937–1939*. Edited by Peter de Mendelssohn. Frankfurt am Main: S. Fischer Verlag, 1980.

T4   Thomas Mann, *Tagebücher 1940–1943*. Edited by Peter de Mendelssohn. Frankfurt am Main: S. Fischer Verlag, 1982.

TB   Tobias Boes. *Thomas Mann's War: Literature, Politics, and the World Republic of Letters*. Ithaca, NY: Cornell University Press, 2019.

V   Hans Rudolf Vaget. "'The Best of Worlds': Thomas Mann in Princeton." *The Princeton University Library Chronicle* 75 no. 1, 9 (January 2013): 9–37.

VA   Hans Rudolf Vaget. *Thomas Mann, der Amerikaner: Leben und Werk im amerikanischen Exil 1938–1951*. Frankfurt am Main: S. Fischer Verlag, 2011.

Introduction

Thomas Mann, heralded as "the greatest living man of letters" by his publisher Alfred A. Knopf, spent the first two and a half years of his extraordinary American exile, between September 1938 and March 1941, in Princeton, New Jersey. In a recently published book, *The Mind in Exile*, I set out to describe Mann's life and work in Princeton,[1] but that account misses a decisive dimension—Mann's participation in a circle of friends, Illuminati all, that was subsequently to be accredited as the "Kahler Circle."[2] Outside of Princeton, the existence of this constellation was known only to a happy few—for one, Carlos Fuentes, the eminent Mexican diplomat, novelist, and critic.

In 1978, Fuentes moved with his family to Princeton, a town he admired for its "tranquility." His writing day included an afternoon walk: "I always follow a triangular pattern [. . .] . I go to Einstein's house on Mercer Street, then down to Thomas Mann's house on Stockton Street, then over to Herman Broch's house on Evelyn Place."[3] But Fuentes's description includes mistakes more grievous than the misspelling of the name of Hermann Broch, the Austrian émigré philosopher and novelist. In 1978, some four decades after Mann's exile in Princeton, the spacious villa on Stockton Street was no longer "Thomas

---

[1] Stanley Corngold, *The Mind in Exile: Thomas Mann in Princeton* (Princeton, NJ: Princeton University Press, 2022).

[2] For the "Kahler Circle," see the instructive Wikipedia entry under its German title "Kahler-Kreis." Julie Melby writes, "The Kahler's Princeton home at One Evelyn Place became known as *Kahler-Kreis* (Kahler-Circle), where German intellectuals gathered, including Albert Einstein, Mann, Erwin Panofsky, Ben Shahn, and Hermann Broch." "Recently in *Ephemera* Category: Antoinette von Kahler's Decorative Ribbons," "Graphic Arts," "Exhibitions, Acquisitions, and other Highlights from the Graphic Arts Collection, Princeton University Library," https://www.princeton.edu/~graphicarts/ephemera/index3.html.

[3] Carlos Fuentes, "Carlos Fuentes, The Art of Fiction No. 68." *The Paris Review* 82 (Winter 1981), https://www.theparisreview.org/interviews/3195/carlos-fuentes-the-art-of-fiction-no-68-carlos-fuentes.

Mann's house": it housed a spirit (*Geist*) very opposite to Mann's "erotic irony"—namely, somewhat ironically, the Aquinas Institute, Princeton University's Catholic Campus Ministry. Furthermore, "the house on Evelyn Place" did not belong to Broch; for seven years, Broch occupied a small apartment under a mansard roof in this house owned by a "universal mind," the historian, essayist, and polymath Erich Kahler (originally Erich von Kahler)—Thomas Mann's great friend and host to the eponymous Circle.[4] Indeed, Mann had urged Kahler to flee Europe and immigrate to Princeton in 1938, valuing his companionship. But Fuentes's geometric mapping of this constellation of talents—their propinquity of mind and body—is very vivid, so let us enjoy it.

Now, Kahler, Broch, and Thomas Mann—the latter, let it be said, less so—were friends of Albert Einstein, who had lent Kahler the money to buy the house at One Evelyn Place, the Nazis having confiscated Kahler's substantial possessions in Munich. And just as Kahler has gone unmentioned in Fuentes's anecdote, so has Kahler's memory at large—ergo, it is no small part of this present project to awaken it. Fuentes's "triangular walk" might fairly be called the "Kahler Triangle," in association with the "Kahler Circle." Between 1938 and Kahler's death in 1970, as we have heard, his house boasted, at regular intervals, such guests—good friends and acquaintances—as, indeed, Thomas Mann and Albert Einstein and fellow scholars from the Institute for Advanced Study, where Kahler was himself a guest in 1949, and many others.

In this book, I address the nascent history of the Kahler Circle in the years of Mann's presence in Princeton, i.e., 1938–41; this circle of friends does not acquire the cachet of the regally named Kahler Circle until decades later. By spring 1941, Mann had already left Princeton for Pacific Palisades—for "Weimar on the Pacific," another, even more spectacular constellation of German-speaking exiles, figures of greatness including no less than Mann, as a central presence, together with Arnold Schönberg, Theodor Wiesengrund Adorno, Bruno Walter, Franz Werfel, Erich Wolfgang Korngold, and many more. That circle was briefly reimagined, only some weeks before this writing, by Alex Ross, the Wagner scholar, in a dramatically titled *New Yorker* piece, "The Haunted California Idyll of German Writers in Exile."[5] But my concern is with this circle of émigré intellectuals in Princeton hitherto little

---

4   Anna Kiel, *Erich Kahler: Ein "uomo universale" des zwanzigsten Jahrhunderts—seine Begegnungen mit bedeutenden Zeitgenossen: Vom Georgekreis, Max Weber, bis Hermann Broch und Thomas Mann* (Bern: Peter Lang, 1989).
5   March 9, 2020, https://www.newyorker.com/magazine/2020/03/09/the-haunted-california-idyll-of-german-writers-in-exile.

explored, meaning to confirm the beginnings of a Princeton Circle as a prelude to the celebrated "Weimar on the Pacific."

In the years of Mann's Princeton exile, the Circle included, besides Mann, Einstein, and Broch (who was *Kahler's* best friend), Mann's son-in-law Giuseppe Antonio Borgese (1882–1952), a frequent visitor from the University of Chicago and an active intellectual correspondent, as well as such local lights as the composer and musicologist Roger Sessions (1896–1985), who taught at the University, as did the physicist Allen Shenstone (1893–1980), of whom Mann was particularly fond. Shenstone's wife Mildred (Molly, d. 1967) was a special favorite of Mann's wife Katharina (Katia, b. Pringsheim, 1883–1980). W.R.S. Garton, an eminent spectroscopist and author of a brief biography of Allen Shenstone, captures the spirit of the time:

> The whole social and cultural relations enjoyed in Princeton in the latter half of the 1930s seem to have been at a high level. For example, Shenstone refers to a dinner party about 1938–39, at which the guests were Einstein, Enrico Fermi, T. Mann, and H. N. Russell. The Shenstones' relations with the Mann family, which came to Princeton in 1938, were especially close, and Molly volunteered to be honorary secretary to Thomas, who needed such assistance from an English-speaking person who knew German.[6]

The Circle, as noted, also included many solid acquaintances from the Institute for Advanced Study, among them the archaeologist Hetty Goldman (1881–1972);[7] the mathematician Hermann Weyl (1885–1955) and his wife, the philosopher Helena Weyl (1893–1948); the mathematical logician Kurt Gödel (1906–1978); and, importantly, H[elen]-T[racy] Lowe-Porter (1876–1963), Mann's inspired but often criticized translator, and her husband, the Russian-Jewish-American paleographer Elias Avery Lowe (1879–1969), who also held a permanent position at the Institute. Einstein and the Shenstones were special friends, as they lived on Mercer Street in houses just opposite to each other. In regard to Helen Lowe-Porter and Elias Lowe, it may be of interest that their daughter Frances Beatrice Lowe became the wife of James Fawcett— president of the European Commission on Human Rights from 1972 to 1981—and mother of the painter Charlotte Johnson Wahl. Charlotte Wahl in turn was well recognized at Princeton in the 1960s and 1970s as a talented artist and the wife of the late Professor of History Nicholas

6   W.R.S. Garton, "Allen Goodrich Shenstone. 27 July 1893–16 February 1980," *Biographical Memoirs of Fellows of the Royal Society* 27 (Nov. 1981): 517.
7   See the account of her splendid creativity on the website of the Institute for Advanced Study, https://www.ias.edu/hetty-goldman-life.

Wahl, and indeed, afterwards, in wider circles, as the mother of the prime minister of the United Kingdom *Boris Johnson*. In plain words, Boris Johnson is the great-grandson of Thomas Mann's translator: here is one of the many ongoing resonances that Thomas Mann's Princeton exile continues to sustain today.[8]

In subsequent decades, until Erich Kahler's death in 1970, other notables would hold inspired conversations at his home, among them, the medieval historian Ernst Kantorowicz (1895–1963);[9] from a tangential field, a visitor no less remarkable than Martin Buber (1878–1965); and, from another tangent, the Lithuanian-born painter Ben Shahn (1898–1969) who, in 1962, received an honorary doctor's degree from Princeton University. Kahler himself was to be so honored in 1969. For almost thirty years, until his death in 1970—with his partner Alice (Lili) and, from 1969, his wife—Kahler presided over the house at Evelyn Place, which, "as a result of the intellectual gatherings there [. . .] was given the nickname 'Little Parnassus' by a young friend of Kahler," the poet Charles Greenleaf Bell.[10]

---

[8]   Incidentally, H-T. Lowe-Porter, her daughter Frances, and her daughter Charlotte Wahl Johnson are not the only female ancestors of Boris Johnson to have recently come into public view. There is also Boris Johnson's great-great-great-great-great-great grandmother, recently discovered in Basel as a "syphilis-ridden mummy." *The Sun*, https://www.thesun.co.uk/news/9566933/boris-johnsons-mum-charlotte-johnson-wahl/.

[9]   In the years following Kantorowicz's move from Berkeley to Princeton in 1951, he "spent a particularly great amount of time with old friends who lived in Princeton: Theodor Mommsen and Erich Kahler (who divorced Fine in 1940 and now was married to a charming and vivacious Viennese woman [Alice ('Lili') Loewy née Pick]." Robert E. Lerner, *Ernst Kantorowicz—A Life* (Princeton, NJ: Princeton University Press, 2017), 337.

[10]   "Preservation Awards from Historical Society," *Town Topics*, August 4, 1993. The poet Charles Greenleaf Bell was the youngest of the persons of intellectual distinction to contribute to a beautifully produced book presented to Kahler on his sixty-fifth birthday. Bell's is the first of seventeen laudations, including texts by Thomas Mann and Albert Einstein. See *Erich Kahler*, edited and in part translated by Eleanor L. Woolf and Herbert Steiner (New York: Eleanor L. Woolf, 1951). In re Kahler's home, "the Historical Society [of Princeton] has announced its fifth annual Preservation Awards in recognition of local building projects completed during the past year. The awards are given to projects in which the owners have expended significant care and effort in historic preservation. 1 Evelyn Place, at the corner of Evelyn Place and Nassau Street, was recognized as an appropriate Speculative Rehabilitation Project. [. . .] The house is a circa-1907 example of the Dutch Colonial revival style and is located in the Jugtown National Register Historic District. [. . .] The house was once home to Eric [sic] Kahler, the noted German writer, philosopher and historian. Kahler came to Princeton at the urging of Thomas Mann and lived at 1 Evelyn Place from 1942 until his death in 1970. Kahler's circle of friends included Albert Einstein, as well as other notable scholars and artists." Web address as above.

The political scientist David Kettler is well aware of the power of this circle, which he terms an "enclosure." Citing Kahler's biographer Gerhard Lauer, Kettler observes:

Kahler never ceased to regard himself as the true prophet of the "conservative revolution" that was to be the timeless antithesis to the critical disorder of the times. He lived in and for that mission, all the more if it was hopeless. In his curiosity, in his generosity, in his kindliness, he was able to befriend many people who nevertheless remained strangers to his designs. What he lacked, because of the fixation on German Bildung integral to the intellectual position to which he was committed, because of his age, and because of his enclosure within an outpost of exile at Princeton whose boundaries were reinforced by the symbolic significance ascribed to its prime inhabitants—notably Mann, Einstein, and Broch—was the capacity to negotiate intellectual reciprocity with American peers.[11]

In this book about Thomas Mann in Princeton and his circle of friends, with its suggestion of the cross-connections in their life and work in the years 1938–41, I hope to summon up what the Mann scholar Heinrich Detering has called "the intellectual atmosphere of an extraordinary place and constellation [. . . for] its significance is not only historical but also contemporary. In a time of an extremely troubling transatlantic alienation, we are reminded of an alliance of European and American intellectuals and traditions that might be an inspiration for the present."[12]

The core of these exchanges is Mann's conversations with Erich Kahler and Hermann Broch—his conversations with Albert Einstein were, regrettably, few and far between (see chapter 5, *infra*). We have very little evidence of his conversations with any of his other acquaintances. And ever since Mann's pet poodle Niko, to whom he was deeply attached, was attacked by Erwin Panofsky's "nasty poodle"

[11] David Kettler, "Symbolic Uses of Exile: Erich Kahler at the Ohio State University," in *Exile and Otherness: New Approaches to the Experience of the Nazi Refugees*, ed. Alexander Stephan (Bern: Peter Lang, 2005), 309. Kettler is referring to the work of Kahler's biographer Gerhard Lauer, *Die verspätete Revolution—Erich von Kahler: Wissenschaftsgeschichte zwischen konservativer Revolution und Exil* (Berlin: de Gruyter, 1995).
[12] An unpublished report invited by the Princeton University Press.

(T4 5), it is certain that there was very little further intercourse between them.[13] Panofsky and Einstein, on the other hand, were good friends.[14]

The more serious matter is the (tenuous) relation of Mann and Einstein, explored in detail in chapters 5 and 6, *infra*. In the past, Mann was intrigued by relativity theory: the famous chapter "Snow" in *The Magic Mountain* can be understood as Mann's complementary time-experiment.[15] The *Joseph* tetralogy begins: "Deep is the well of the past [*Tief ist der Brunnen der Vergangenheit*]."[16] But there were no café afternoons for them: each was immersed in the special conditions that exile imposed on their individual lives—an affair of survival as independent writers (*freie Schriftsteller*) and scholars, in some cases, without a fixed professional abode.

It is not that conversations about time did not take place in Princeton in the years 1938–41: they did, but rather between Einstein and Gödel, viz., Gödel's notorious pronouncement that time does not exist.[17] Add to these conversations such emergent perspectives as Kantorowicz's view on historical explanation that allegedly removes the factor of time. Regrettably for our compass, Kantorowicz was not bodily present in Princeton until 1951, when, after a friendship with Kahler of many decades, Kantorowicz could now visit him; they remained friends despite Erich's knowing full well that his first wife Josefine ["Fine"] had been Kantorowicz's lover even during his marriage. Kahler and Kantorowicz shared conservative sympathies: they rued the fate of a conservatively understood human essence, an essence threatened—indeed, all but obliterated—in evil times. This is a topic of Mann's, Broch's, and Einstein's political and philosophical-anthropological writings as well, especially in their correspondence with Kahler. It is Kahler's obsessive theme, as we shall see, especially in his books *Man the Measure* and *The Tower and the Abyss*.

Mann, Kahler, Broch, Borgese . . . : all were bent on discerning the shape of any hope—individually, socially, or politically conceived—of a restoration of the best in humankind in the wake of fascist rule. All

---

[13]   The point is confirmed by conversation with Panofsky's widow, the art historian Gerda Panofsky.

[14]   Jamie Sayen, *Einstein in America* (New York: Crown, 1985), 126.

[15]   Armando Caracheo, "The Measurement of Time: Mann and Einstein's Thought Experiments," *Configurations: A Journal of Literature, Science, and Technology* 25, no. 1 (2017): 29–55.

[16]   Thomas Mann, *Joseph and His Brothers*, tr. John E. Woods, Everyman's Library (New York: Alfred A. Knopf, 2005), 3; *Joseph und seine Brüder: Vier Romane in einem Band*, Fischer Klassik Plus, Kindle edition (Frankfurt am Main: S. Fischer Verlag, 2009), loc. 111 of 26516.

[17]   Palle Yourgrau, *A World without Time: The Forgotten Legacy of Gödel and Einstein* (New York: Basic Books, 2004).

dwelt inevitably on the experience of exile—for many, basically ruinous, and for all, deeply disturbing—particularly in the United States and not excluding Princeton. We can discern other dominant themes in this Circle: the irritating success of the Nazi movement in Germany; the diabolical genius of Hitler; the lure of fascism; the psychosis of mass man; the demoralizing collapse of a democratic opposition; the American, German, and Italian character—all discernible in members' books, essays, speeches, and letters.

My chief concern, however, is to situate the presence of Thomas Mann in this colloquium of scholars and writers, discovering, where possible, the suggestions he would have received from them. This enterprise has its limits, which are not uninteresting. The first concerns Mann as a writer of fiction. While absorbed in writing his novels—which in Princeton were chiefly hermetic and self-enclosed—Mann was deaf to the concerns of his few acquaintances, whom he tended to regard as audiences for reading finished work aloud. In a letter to Kahler, sent shortly after Mann's new situation, in 1941, at Pacific Palisades, Mann laments having had no news of him and adds that he is "piling one page *of Joseph* [*the Provider*] upon the other" and then reading them aloud "to Erika and my wife for hours, and once again 'dear Erich' was very much missed" (EF 49–50). If, when Mann lived in Princeton, Kahler and the Circle had been competent Hebraists or Egyptologists, we would have a different story to tell. As we know, the novels that Mann was concerned to finish in Princeton were *Lotte in Weimar* and the fourth volume of *Joseph and His Brothers*. He also did write most of a novella, an Indian romance, *The Transposed Heads*, as something of a diversion inspired by his reading of ancient Indian stories. On beginning to write his books, he was certainly open to the work of other thinkers. In the case of *Lotte*, Goethe's dreamy speech likening the fate of the Germans to that of the Jews—both peoples greatly admired and greatly despised—is indebted to Erich Kahler's 1933 monograph *Israel unter den Völkern* (Israel among the nations), which Mann had read enthusiastically.[18] And *The Transposed Heads* was plainly inspired by a book by Heinrich Zimmer, the son-in-law of Hugo von Hofmannsthal, titled *Die indische Weltmutter* (the Indian world-mother), which Mann read in late fall 1939. But once in the throes of composition, Mann was unreceptive, his pores closed, and so there is no mention whatsoever in his Princeton diary or in his correspondence with Erich Kahler and Hermann Broch of his incorporating in his novels the remains of their evenings' conversations.

18   Hans Rudolf Vaget, "Deutschtum und Judentum: Zu Erich Kahlers Bedeutung für Thomas Mann," *Deutsche Vierteljahrsschrift für Literaturwissenschaft und Geistesgeschichte (DVjs)* 86, no. 1 (March 2012): 159.

A remote exception to this point is a notation in Mann's diary that in the course of writing *The Transposed Heads*, he received a couple of "Indian books" from Kahler, but Mann's note does not mention any of Kahler's words accompanying the gift (T4 20).

The conception of the two major novels—*Lotte* and *Joseph*—was defined by forms and ideas and plot elements already well embedded in them. Even before arriving in Princeton, Mann had written six chapters of *Lotte in Weimar*, having begun this project in 1936 while in exile in Switzerland. The trajectory of *Joseph the Provider*, the final volume in the tetralogy, was shaped, of course, by the preceding three volumes, not to mention the Hebrew Bible, though added to by scholarly works from the university library and Mann's personally keen interest in the political fortunes of his much admired President Roosevelt—in plain words, the New Deal. Of the three novels, only *The Transposed Heads* was written from a fresh start in Princeton, but that play of opposite pairs—physical beauty versus spiritual prowess—even in this esoteric context, had already been established in Mann's earlier stories, most vividly in *Tonio Kröger*. This fact was not lost on Mann's patroness in the United States, Agnes Meyer, who wrote to Mann shrewdly about the conclusion to the novella, in which the love of the three protagonists is consummated in a funeral pyre. Here, she remarked, Tonio, Hans, and Inge, the protagonists of "Tonio Kröger," "had now been united in an Indian death."[19] And so, we will find no traces in Mann's novels of the independently achieved literary and critical work of Kahler, Broch, and Einstein in Princeton: they are works driven by their own engines. *However . . .*

Mann's ongoing political and polemical work is another story; his writings were deeply affected by contact with other Princeton refugee scholars. His past political views, of course, are not negligible here; but their thrust is defined once and for all by his turn away from an earlier apolitical cultural conservatism to a militant nationalism and then, in the 1920s and thereafter, to a cosmopolitan liberal humanism—viz., militant democratic socialism—driven importantly by fury at the fate inflicted on him by the Nazis.

The main extrinsic impulses embedded in all Mann's political writings during the Princeton period arrive from the world-historic convulsions of the time, heard on the radio or read in newspapers or told by visitors and acquaintances. These impulses were abetted by the works of such savants as Lewis Mumford, Harold Laski, and Herbert Read, among others, which Mann, a formidable reader—and

---

[19]   Agnes Meyer's comment is cited in Klaus Harpprecht, *Thomas Mann—Eine Biographie* (Reinbek: Rowohlt, 1995), 1161.

presumably on the advice of Kahler—never failed to consult. All this information was filtered through conversations with the leading members of the Circle: Mann's *entire* political education was furthered by his decades-long contact with Kahler, almost a member of Mann's family, as well as, more recently, Broch and Borgese. On their consanguinity of thought, Gerhard Lauer has remarked of Kahler's manuscripts of the 1920s and 1930s—*Israel unter den Völkern* (Israel among the nations) and *Der deutsche Charakter in der Geschichte Europas* (*The German character in the history of Europe*)—that "both books, like Kahler's subsequent essays on German politics, history and art, show an astonishing intimacy with the thought of Thomas Mann on their difficult rapprochement with modernity." The similarity is so great, Lauer adds, that it makes difficult his task of writing a unique account of Erich Kahler's thought in the years of his exile—and not of Thomas Mann's![20] At one point the Mann scholar Tobias Boes cites a later radio address from 1943 in which Mann declares:

> European listeners! I speak to you as one of you, *as a German who has always considered himself a European*, who knew your countries and cultures and was deeply convinced that the political and economic conditions of Europe were outdated, this division into arbitrarily bordered states and sovereignties that has brought about the misfortune of the continent.[21]

Imagining a concern of Mann's listeners, Boes asks, "What gave him the authority to make such sweeping pronouncements on political and economic matters, when his own expertise was clearly confined to the cultural sphere?" (TB 191). An answer: the Princeton enclosure, for one; the intellectual fortification of Mann, Kahler, Broch, and Borgese— "pronouncements" from this salient of republican democracy, which vibrated in Mann's memory even in California.

One caveat, however: the essential similarity between the minds of Kahler and Mann also included sporadic critical opposition. Mann sharpened his politics of rational republicanism on the whetstone of Kahler's sometimes maddening appreciation of events in Nazi Germany. Kahler's recognition of the "positive" aspect of Nazism derives, following Lauer, from his earlier signature "vitalistic, radicalized historical relativism, for which all historical occurrences are the indifferent expression of that one life beyond good and evil."[22] On

---

20   Lauer, *Die verspätete Revolution*, 274–75.
21   "[European Listeners!]," GW XIII: 747; emphasis added.
22   Lauer, *Die verspätete Revolution*, 275.

the matter of a necessary federation of European states, however, they were of one mind.

Kahler, we learn from his correspondence with Mann, "adapted rapidly to America and acquired a remarkable command of English [and] often took the lead in interpreting American conditions to Mann. Kahler's preoccupation in his historical studies with the evolution of human consciousness," which we will soon address, "made him one of the foremost interpreters of Mann's fiction—which in turn exemplified and helped to shape some of Kahler's theories" (EF viii). But the fiction, unlike the dream, preexisted its interpretation.[23]

To my grief and chagrin, the work of Kahler and Broch, who were lifelong friends, today scrape together an only mean, much-diminished existence in the memory of even German professors of literature and intellectual history. It was not for any lapse of consideration on Kahler's part that this became the case: in 1953 he edited Broch's poems and a decade later published an entire monograph on *Die Philosophie von Hermann Broch.*

However intriguing the idea, a book that would address *everything* that Mann and Kahler and Broch and Borgese and Einstein shared and accomplished during this period would exhaust the resources of author and publisher and exceed any reasonable expectation of the stamina of even the exceptionally motivated reader. But here are some strong beginnings: let us hear now about Mann and Erich Kahler and Mann and Hermann Broch and thereafter about Mann and Albert Einstein in Princeton.

---

[23] "Whoever dreams interprets as well [. . .]. But ultimately and by nature every man is the interpreter of his own dream and so has his dream interpreted only for the sake of elegance. I wish to reveal to you the secret behind our dreaming: the interpretation precedes the dream and what we dream issues from the interpretation." *Joseph*, 1103. "Wer da träumt, der deutet auch [. . .]. Im Grunde aber und von Natur ist jedermann seines Traumes Deuter, und nur aus Eleganz läßt er sich mit der Deutung bedienen. Ich will euch das Geheimnis der Träumerei verraten: die Deutung ist früher als der Traum, und wir träumen schon aus der Deutung." *Joseph* (Fischer Klassik Plus), Kindle, loc. 19499 of 26516.

One Thomas Mann in Princeton

The life of Thomas Mann himself, and not merely of Joseph, the hero of Mann's grand tetralogy *Joseph and His Brothers* (1933–43), turns out—to an extraordinary extent—to fit the pattern of the fugitive hero in biblical and ancient Near Eastern narrative. The authority for this surprising statement comes from the epochal discovery made by the scholar Edward Greenstein of the University of Bar-Ilan (Israel). "Tales of individuals who must leave their homeland and survive a precarious exile before returning in triumph are widespread in world literature. However, the 'fugitive hero pattern,' as reflected in biblical and extra-biblical narratives, appears to be specific to the cultures of the ancient Near East."[1] The life of Thomas Mann appears to be an exception in belonging to the culture of the modern West. "The pattern," writes Greenstein,

> consists of fourteen basic features: (1) The hero is a younger or youngest brother. (2) There occurs a political and/or personal crisis. (3) The hero flees or is exiled; (4) enjoys the support of a female protector; (5) marries the daughter of his host in exile; (6) assumes a position of responsibility in the host's household; (7) has a divine encounter (often divination or revelation); (8) and is joined by kin. (9) There is a seven-year period (usually in exile). (10) The hero repels an attack (or attacks); (11) takes spoils or plunders; (12) returns home; (13) is restored to a position of leadership and/or honor; (14) and establishes or renews a cult.[2]

Consider, now, the life, tribulations, and glory of Thomas Mann in light of this pattern. (1) Mann is the younger brother of Heinrich Mann.

---

[1] Edward L. Greenstein, "Moses and the Fugitive Hero Pattern," *The Torah*, December 27, 2018, 2.

[2] Ibid. This formulation of the fourteen features of the pattern is a lightly edited version of the original. This new version was read by Professor Greenstein at a workshop "Migration and the Bible," Princeton University, March 3, 2019.

(2) His German homeland suffers a political crisis in 1933, with the Nazi seizure of power: Mann will become persona non grata. He is personally affected, most acutely when, while abroad in Switzerland, he is deprived of his German citizenship. (3) In 1938, he flees to America,[3] where he enjoys (4) the support of a powerful female protector, Agnes E.[rnst] Meyer, the wife of the wealthy publisher of the *Washington Post*. She realizes her plan to have Mann become a lecturer in the humanities at Princeton University on a generous salary. At one point Mann writes to her: "Believe me, the most sincere statement in the book *The Beloved Returns* (*Lotte in Weimar*) is what I have the old fellow [Goethe] think about 'all human work, deed and poem': it is 'rubbish' without the love that comes to its aid and the partisan enthusiasm that props it up.[4] Well, women are great in that they 'participate from above,' as it's said in Faust; they are our redeemers and bring about the realization of what's inadequate."[5] (5) Mann does not marry the daughter of his host in exile, being already married; but a reflection of this deed informs Mann's early exile. A European scholar, novelist, and literary critic and author of highly articulate antifascist tracts ("The City of Man")—Giuseppe Antonio Borgese,[6] with whom Mann is well acquainted—marries Mann's youngest daughter Elisabeth. Mann is

---

3   Thomas Mann, "We are starting our 'homeward' journey to Princeton on September 15 [1938]" (BR.H 216). "Wir treten die 'Heim'-Reise nach Princeton am 15. September an" (BR.HG 295).

4   "Was ist denn all Menschenwerk, That [*sic*] und Gedicht, ohne die Liebe, die ihm zu Hilfe kommt, und den parteiischen Enthusiasmus, ders zu was aufstutzt?" (LW 291). In the diminished Lowe-Porter translation: "What does all man's work amount to, either the deeds or the poetry-writing, without love, and the stimulus of taking sides?" (LWA 291).

5   In a telegram sent to Agnes Meyer on January 18, 1939, Mann wrote: "You are my good angel" ("Sie sind mein guter Engel"; Br.M 143). Lines cited above are from his letter to Agnes Meyer of January 5, 1940: "Glauben Sie mir, das aufrichtigste Wort in dem Buch [*Lotte im* Weimar] ist, was ich den Alten denken lasse über 'all Menschenwerk, Tat und Gedicht,' dass es nämlich, 'ein Dreck ist' ohne die Liebe, die ihm zu Hilfe kommt, und den parteiischen Enthusiasmus, der's zu was aufstutzt. Nun, darin sind die Frauen gross, sie 'nehmen von oben teil,' wie es im 'Faust' heisst, sie sind unsere Erlöserinnen und machen, dass das Unzulängliche Ereignis wird" (BR.M 193–94). The conclusion to this extract adapts lines from the final strophe of *Faust*: "Das Unzulängliche / Hier wird's Ereignis" ("What fails ineluctably . . . here it was action"); *Goethe's Faust*, tr. Walter Kaufmann (New York: Random House, 1961), 503.

6   In a letter to his brother Heinrich (November 26, 1939) congratulating him on *his* marriage, Mann tells Heinrich of another marriage, that of "our little Medi [Elisabeth]," suggesting that she, "with the man who has now become her husband, G. A. Borgese," might stand in "urgent need of blessings. [. . .] Medi has

dismayed by what he feels is his daughter's subconscious identification of her new husband with himself, her father (at the ceremony, he weeps "from bad nerves" [*vor Nervenschwäche geweint*]; H 1133). To the extent that Mann "as the greatest living author" has been rapidly assimilated to a position of considerable authority in America and become "an object of national pride,"[7] meanwhile self-identifying as an American—and to the extent that Mann may be identified with Borgese—although not every reader will want to accompany me in making this connection—Mann has, so to speak, married the daughter of his host in exile. Other features of the fugitive hero "pattern" apply more directly, even astonishingly so. We have seen Mann assume (6) "a position of responsibility in the host's household," speaking throughout strenuous lecture tours across the country to audiences of thousands as a prime exponent of the values of American democracy. (7) In the matter of whether Mann, as this hero, has "a divine encounter (often divination or revelation)," it may be hyperbolic to describe his literary impulses this way; but during his exile he writes inspired works, especially his "wildest" book, *Doctor Faustus*, which centers on a scene of diabolical inspiration, giving rise to a version of twelve-tone musical composition.

---

married her antifascist professor, who at the age of fifty-seven [Mann is sixty-four] probably no longer expected to win so much youth. But the child wanted it and brought it off. He is a brilliant, charming, and excellently preserved man, that must be granted, and the bitterest hater of his Duce, whom out of pure nationalism he regards as the worst of the worst. [. . .] But at the same time, he is an enthusiastic American" (BR.H 229). "[Heinrichs Vermählung] besiegelt ein wohlerprobtes Verhältnis, das der dringlichen Segenswünsche nicht mehr so sehr bedarf wie das unserer kleinen Medi zu ihrem nunmehrigen Gatten G.A. Borgese. [. . .] Medi hat ihren antifascistischen [*sic*] Professor geheiratet, der mit seinen 57 Jahren nicht mehr daran gedacht hätte, soviel Jugend zu gewinnen. Aber das Kind wollte es und hat es durchgesetzt. Er ist ein geistreicher, liebenswürdiger und sehr wohlerhaltener Mann, das ist zuzugeben, und der erbittertste Hasser seines Duce, den er aus purem Nationalismus für den Allerschlimmsten hält. [. . .] Er ist aber dabei ein überzeugter Amerikaner [. . .]" (BR.HG 312). The birth of their first child, which was delayed, led Mann to write to Heinrich, on December 8, 1940, "I had the clear feeling that it was just our presence that put off the delivery, whether from the distraction *or some sort of embarrassment,* so that it was probably simply the right thing to do for us to discreetly turn our backs" (BR.H 241; emphasis added). "Ich hatte aber das deutliche Gefühl, daß gerade unsere Anwesenheit die Befreiung verzögerte, sei es durch Zerstreung oder irgend ein Embarassement [*sic*], so daß es wahrscheinlich nur richtig war, daß wir diskret den Rücken wandten" (BR.HG 328).

7   Letter of Stefan Zweig to Waldemar Jollos (February 25, 1939), in *Thomas Mann–Stefan Zweig, Briefwechsel, Dokumente und Schnittpunkte,* ed. Katrin Bedenig and Franz Zeder (Frankfurt am Main: Vittorio Klostermann, 2018), 339.

(8) Mann, the hero, is indeed joined by his kin—his six children, foremost his favorite, Erika, who returns from England, where she has been working for British intelligence, and Golo, who is rescued from parlous circumstances in Europe. (9) The pattern of the fugitive hero requires a seven-year period, usually of exile: the number fits perfectly the interval between Mann's immigration in 1938 and the end of the world war in 1945, when he is entreated by many to return to Germany despite his having acquired American citizenship the year before.[8] But he will not return permanently, (10) "repelling" his attackers in Germany, who are caustic about his having assumed American citizenship while the self-styled best of them, as being unsympathetic to the regime, had to endure a painful "inner emigration." (11) The spoils he "will be bringing home" are the complete *Lotte in Weimar*, *The Transposed Heads* (*Die vertauschten Köpfe*), the fourth *Joseph* novel, *Doctor Faustus*, and other works that could not have been written or with few exceptions read in Europe, let alone in Germany, during the Nazi reign of terror. (12) Thereafter, in 1949, the hero returns to his homeland and travels through both Allied and Soviet zones, attending celebrations in Frankfurt am Main and Weimar in honor of Goethe's 200th birthday. (13) He is honored in Frankfurt with the Goethe Prize, and his attendance amounts to the statement that "German culture extends beyond the new political border."[9] In 1952 he finally leaves his American exile and returns to his home before his emigration, to neighboring Switzerland; and yet where he is, it is said—*he* has said!—there is

---

[8]   The crucial seven-year period makes a literal appearance in Mann's reflections, in a letter to his brother, on Roosevelt's election to a third term. "The first really joyful and satisfying turn in seven years or longer. Nothing but setbacks up till then. So, I had scant belief in it, feeling that, as an event, it would fall outside the frame of our epoch. Now we learn that the frame is broader after all than was thought. Good instincts guided the American populace: a fortunate backwardness, if you will. Victory is accordingly only a matter of time, if a very long time. A fourth term will probably be necessary." Letter of November 14, 1940 (BR.H 238). "Die erste Freude und Genugtuung seit sieben Jahren und länger. Nichts als Nackenschläge bis dahin. Mein Glaube war denn auch gering, und ich fühlte, daß das Ereignis gewissermaßen aus dem Rahmen der Epoche fallen würde. Nun, dieser Rahmen ist eben doch weiter, als man gedacht hatte. Ein gesunder Instinkt hat das amerikanische Volk geleitet, wenn man will: eine glückliche Rückständigkeit. Der Sieg ist hiernach wohl nur noch eine Frage der Zeit, wenn auch einer sehr langen. Wahrscheinlich wird ein 4th term nötig sein" (BR.HG 325). This virtual victory, after seven years, marks the moment of a *turn*, in which Mann can imagine a return to an older state of life, in Europe.

[9]   The anonymous author of the solid essay "Thomas Mann," in Wikipedia, https://en.wikipedia.org/wiki/Thomas_Mann#Novels, last modified August 19, 2021, at 01:58 UTC.

authentic Germany.[10] (14) Does Mann establish a cult? In the long view, after his reputation suffered several vicissitudes, his work continues to produce a vast library of critical study by countless devotees; and as we have seen, on the example of Princeton, he is alive in seminar rooms throughout the academic world.

In his amended essay, Greenstein writes, "In the Hebrew Bible the pattern is found in nearly all the major narratives: Jacob, *Joseph*, Moses [. . .]" (emphasis added). What a wonderful concatenation of thoughts about Mann and his work arises here: Mann controlled the Joseph narrative; but he was possessed by Joseph's myth, larger than his life. He would have been deeply pleased by this coincidence.[11]

A Mosaic of Stances

Das Neue Tage-Buch versus Runa
What follows is a conspectus of some of the more striking and representative of Mann's views on the European political crisis during his Princeton years. An immediately intriguing item jumps out of a diary entry for July 1, 1939, in which Mann cites an "unpleasant (*mißliebiger*) article" in "TB"—the journal *Das Neue Tage-Buch*, no. 27 (1939). What is this unpleasantness all about? The piece reports an exchange of letters between communist writers in Zurich dealing with a Stalinist attack on Mann for his apparently having equated, in his American lectures, Nazism and communism. The origin of this complaint, according to Mann, is a *false* report in *The New York Times* and *New York Herald Tribune* about a talk he gave on May 29, 1939, on receiving an honorary doctorate at Hobart College in Geneva, New York. The editor of Mann's diaries, Peter de Mendelssohn, clarifies this affair, as follows: *Das Neue Tage-Buch* had printed a long *anti-Stalinist* polemic under the title "These Fighters" and included Thomas Mann. It had then supported him *against* an attack by Stalinist communists for his renegade anti-Stalinism. "It is true," writes de Mendelssohn,

---

[10]   At a press conference on the day of his arrival in New York on February 21, 1938, Mann remarked, "Where I am, there is Germany." This often-quoted claim is tempered by the next: "I carry *my* German culture in me" (emphasis added). *The New York Times*, February 22, 1938, 13 (cited in TB 3). An ungrounded consensus as to the German translation (e.g., https://kuenste-im-exil.de/KIE/Content/DE/Personen/mann-thomas.html) is, "Wo ich bin, ist Deutschland. Ich trage meine deutsche Kultur in mir."

[11]   These pages were previously published in 2021 as "A Near-Eastern Template for the Life of Thomas Mann," *Academia Letters*, Article 568, https://doi.org/10.20935/AL568.

that for a time Mann had paid homage to some sort of crypto-Stalinism, but he had long since seen through this delusion, and now he was getting his own back from the Communist *Rundschau-Nachrichten-Agentur* (*Runa*) in Zurich. *Runa* published a vituperative piece, calling him a "reactionary ignoramus." This article, in turn, was based on a report in the *New York Times* on Thomas Mann's speech on "The Problem of Freedom" at Hobart College, Geneva (NY), in which he had said that Nazism owed its "principal success to the 'fiction' that it was established as a bulwark against communism."

The *Times* article cites Mann as saying,

National Socialism is nothing but Bolshevism: they are hostile brothers of whom the younger has learned almost everything from the elder, Russian brother. It is quite certain that the expropriation of the Jews is only a prelude to more comprehensive acts of this sort, which will be wholly free of any race-ideology.[12]

As a result, de Mendelssohn concludes, *Runa* declared that "Thomas Mann [. . .] is a swindler and a crypto-fascist (*ein faschistischer Spiegelfechter*)" (T3 814).

In a subsequent diary entry, on July 15, 1939, Mann does not appear to take the affair very seriously, writing, "Yesterday, an amusing letter from Erika: Moscow's indignation at the Zurich attack [by *Runa*] against me."[13] It would appear that Moscow wants Mann on Stalin's side at any cost and does not object to "Bolshevism" being equated with Nazism.

Now, it could be a puzzle to understand why Stalin's "Moscow" does *not* support *Runa*'s attack on Mann for calling its policies Nazism's brother. We are one month before August 23, 1939, the signing of the Nazi-Soviet Non-Aggression Pact. One solution to this riddle reads: Were Moscow to attack the eminent opponent of the Nazi regime, it might—might it?—weaken its hand in the run-up to the pact by prematurely siding with the Nazi regime. It would make friends with Germany by attacking a common enemy and in this sense relieve Germany, in one small way, of needing to make further concessions to

---

[12] "Hobart Confers Degree on Mann: Makes Him Doctor of Letters after His Commencement Address Assailing Nazis," *The New York Times*, May 30, 1939, B 22.

[13] "Gestern amüsanter Brief Erikas: Moskauer Indignation über den Zürcher Angriff auf mich" (T3 435).

win that friendship. In this vein Mann had also said, according to the *Times*, that "Moscow" and the Nazis were *hostile* entities. The adjective contributes to this line of reasoning. Moscow might find it profitable to keep a superficial tension alive between the two totalitarian states. And so, Erika and Thomas can have found it amusing to see this hypocrisy at work, as if Moscow had the slightest real interest in protecting the empirical existence of Thomas Mann.

On the other hand, for a quite opposite reason—disdaining all such tactical subtleties—Moscow may simply have been pleased by the literal claim that, in this run-up to the German-Soviet Nonaggression Pact, National Socialism and Bolshevism belong together—brothers in the party of revolution. But this hypothesis misses the excoriating tone of Mann's comparison.

Finally, there is the somewhat jejune view that Moscow was or preferred to remain behind the times, pushing aside Mann's new formulations at Hobart and recalling his fervor for a genuine socialism not excluding Stalinism. I supply all these speculations in the hope that they may be stimulating.

The most persuasive solution to Moscow's support of Mann will finally be Mann's own: it arises from a closer reading of Mann's speech than the *Times* supplies. In fact, unlike the *Times*'s truncated version, the speech nuances the relation of Nazism and Bolshevism in Bolshevism's favor. Yes, "they are one," but only in selected respects. (Since Mann's actual *English* version of this often revised and often delivered essay on "The Problem of Freedom" is not extant, we must go to the German text for verification, assuming that, in his speech at Hobart, Mann preserved the original thrust of this delicate ideological equation.)

What other nuances are omitted by the *Times*? It reports Mann as saying that Nazism owed its "principal success to the 'fiction' that it was established as a bulwark against communism." This formulation could be misleading. There is nothing fictitious about its having been established, whether as a bulwark against communism or not. What is properly fictitious is Nazism's claim that it would indeed function as a bulwark against Bolshevism when, as Mann would have us see, in many respects, but not all, it is one with Bolshevism. For,

> precisely in the matter of economics, National Socialism is nothing but Bolshevism: they are hostile brothers of whom the younger has learned almost everything from the elder, Russian brother— *only not its morality*; for its [National Socialism's] socialism is morally inauthentic, mendacious, and contemptuous of human beings. [. . .] And precisely when one takes the notion of Bolshevism in its popular, mythical meaning, as the epitome of terror and frenzied destruction, I [TM] would not know which

images would better fit in with it than those that the *German* pogrom (*Reichskristallnacht*) has produced.[14]

Mann scarcely praises Bolshevism, but he is temperate in his criticism, unlike his assault on the Nazis. Soviet communism is not *immediately* damnable in its relation to a democratic socialism: "The essential contradiction of Bolshevism to what we call social democracy, to a *conscientious freedom*, is today not clear enough to grasp and not strong enough to emphasize."[15] Moscow might have found these relativizations attractive and to its—and Mann's—credit. In this light, it was altogether predictable that when, some two years later, on June 22, 1941, the Germans invaded the Soviet Union, Mann would once again be put high up on Moscow's *approved reading list of progressive authors!* The crux: As long as Moscow was not "at peace" with the Nazis, both before and after the Nonaggression Pact, Mann's name, like that of Abou ben Adhem, "as one that loves his fellow men [. . .] led all rest."[16]

Meanwhile, nothing about his Hobart talk could be regarded by any sound mind as favorable to fascism: the charge of Mann's being a "crypto-fascist" is grotesque enough also to have inspired his (wry) amusement. In the later years of his American exile, as we know, he would suffer for his alleged communist sympathies. And when, as on several occasions, he was accused of having published anti-democratic opinions, it was with regard to writings from the time of the First World War—before German fascism had shown its twisted face.

Some weeks later—shortly before his return from his trip to Europe— Mann learned of the devastating German-Soviet Nonaggression Pact of August 23, 1939. He then wrote a note in his diaries in which a gleam of his socialist fervor can be descried: "Hitler has managed to throw the moral fronts into chaos, has prevented a union of socialism and democracy into a free world that is not only conservative. The world of

---

14   Emphasis added. "Gerade in wirtschaftlicher Beziehung ist der Nationalsozialismus nichts anderes als Bolschewismus: es sind feindliche Brüder, von denen der jüngere von dem älteren, russischen, so gut wie alles gelernt hat—nur nicht das Moralische; denn sein Sozialismus ist moralisch unecht, verlogen und menschenverächterisch.[. . .] und gerade wenn man den Begriff des Bolschewismus in seiner populären, mythischen Bedeutung, als Inbegriff des Schreckens und rasender Zerstörung nimmt, so wüßte ich nicht, welche Bilder sich besser mit ihm decken sollten als diejenigen, die der deutsche Pogrom gezeitigt hat." *Das Problem der Freiheit* (GW XI: 966–67).

15   "Der Wesensgegensatz des Bolschewismus zu dem, was wir soziale Demokratie nennen, zu einer *gewissenhaften Freiheit*, ist heute nicht klar genug zu erfassen und nicht stark genug zu betonen." Ibid., 965.

16   Leigh Hunt, "Abu ben Adhem," https://www.poetryfoundation.org/poems/44433/abou-ben-adhem.

the future—or so it seems—and the world of the past are now
confronting each other.—The decision to make a pact with bolshevism
probably originated with Goebbels. [. . .] [The ideal of a] socialistically
tinted freedom believed it could count on Russia and has erred" (D
335).[17] On September 1, 1939, a week after Germany had signed the
Nonaggression Pact with the Soviet Union, Germany invaded Poland
and began the Second World War. In his diaries the next day, Mann
addressed his degenerate "brother" Hitler: "If this unholy man had a
spark of the 'love of Germany,' which has allegedly inspired his crimes,
he would put a bullet in his brain and bequeath [the order] to withdraw
from Poland."[18] As if this point required emphasizing, Mann *hated*
Hitler beyond saying, even though he experimented with the view, in a
piece called "A Brother," that a strange likeness existed between them
as once estranged bohemian *artists*.[19]

There was further dreadful news a week later, on September 11 (!):

A radio message reporting a Russian partial mobilization has
excited far-reaching, worried thoughts about the course of the

---

[17] "Aber die Verwirrung der moralischen Fronten ist gelungen, das Zusammengehen
von Sozialismus u. Demokratie als nicht bloß konservative Freiheitswelt
verhindert. Es stehen sich nun—wenigstens scheinbar—eine Welt der Zukunft u.
eine der Vergangenheit gegenüber.—Der Entschluß, mit dem Bolschewismus zu
paktieren, stammt wahrscheinlich von Goebbels. [. . .] Die sozialistisch gefärbte
Freiheit glaubte auf Rußland zählen zu können und hat sich geirrt" (T3 456–57).

[18] "Hätte der unselige Mensch einen Funken der 'Liebe zu Deutschland,' aus der
er angeblich seine Untaten begangen, so würde er sich eine Kugel in den Kopf
schießen und hinterlassen, daß man aus Polen abziehe" (T3 463–64).

[19] As I note in chapter 3 in *The Mind in Exile*, "Mann composed this astonishing tour
de force in 1938. It was published a year later in English in *Esquire* magazine with
the title 'That Man Is My Brother' and, in an extraordinary temporal and spatial
sequence of events, reprinted almost immediately thereafter in German, in a Paris-
based German exile newspaper. 'That man'—'my brother'—is Hitler!" The
intellectual historian Martin Jay urges us to consider "the nuanced analysis of how
much Mann might have 'hated' Hitler, in Hans Blumenberg's *Rigorism of Truth*
[Ithaca, NY: Cornell University Press, 2015]. Blumenberg claims that Mann was
'not a genuine enemy of Hitler' and says his 'enmity has something of apostasy
about it and of the need to prove oneself, of the overeagerness of the convert who
is keeping watch over the others [to make sure] that they too are good enemies'
(p. 61)." Martin Jay, "Commentary," a private communication (May 12, 2021).
However, Mann himself makes clear in his essay "A Brother" that his hatred
has an element of "apostasy," based on a brave acknowledgment of a (residual)
affinity of character between him and his "brother." At one time, *both* were
marginal, fantastical bohemian-artists. And it is moot that his plain distress at
Kahler's fixation on Hitler must be viewed as a reprehensible "overeagerness of
the convert." Mann's political speeches are devastatingly clear in displaying the
grounds of his revulsion—the concrete crimes of the Hitlerite regime.

war. Will the regime be overthrown? In Germany, a profound revolution took place, which, with its "national allure," based on all older concepts of Germanism, completely denationalized the country. Nazi Bolshevism has nothing to do with Germanism. This barbarism very naturally found contact with its seemingly opposite Russia. If this bloc of nearly 300 million people holds, it is almost unthinkable that "civilization," which in a long war does not remain what it was, could defeat it to the degree of setting its conditions. What has happened in Germany is not likely to be reversed. The future is very dark.[20]

On the very day of his return to Princeton, September 19, weary and distraught, Mann continued his meditation and wrote down a possibly unstudied thought: "What I anticipate and hope for is that Germany might become the battleground for the struggle between Russia and the Western powers, with a communist revolution and the overthrow of Hitler."[21] It is unlikely that Mann was using the word "communist" in a rigorous sense; and quite possibly with the intention of clarifying his thought that evening, he studied Berdyaev's *Sinn und Schicksal des russischen Kommunismus* (retitled in the English translation as *The Origin of Russian Communism*).

Typical Anxiety

Another day, October 6, 1939, typical at the Manns at this parlous time, would unfold anxiously:

Katia had got up at six in the morning to listen, with bated breath, to Hitler's "Reichstag speech." *Nascitur* ["to us is born"], etc. But

---

[20]   "Radio Meldung russischer Teil-Mobilmachung, die mir weitläufig-sorgenvolle Gedanken über den Verlauf des Krieges erregte. Wird das Regime zu stürzen sein? In Deutschland hat eine tief greifende [*sic*] Revolution stattgefunden, die das Land, bei 'nationaler' Allüre, nach allen älteren Begriffen von Deutschtum, völlig *ent*-nationalisiert hat. Der Nazi Bolschewismus hat *nichts* mit Deutschtum zu tun. Die neue Barbarei hat sehr natürlich den Kontakt mit dem scheinbar entgegengesetzten Rußland gefunden. Steht dieser Block von annähernd 300 Millionen Menschen zusammen, so ist es fast undenkbar, daß die 'Civilisation,' die in einem langen Kriege auch nicht sie selber bleibt, ihn so besiegen könnte, daß sie ihre Bedingungen stellen kann. Das Geschehene in Deutschland wahrscheinlich nicht rückgängig zu machen. Die Zukunft sehr dunkel" (T3 469).

[21]   The passage continues: "The downfall of the regime and severe punishment of the guilty country is basically all that I could wish for" (D 342). "Was ich erwarte und erhoffe ist: Deutschland als Kriegsschauplatz beim Kampf zwischen Rußland u. dem Westen, kommunistische Revolution und Untergang Hitlers darin. Der Untergang des Regimes unter schwerer Heimsuchung des schuldigen Landes ist im Grunde alles, was ich wünsche" (T3 474).

this mouse is a dangerous vermin. This dirty rogue wants to be released from the war to gain time and subjugate everything through well-established "peaceful" means. Not the smallest handle for the democracies for a peace with honor. Infallibly, the war must go on—an anachronism, forced by a criminal who wanted limitlessly to blackmail a state of Europe that mentally/ spiritually excludes war.[22]

A letter Mann sent on January 16, 1940, to Agnes E. Meyer, his patroness, with whom he maintained a steady correspondence full of substantial content, contains one of his clearest statements about the rise of Hitlerism:

I am speaking of the complexity and two-facedness of life that cannot be broken down into "good" and "evil," but is mostly good and evil at once; and suddenly evil emerges from goodness with a ghastly grimace. That in Hitlerism the "deep," the "supra-political," anti-rationalist, and anti-civilizational Germany has become extremely malignant, and that it—that is, Hitlerism—must be beaten, we are probably in agreement. This means practically that Germany must be defeated [. . .] for against all our hopes, the unfortunate German people with all their intelligence and vitality are giving their all for the régime and will not break away from it until their last breath.[23]

This fact was deplorable; Mann's deepest hope had been that Hitler would be overthrown before any world war. Earlier, on May 14, 1939,

---

22 "K. war morgens um 6 aufgestanden, um Hitlers mit angehaltenem Atem erwartete 'Reichstagsrede' zu hören. Nascitur, etc. Doch ist die Maus ein gefährliches Ungeziefer. Dieser schmutzige Gauner möchte aus dem Krieg herausgelassen werden, um Zeit zu gewinnen und mit den bewährten 'friedlichen' Mitteln alles zu unterjochen. Nicht die kleinste Handhabe für die Demokratieen [sic] für einen Frieden in Ehren. Unfehlbar muß der Krieg weitergehen—ein Anachronismus, erzwungen von einem Verbrecher, der einen Zustand Europas, der den Krieg geistig ausschließt, grenzenlos erpressen wollte" (T3 483).

23 "Ich spreche einfach von der Kompliziertheit und Zweigesichtigkeit des Lebens, das sich nicht in 'gut' und 'böse' auseinanderlegen lässt, sondern meistens gut und böse auf einmal ist und plötzlich das Böse aus dem Guten als grässliche Fratze hervortreten lässt. Daß im Hitlertum das 'tiefe,' das 'überpolitische,' antirationalistische und anti-civilisatorische Deutschland äußerst bösartig geworden ist, und daß es—das Hitlertum—geschlagen werden muss, darüber sind wir uns ja wohl einig. Auch dass dies praktisch heißt, dass Deutschland geschlagen werden muss [. . .] denn gegen all unser Hoffen legt sich das unselige deutsche Volk mit all seiner Intelligenz und Lebenskraft für das Régime ins Zeug und wird sich nicht von ihm lossagen ehe ihm selbst der Atem ausgeht" (BR.M 195).

he had written to his brother Heinrich, "War can be averted only if the Germans make an end of Hitler. If it is not averted, any hope for a peace that will not once again contain the seeds of a new war depends upon the Germans repudiating the regime *before the defeat.*"[24] His January 16, 1940, letter to Agnes E. Meyer continues this reflection:

> It is far from over yet, it will cost the opponents terrible sacrifices to bring it to this point, yes, my personal opinion is that the colossal Russian-German bloc will not be defeated without America's entering the war and providing a counterbalance. (No fear that I will broadcast my opinion.) But today in this country there is already a tendency to pity Germany for the injustice that the Allies could inflict on it after their victory, when, for the time being, it is Germany that with all its might commits injustices and covers itself with almost indelible guilt. I wish things were so far along that the Allies were somehow capable of committing injustices, but perhaps they may never get into this parlous situation. The other danger, that Hitler will win, seems to me the immediate threat—and in this case America will have a grace period of perhaps two years until it is all over with its freedom. The compassionate Americans will still long for their shallow rationalism once anti-civilization is on the loose.[25]

In a letter to Meyer some months later, on March 22, 1940, Mann considered the few options available to the remaining democracies and

24   BR.H 224. "Nur wenn die Deutschen mit Hitler ein Ende machen, kann der Krieg vermieden werden. Nur wenn,—sollte er nicht vermieden werden,—die Deutschen *vor der Niederlage* dem Regime die Gefolgschaft verweigern, dürfen wir auf einen Frieden hoffen, der nicht die Keime des neuen Krieges schon wieder in sich trägt" (BR.HG 306).

25   "Es ist noch lange nicht soweit, es wird die Gegner fürchterliche Opfer kosten, es dahin zu bringen, ja, meiner privaten Meinung nach wird der kolossale russisch-deutsche Menschenblock überhaupt nicht zu besiegen sein, ohne dass Amerika in den Krieg eintritt und einen Ausgleich schafft. (Ich werde mich hüten, diese Meinung laut werden zu lassen.) Aber in diesem Lande ist eine Neigung, Deutschland heute schon wegen des Unrechts zu bemitleiden, dass die Alliierten ihm nach ihrem Siege zufügen könnten, wo es doch vorläufig Deutschland ist, das aus allen Kräften Unrecht tut und sich mit fast untilgbarer Schuld bedeckt. Ich wollte, es wäre erst so weit, dass die Alliierten nur irgend in der Lage wären, Unrecht zu tun, aber vielleicht kommen sie nie in diese gefährliche Lage. Die andere Gefahr, dass Hitler siegt, scheint mir die unmittelbarer drohende,—und in diesem Fall wird Amerika eine Schonfrist von vielleicht zwei Jahren haben, bis es auch mit seiner Freiheit zu Ende ist. Die mitleidigen Amerikaner werden sich noch nach ihrem seichten Rationalismus zurücksehnen, wenn hier erst die Anti-Civilisation los ist" (BR.M 195–96).

wondered whether "America really want[s] a negotiated peace with the
dirty swindler, who is now once again throwing out the conservative-
anti-communist bait while letting Nazi-Communist propaganda do
more to confound and paralyze the world."[26]

War and Christianity

Mann hardly restricted his political sensibilities to letters and diary
entries. He was, of course, an engaged public speaker, intending again
and again to alert his American public to the barbarism in Europe that
would sooner or later forcibly threaten this country. In his heart of hearts,
he wanted America to go to war against Hitler, but he could not be too
explicit in stating this unpopular opinion. He speaks directly of this *hope*
on September 3, 1940, in a letter to Agnes Meyer: "One really *hopes* anew.
England's resistance is admirable, and this country will help it the better
it helps itself. I believe that, whether Wilkie or FDR—if England holds out
into the winter, we will have America at war in the spring, and I believe
that would result in the almost immediate overthrow of the Nazi
regime."[27] Some months later, on November 26, Mann wrote in his diaries
a rather brutal and unexpected commentary on the urgent theme of
revolution in the Fascist states. The topic has been conveyed to him by a
letter from an (unidentified) emigrant by the name of Schwarzert. It reads:

The preparation of a constructive revolution from the outside
[. . .]. The inner one can only be anarchic, [an affair of] blood and
revenge. In my opinion, it must take place first; only in this way is
it logical and a lesson forever. A cleaning out is necessary, which
is not something for the successor government: what has
happened can only be atoned for and washed away with streams
of blood.[28]

---

26 "Wünscht Amerika wirklich einen Verständigungsfrieden mit dem schmutzigen
Betrüger, der jetzt wieder einmal den konservativ-antikommunistischen Köder
auswirft, während er die Nazi-kommunistische Propaganda ein Weiteres tun
lässt zur Verwirrung und Lähmung der Welt?" (BR.M 199).
27 Emphasis added. "Man hofft ja überhaupt aufs neue. England's resistance is
admirable, and this country [the preceding seven words are in Mann's English]
wird ihm helfen je besser es sich selber hilft. Ich glaube, ob Willkie oder F.D.R.,—
wenn England sich bis in den Winter hält, haben wir im Frühjahr Amerika im
Kriege, und das würde meiner Überzeugung nach den fast unmittelbaren Sturz
des Nazi-Regimes zur Folge haben" (BR.M 232).
28 "Die Vorbereitung einer konstruktiven Revolution von außen. Die von innen
kann nur anarchisch, Blut und Rache sein. Nach meiner Meinung muß sie es erst
einmal sein, nur so ist es folgerichtig und eine Lehre für immer. Ein Aufräumen ist
nötig, das nicht Sache der Folge-Regierung sein kann, und was geschehen kann
nur mit Strömen von Blut gesühnt und hinweggewaschen werden" (T4 184–85).

What words would bring about the right political change—or, at the least, not inhibit in Mann's audience a felt need for *American intervention*? Mann's observant biographer Janet Flanner noted, in fall 1941, that "Mann has no deistic conviction, but lately he has put a veneer of Christianity upon the lectures he has been giving on tour."[29] Flanner might have pointed to such passages, in stilted English, as are found in "War and Democracy," a lecture to which Meyer objected for its militancy and the breadth of its political engagement:

> But logic has not a final nor [*sic*] the highest validity for Life, and in ethic requirements of man, freedom and equality are not a real contradiction. The contrast between them is resolved in that which transcends and relates both of them, namely in Christianity.
>
> Christian humanity has combined the individual and the social principles in a way that is emotionally unassailable and wholly natural. The value and dignity which it bestows upon the individual, the human soul in its immediate relationship to God, are not contradicted by the equality of all before God. It is in the statute of "Human Rights," this Christian heritage of the great bourgeois revolution, that both principles, the individualistic and the social, freedom and equality, are combined and justify each other.[30] The Christian conception of the world denies that freedom and equality constitute an irreconcilable contrast. It accepts as necessary truth that a human synthesis, a reasonable and just synthesis, must be possible between freedom and equality, individual and society, the person and the collectivity—acknowledging that both demands include great *values* and great *dangers*.
>
> (T4 1046–47)

Flanner does not venture extra-intellectual motives for Mann's application of this veneer—a dubious historical disquisition on the origin of Western democracy and the alleged contribution of Christianity to it (Christianity's "universalism"?)—but I shall. It is a prudent political tactic meant to aid Mann's goal: to have America enter the war on the side of England and the crushed Western democracies. He wishes to make it clear that the reason for America's entry is not to rescue the

---

[29]   Flanner, "Goethe in Hollywood," *New Yorker*, part 1 (December 13, 1941), 32.

[30]   On the vexed issue of the Christian contribution to postwar human rights discourse, see Samuel Moyn, *Christian Human Rights* (Philadelphia: University of Pennsylvania Press, 2015).

Jews of Germany or otherwise fight a war on behalf of the German-Jewish émigrés in America: American Christians need not suspect a personal interest in his advocacy. (Mann's wife Katia was Jewish, as well as, of course, her brother, the formidable physicist Peter Pringsheim, not to mention Erich Kahler, Hermann Broch, and Albert Einstein.) Moreover, Mann's professed Christianity has the effect of additionally detaching Mann the individual from the Nazi identification of him as a Jew or Jew-sympathizer, meant of course as a lethal defamation. This is not a far-fetched hypothesis, as consider this one event reported in his diary, "A card, a vile slander, in the mail, in a Jewish jargon, with the presumption that I had caused the English bombardment of Weimar—as Gumpert told me; I would not have read it, just that the sender was spitting 'contemptuously into my face.' The reason is the reviews of *Lotte in Weimar.*"[31]

The Home Front

Mann was politically engaged *at home* in Princeton as well. "I shall always go home," one refugee friend of his has said, "to the house of Thomas Mann in whatever land. There our sadness as aliens is admitted; our homesickness is admitted, our sometimes-outbursting love for German language and music—these are admitted. He is our most important, consoling figure. His writing, his art, his wisdom, his life have not been doomed by human circumstances."[32]

A diary entry written earlier, in the first long year of his stay in Princeton, in 1939, points to the way that a hospitable Mann could welcome visitors. On October 11, he jots down the brief phrases "*Dr. Lothar* for lunch from New York to discuss his 'Princeton Theater'-Plan. Pledged support."[33] We are lucky to have the memoirs of Ernst Lothar, the émigré Austrian novelist and theater director, which recount, in convincing detail, Lothar's visit to the Manns': "I suddenly find myself standing in front of my host, whose perfect art of [literary] representation, at once grounded and cryptic (*gegründet-hintergründig*)—and, likewise, his perfect feeling for detached irony—I have admired up to the present day." Lothar continues:

"Scheußliche Schmähkarte unter der Post, jüdelnd, mit der Vermutung, dass ich das Bombardement von Weimar durch die Engländer veranlaßt hätte,—wie Gumpert mir erzählte; ich hatte es nicht gelesen, sondern nur, dass der Sender mir 'verachtungsvoll ins Gesicht spucke.' Der Anlaß sind die reviews über 'Lotte in Weimar'" (T4 144).

[32] Flanner, "Goethe in Hollywood," part 1, 35.

[33] "Zum Lunch Dr. *Lothar* aus New York zur Besprechung seines 'Princeton Theater'-Plans. Unterstützung zugesagt" (T3 486).

He received me, although I had come unannounced, without
hesitation, came toward me in the bright house with hands
outstretched, and turned the quarter-of-an-hour visit that I'd
planned into a half-day's visit, including lunch and afternoon tea
and, despite his being so much in demand, displayed a paternal-
fraternal concern for my fate—the common fate, he declared, of
outcasts from the German spirit (*Geist*).

I thank that half-day in summer [actually, in fall] for more than
sincere encouragement—I thank him for rejecting all thoughts of
a [hypothetical] "Or? . . ." and feel the urgent need now to state
my thanks.

In a conversation lasting several hours, my immediate distress
occupied the foreground. But there were two things, Thomas
Mann said, that he considered inadmissible, indeed, contemptible
for an émigré writer: one, to change his language like a piece of
worn-out clothing and write in an inappropriate, hence, arrogantly
assumed one. And two: not to write anymore. It was our duty—
he, I, all those to whom the German language had been given—to
write in it. We had no choice. We too were obliged to serve, and
this—it was his expression—would be our "wartime service"; we
too had to fight a war against Hitler with the weapon of the
German word, which did not by any means have to be polemical
but instead must hold fast to what had to be preserved.[34] He
anticipated the objection that I did *not* make: such a fight would
be incomparably easier for a Nobel Prize winner; but there was no
being excused from a sort of counter-espionage (*Abwehrdienst*)—
that was the word he used: "non datur"; he cited, as did my
father in his time, the Latin [which is to say: *tertium non datur*:
you have no other option!]. One must—every one of us—must
hammer home the thought—he made us understand this, with
a schoolmaster's delight in precepting, for which we called him
the "Praeceptor Germaniae"—that spiritual desertion would be
even less excusable than physical. "You have no other option!
No other option!" he repeated sternly. Run away, after you
had escaped? A shame! Whether he would return [to Germany],
he did not know; but concerning the abuse done to the German

---

[34]   This turn of thought was familiar to Thomas Mann, who, during the First World
War, pronounced his *Reflections of a Nonpolitical Man* "a form of 'intellectual
military service' ['Gedankendienst mit der Waffe'] in the struggle of German
Kultur against French and British 'civilization.'" *Reflections of a Nonpolitical
Mann*, tr. Walter D. Morris (New York: Ungar, 1983), 1, (translation modified)"
(cited in TB 53). *Betrachtungen eines Unpolitischen*, GW XII: 9.

spirit [. . .] he knew this: he would help to wash it off. And that is something I too must do. Whence, he then just tossed out the challenge: "Did I not have the courage, since I was in fact committed to the theater, to put on plays in German in New York—still better: in Austrian German, for which I had the competence?" One had to begin somewhere. I might make that beginning. [. . .] When I returned [to New York] that evening, Adrienne [my wife, a leading actress] and I decided to set up an Austrian theater.[35]

Consider, finally, this historical analogy. Around 1910, Max Brod, fresh from his conversion to an active Judaism, having been inspired by a talk given in Prague by Martin Buber, wrote in the Zionist weekly *Selbstwehr*, "It is the mission of the Jewish-national movement, Zionism, to give the word 'nation' a new meaning."[36] But it would be the Nazis who would give the words "Jewish" and "nation" a new meaning, producing, in the slightly luckier case, a nation of miserable exiles. One finds this very formulation in Mann's diaries. Noting a comment made by his son, Mann remarks: "The émigrés are like a nation that considers me as its ambassador."[37] An entire history, a terrible tragedy, is encompassed in these few lines.

Ernst Lothar's report of his visit corroborates Klaus Mann's surmise: it represents Mann as a lead figure, an inspiration, not only for Lothar but also for a great many other German exiles in America. Mann might serve *us* as well, in inspiring *our* creative answer to the abuse done today to the *democratic* spirit. Then we would owe this encouragement to Mann's hospitality to Lothar. Not every one of Mann's visitors, however, could count on so intimate a participation in his troubles and so positive an outcome. There was an intuitive triage at work. Consider the visit of Stefan Zweig by contrast. Over the years, Mann and Zweig—the very prolific, extremely successful Austrian-Jewish writer—had maintained a respectful and supportive correspondence. When Zweig finally made his way to America, Mann wrote of his eagerness to receive him—for lunch on January 4, 1939, at about 1:30. Zweig was carrying many moral burdens; aside from the pains of his own emigration—that continual "disturbance," that "loss of balance"—he was seeking help

---

35   Ernst Lothar, *Das Wunder des Überlebens: Erinnerungen und Ergebnisse* (Vienna and Hamburg: Paul Zsolnay Verlag, 1961), 141.

36   Max Brod, cited in Benjamin Balint, *Kafka's Last Trial: The Case of a Literary Legacy* (New York: Norton, 2018), 53.

37   "Die Emigranten gleichen einer Nation, die mich [Thomas Mann] als ihren Gesandten betrachtet" (T4 117).

from Mann for Lavinia Mazzucchetti, Mann's Italian translator. He obtained less than he had hoped for. He wrote to a friend,

> It would be Thomas Mann, of course, who could do the most—
> Mann, who is really all-powerful here [in America] and has the
> widest influence in the widest circles. He has an unprecedented
> position and not only in literature but perhaps an even stronger
> one owing to his opposition to Nazism and his struggle for
> democracy, which is the alpha and omega of the whole country. It
> was just hard for me to get hold of him; I spoke to him only twice
> and always in the turmoil of other people or family.[38]

Despite his rapidly gained prestige, it was never an easy matter for Mann, as Hans Rudolf Vaget observes, to cope with "the heartache of exile," which he "considered a 'fatal error'—a grave stylistic mistake on the part of History—that he only grudgingly accepted."[39] On the whole, however, as we shall see, the years of exile provided him (to speak with Milton's *Samson Agonistes*) with a "new acquist of true experience," leading to "a widening out and heightening of his self-image as a writer and as a German." In this new perspective, "national views and valuations lost their old validity, spurred on by an irrepressible thought . . . 'If only I had been born into Anglo-Saxon culture!'" (Mann envied the worldwide fame and canonical solidity in particular of Joseph Conrad and T. S. Eliot.) In now taking up arms for "the other Germany," Mann was entering the wider moral, intellectual, and literary sphere of a "world bourgeoisie" (Weltbürgertum), which implies the repudiation of an older Germanness focused on Goethe and Wagner as models.[40]

The Princeton Experience

The question that now concerns us particularly is how much of that "new acquist of true experience" took place in Princeton. Elsewhere,

---

[38] "Am meisten könnte natürlich Thomas Mann tun, der hier [in Amerika] wirklich allmächtig ist und weitesten Einfluß in weitesten Kreisen besitzt. Er hat hier eine Position ohnegleichen und nicht nur vom Literarischen her, sondern vielleicht noch stärker durch sein Auftreten gegen den Nazismus und seinen Kampf für die Demokratie, der ja hier das Alpha und Omega des ganzen Landes ist. Es war nur recht schwer für mich, seiner habhaft zu werden, ich sprach ihn gerade zweimal und immer im Tumult von Menschen oder Familie." Stefan Zweig, letter to Waldemar Jollos (February 25, 1939), in *Thomas Mann–Stefan Zweig*, 97.

[39] Hans Rudolf Vaget, "Thomas Mann und die amerikanische Literatur: Eine Skizze," in *Thomas Mann in Amerika*, ed. Ulrich Raulff and Ellen Strittmatter (Marbach am Neckar: Deutsche Schillergesellschaft, 2019), 37. The embedded phrase is from V 27.

[40] Vaget, "Thomas Mann und die amerikanische Literatur," 37–38.

Vaget points out that whatever gains he made in Princeton, they were achieved at a cost: "Under these circumstances [primarily, the enervating news of Hitler's successes], it is not surprising that the literary harvest of the Princeton years, when compared with the preceding years in Switzerland and the ensuing years in Los Angeles, was meager" (V 29). One should take note of Vaget's phrase "*literary* harvest," which excludes Mann's first five polemical radio broadcasts for the BBC (published under the title of *Listen Germany!*)[41]—works that, however brief, are certainly of high literary quality—along with copious essays and speeches on the grave political issues of the time, including "This Peace," "The Problem of Freedom," and "This War." All these works were published by Knopf: I have looked at them in some detail in *The Mind in Exile*. I think it has been rewarding to do so: even in inadequate translation, they display Mann's breathtaking rhetorical prowess. These essays, moreover, are not entirely accidental accompaniments of the European crisis: they are, in Mann's own words, essential parallels to his literary work. In his speech to Princeton undergraduates "On Myself" on May 2, 1940, Mann alluded, first, to the catastrophe of the First World War,

which interrupted my work for years on "The Magic Mountain." During the war I wrote the "Reflections of a Non-Political Man," a work of painful introspection in which I intended to "have it out" with the war and its problems. Yet it also became an indispensable preparation and relief for my artistic work, particularly for "The Magic Mountain," as it turned out later. I have remained true to this inclination to unburden fictional enterprises of thought content by essayistic "parallel actions"— indeed, I do not hesitate to consider this critical-polemical aspect as an inalienable and essential ingredient of my being—and not only a matter of sense of duty.[42]

The politically accentuated portrait of Goethe in *Lotte in Weimar*, for one, is written in tandem with Mann's polemical speeches and his Princeton lectures on Goethe's *Faust* and *The Sufferings of Young Werther*, which are also discussed in *The Mind in Exile*. To appeal, once more, to Vaget's biographical judgment, he later adds to his remark about Mann's "meager literary harvest" words that would be difficult to improve on and are here quoted in full:

---

41   Thomas Mann, *Listen Germany! Twenty-Five Radio Messages to the German People over BBC* (New York: Knopf, 1943).
42   Thomas Mann, "On Myself" (unedited version) (B 153).

The Princeton years were an astonishingly active and productive period of Mann's life. If the literary harvest of those two and a half years was, for him, modest [. . .] there can be no doubt that it was during the period in Princeton that Thomas Mann cemented his position as Germany's preeminent literary figure, came to prominence as the most vocal and passionate opponent of Hitler in America, and, by dint of his remarkable political clairvoyance and moral strength, assumed the role of the undisputed leader of the "Other Germany"—a role he would maintain during the longest and darkest years in the history of his native country.

(V 31–32)

In this matter of Mann's hospitality to other exiles, many of whom also took up arms on behalf of the "Other Germany," it would be good to know what sorts of welcome were exchanged between Mann and the other great minds who were his neighbors in Princeton—Erich Kahler, Hermann Broch, and Albert Einstein, above all. In the latter case, we shall be left wishing for more. In a blunt word, Einstein did not like Mann's company. But this is a topic for another chapter. Meanwhile, let us look at the life and work of a scholar who cherished Mann's company, and Mann, his—Erich Kahler.

Two Erich von Kahler: Mann's Great Friend

A genius of place inhabits Erich Kahler's sitting-room in Princeton. The book-lined walls, the tables covered with books, the pictures in the room, argue a high and specific legacy. Even if only this book-crowded space survived, the historian of ideas and feelings could, in some measure, reconstruct a lost world. It is that world of Central European humanism which Nazism and Stalinism have all but obliterated, and of which Erich Kahler is one of the distinctive, vitalizing survivors.

—George Steiner

I feel the need to say how much we wish that we had you here together with us during this period of agonizing and numbing expectation. It is painful and constricting that we should be so far apart now of all times.

—Thomas Mann

From California, Thomas Mann wrote a grand encomium to Erich Kahler on October 14, 1945, Kahler's sixtieth birthday:

Erich von Kahler [. . .] is one of the most intelligent, refined, and abundant minds at work today, one of the most benevolent, sensitive, and helpful hearts that beat today. Not all too many know this; the split in his life brought about by the German catastrophe of 1933, by exile, this wandering about in foreign lands, has held back and delayed the fame that would have grown unfailingly and increasingly if Germany had stayed sane. But in the course of time this fame will come to him, certainly; and it is a genuine pleasure for me to testify publicly too, on the soil of the German spirit, in this journal [*Deutsche Blätter*], to the value of this exceptional man, and offer him my congratulations, in which I include all the thanks that my life owes him for his grand effort on behalf of truth and goodness and all the pride I take in being allowed to call him friend, comrade, and brother.[1]

Erich Kahler—until his immigration to the United States, in November 1938, Erich *von* Kahler—was, as we now know, a central figure in the Princeton "enclosure" of émigré intellectuals. Born in Prague (of the Austro-Hungarian Empire) on October 14, 1885, Kahler lived there for fifteen years as a contemporary of Franz Kafka, who was two years older. They did not meet, chiefly because Kahler was homeschooled and thereafter moved in the circles of the *haute bourgeoisie*. After many sojourns and way stations—Vienna, where he studied philosophy; Wolfrathshausen near Munich, where he was active as a freelance scholar, public intellectual, and increasingly casual adherent of the Stefan George Circle; Ascona and Zurich, where he fled from Nazi persecution—he finally settled in Princeton, where, after more than three decades in residence—writing copiously, thinking deeply— he died on June 28, 1970.

Mann's encomium to Kahler describes Kahler's early biography in rather striking figurative language:

Mysterious Prague, from whose unique historic atmosphere so many fascinating things have arrived in our intellectual-spiritual world—Prague, which has produced Kafka and Werfel [and add on Rainer Maria Rilke], was also his birthplace. Vienna held this youth for a while, but soon—who knows from what need for a harder air, a stricter feeling of life—he went to Germany, to the South, at any rate to Munich; and without subtracting from his style, his expression, anything of the softer, more colorful bloom of the culture of the East, his being was penetrated by the problematic of Germanism [. . .]. He has become, in my opinion,

---

[1]   "Erich von Kahler [. . .] ist einer der klügsten, feinsten und reichsten Köpfe, die heute wirken, eines der gütigsten, wissendsten und zur Hilfeleistung willigsten Herzen, die heute schlagen. Nicht allzu viele sind dessen gewahr; die Spaltung seines Lebens durch das deutsche Unheil von 1933, durch das Exil, das Verschlagenwerden in fremde Welt, hat seinen Ruhm, der unfehlbar stetiges Wachstum gehabt hätte, wenn Deutschland bei Sinnen geblieben wäre, zurückgehalten und vertagt. Auf die Dauer aber ist es ihm sicher, und es ist mir eine wahre Freude, für den Wert des seltenen Mannes zu zeugen und ihm auch öffentlich, auf deutschem geistigem Boden, in dieser Zeitschrift, meine Glückwünsche darzubringen, in die ich allen Dank einschließe, den mein Leben seiner großartigen Bemühung um das Wahre und Gute schuldet, und meinen ganzen Stolz darauf, ihn Freund, Genossen, Bruder nennen zu dürfen" (GW X: 502–3).

today's most knowledgeable and pained, sympathetic analyst of the German character and destiny.[2]

If one reads closely, as does the Mann scholar Bernd Hamacher, one can perceive a likeness between Mann's relation to Kahler and Mann's relation to Kafka. In this way, we have underlined Kafka's relevance to the Kahler Circle (see chapter 6, "Did Einstein read Kafka's *Castle?*" *infra*). Hamacher writes:

Kahler's path from East to West and from South to North (albeit "only" to Munich) is imagined here as a phantasy of adolescence, as the path of development from the female ["the softer, more colorful bloom"] to the male cultural paradigm. It is precisely the fact that this "masculinization" in Kahler's life's journey remains, so to speak, incomplete and arrested, that constitutes its fascination for Mann.[3]

The linking of Kafka and Werfel in Mann's encomium stresses Mann's attraction to a *cluster* of writers of a certain Eastern—that is to say, Austrian—complexion. Mann and Werfel—and I will add Franz Kafka and Erich Kahler to the figure of "Werfel"—"form a constellation [. . .] North and South, Protestantism and Judaism, Lübeck and Prague, Faust and the Golem of Maharal ['Our Teacher, Rabbi Loew']."[4] These polarities, which imagine contrasting sensibilities, types of cognition, and shapes of desire, incite in Mann the strongest sort of attraction (oscillating with reserve), and they are well represented in his fiction.

Kahler was a prolific author of poems, articles, manifestos, and books of intellectual history. Two ethnophilosophical works share pride of

---

2   "Im geheimnisvollen Prag, aus dessen eigentümlicher historischer Atmosphäre der geistigen Welt so viele Faszinationen gekommen sind, das Kafka und Werfel hervorgebracht hat, stand auch seine Wiege: den Jüngling hielt Wien eine Weile, aber früh, wer weiß aus welchem Bedürfnis nach härterer Luft, unlässigerem Lebensgefühl geführt, kam er ins Reich, in dessen Süden, nach München wenigstens, und ohne daß je von seiner Form, seinem Ausdruck der weichere farbigere Kulturschmelz des Ostens sich verloren hätte, durchdrang sich sein Wesen mit der [. . .] Problematik des Deutschtums. Er wurde, nach meiner Meinung, zu dem in unseren Tagen kundigsten und schmerzhaft mitfühlendsten Analytiker des deutschen Charakters und Schicksals" (GW X: 503).

3   Bernd Hamacher, "'Wieviel Brüderlichkeit bedeutet Zeitgenossenschaft ohne weiteres!' Franz Kafka und Thomas Mann—Versuch eines 'Kulturtransfers,'" in Claudia Liebrand and Franziska Schößler, eds., *Textverkehr: Kafka und die Tradition* (Würzburg: Königshausen & Neumann, 2004), 369n34.

4   Michel Reffet, "Thomas Mann und Franz Werfel. Eine deutsch-österreichische Kulturdialektik im amerikanischen Exil," *Studia austriaca* II , ed. Fausto Cereignani (Milan: Edizioni dell'Arco, 1993), 261.

place in the canon of his literary production in the decade before his emigration: *Israel unter den Völkern* (Israel among the nations; 1933) and *Der deutsche Charakter in der Geschichte Europas* (The German character in the history of Europe).[5] In *The Mind in Exile*, I discuss the latter's influence on Mann's sense of the German character as a thing forever engaged in a process of "becoming." On Kahler's seventieth birthday, the philosopher Jacob Taubes praised the two books as admirably independent of party interests and bent on genuine "historical truth." "Kahler shapes the fate of the Jews and the fate of Germany as spiritual figures. They belong together as the two worlds in Kahler's life that he carries within him: [. . .] Israel's apocalyptic view of history and German romantic history (*apokalyptische Geschichtsschau Israels und deutsche, romantische Geschichtswissenschaft*). The Apocalypse taught him the end of history; he owes the German philosophy of history his vision of the organic forms of peoples, whose 'character' takes 'shape' in the course of history."[6]

In 1940, on the brink of the Second World War, Kahler declared his chiefest predilection, a hope of redemption, via the cooperation of whole peoples: "What has to be done to remedy today's misery"— namely, energize the will to advance a transnational federation of nations—"can no longer be done by only this or that individual, nor even by this or that individual *people*, however powerful, but only—and that is the fateful difficulty—of everyone together."[7] The title of one of his later books repeats his main concern: *Die Verantwortung des Geistes*. This is the *responsibility* of the individual mind (or spirit or intelligence) for the well-being of all: this duty must be fulfilled in a mode assimilable and productive for all.[8] "For all" is not an idle phrase: Kahler believed in a fundamental common humanity capable of "searching reflection,"

---

5   *Israel* (Zurich: Humanitas Verlag, 1936); *Deutscher Charakter* (Zurich: Europa Verlag, 1937). A revised, abridged version of the latter was published in English as *The Germans*, ed. Robert and Rita Kimber (Princeton, NJ: Princeton University Press, 1974). Hans Rudolf Vaget was the first to point out the considerable importance for Mann of *Der deutsche Charakter*. See "Kaisersaschern als geistige Lebensform. Zur Konzeption der deutschen Geschichte in Thomas Manns *Doktor Faustus*," in *Der deutsche Roman und seine historischen und politischen Bedingungen*, ed. Wolfgang Paulsen (Bern: Francke, 1977), 200–235.

6   Jacob Taubes, "Erich Kahler. Zu seinem 70. Geburtstag," *Apokalypse und Politik*, ed. Herbert Kopp-Oberstebrink and Martin Treml (Paderborn: Wilhelm Fink/ Brill, 2017), 385–87.

7   "Denn was getan werden muß, um dem heutigen Elend abzuhelfen, das kann nicht mehr nur von dem und jenem einzelnen, nicht einmal mehr von dem und jenem einzelnen Volk, und sei es noch so mächtig, getan werden, sondern nur— und das ist das verhängnisvoll Schwere—von allen zusammen." Erich Kahler, "Was soll werden?" *Mass und Wert* 3, no. 3 (March/April 1940): 302.

8   Erich Kahler, *Die Verantwortung des Geistes: Gesammelte Aufsätze* (Frankfurt am Main: S. Fischer Verlag, 1952).

which he held to be the great axiom of "the Enlightenment." This claim might seem merely speculative, bare of empirical support, but Kahler was Hegelian enough to believe that history advanced through convulsions toward a global increase of human intelligence. Assuring this increase is the special responsibility of an elite, who "would have the task, in our ever more technicized and functionalized world, to keep alive the spiritual as the genuinely human: [. . .] a sense and a care for the universal, for that which is common to the people and to humanity."[9] Kahler's work displays a remarkable continuity through "the utopian metaphorics of the unity of the human race [. . .] the demand for unity of the intellectual disciplines, and the primacy of representation, of 'showing' (*Darstellung*) over analysis."[10] We shall be revisiting this "demand" for unity of the intellectual disciplines, which was enthusiastically shared by Broch and to a certain extent by Einstein, in chapter 4, *infra*, titled "Goethe and the Circle."

Kahler argued his convictions within a dense matrix of plastically demonstrated facts and trenchant concepts of European and American political, economic, and cultural history. He shows, for example, how all dictators are prey to the same convulsive gestures of rule; how *every* liberal democracy has been corrupted by overriding economic interests; how the Nazi dictatorship survived from the start via a total "mobilization" of its people for war; and more.[11]

In Princeton Kahler began composing his chef-d'oeuvre, *Man the Measure: A New Approach to History*, the most prominent cultural product of his thirty years of American exile.[12] To give some notion of why Thomas Mann would have compared Kahler's book to "a majestic 'novel of mankind,'" the Dostoyevsky scholar Joseph Frank, an intimate friend of Kahler in the 1960s and author of the best single short essay on Kahler, cited this sample—a synoptic passage, with its characteristic density and detail:

---

[9]   "Denn diese Elite hätte die Aufgabe, in unserer immer mehr technisierten und funktionalisierten Welt das Geistige und Menschliche lebendig zu erhalten, den gemeinschaftlichen Sinn des Volks- und Völkerlebens." Erich Kahler, "Das Schicksal der Demokratie" [1948], in *Grundprobleme der Demokratie* (Darmstadt: Wissenschaftliche Buchgesellschaft, 1973), 63–64. Cited in Gerhard Lauer, "The Empire's Watermark: Erich Kahler and Exile," in *Exile, Science and Bildung, The Contested Legacies of German Émigré Intellectuals*, ed. David Kettler and Gerhard Lauer (New York: Palgrave Macmillan, 2005), 68–69.

[10]   Gerhard Lauer, *Die verspätete Revolution—Erich von Kahler: Wissenschaftsgeschichte zwischen konservativer Revolution und Exil* (Berlin: de Gruyter, 1995), 298.

[11]   Kahler, "Was soll werden?" 300–302.

[12]   Erich Kahler, *Man the Measure: A New Approach to History* (New York: George Braziller, 1956).

On the socio-political plane, the evolution [of mankind] [. . .] proceeds from the theocratic temple-city to the city and city-state, settling down here below as a mundane community (even the Roman Empire is still a city-state); then, through the intermediary of feudal principalities, which were the first to give non-urban territory some political weight, to territorial estates; from the territorial estates to dynastical and nation-states; from nation-states to fully-developed nations representing the whole of the people; from the nations to civilizational and ideological power-blocs, whole continents or even international units; and finally to the technical, technological prefiguration of a "one world," which is psychologically very far from realization, but which looms as the only alternative that science and technology have presented us to their opposite achievement, nuclear or biological annihilation.[13]

Kahler struggled in all the years of his emigration to hold fast to this more hopeful alternative in the light of the atrocious evidence of barbaric recidivism in his homeland—and in every other country in Europe and its environs. His idée fixe was to imagine that even the calamity of the Second World War could end in the production of a better human type and an enlightened human community, answering to what Gerhard Lauer calls "Kahler's aim of detecting in every downfall (*Untergang*) the transition (*Übergang*) to a better world."[14] This is the idea behind Thomas Mann's rather cryptic notion that via the present triumph of fascism "still unknown but necessary aims and purposes" might be achieved that could well have been produced by infinitely less vicious means.[15]

Before their exile from Europe, many of these German intellectuals had been part of "circles," of "schools"—a point that the historian Volker Breidecker has emphasized. Individual scholars—like Kahler and Panofsky and Kantorowicz—who were able to flee and survive chiefly in the United States—were deprived, with the Nazi destruction of such associations, of the social oxygen of fellow scholars.[16] The nascent Kahler Circle could go only a short way to supplying these needs. Kahler, of

---

[13] Joseph N. Frank, "Erich Kahler and the Quest for a Human Absolute," *Responses to Modernity: Essays in the Politics of Culture* (New York: Fordham University Press, 2012), 122. A second admirable essay on Kahler is by George Steiner, "A Note in Tribute to Erich Kahler," *Salmagundi,* no. 10/11 (Fall 1969–Winter 1970): 193–95.

[14] Lauer, Die verspätete Revolution, 143.

[15] EF 31; "ein Instrument zu noch unbekannten, aber notwendigen Zwecken und Zielen" (BR.K 26).

[16] Volker Breidecker, "Einige Fragmente einer intellektuellen Kollektivbiographie der kulturwissenschaftlichen Emigration," in *Erwin Panofsky: Beiträge des Symposions, Hamburg, 1992,* ed. Bruno Reudenbach (Berlin: Akademie Verlag, 1994), 83.

course, was especially fortunate to be so close—physically and affectionately—to Mann, Einstein, and Broch; Kahler was Mann's closest friend; Einstein and Kahler met frequently, as did Broch and Kahler; and Broch lived above Kahler's head at One Evelyn Place in the years 1942–48, where, doted on as a foster son by Erich Kahler's accomplished mother Antoinette, Broch composed *The Death of Virgil.* Broch's "brother" Kahler helped him translate Virgil into idoneous German meters. Kahler did what he could to inspire a sense of community among the Princeton exiles through his exemplary kindness and civility—his hospitality, steady judgment, and readiness to lend intellectual help.

In late 1945, writing to Thomas Mann in defense of the journal *Deutsche Blätter,* Kahler describes the moral dilemma that had confronted him and other German exiles during all their war years in America. I quote from this later letter because it profiles Kahler's equable, balanced character—his probity and judiciousness—qualities that, along with Kahler's stupendous erudition, Mann—and others—found nourishing and even indispensable. Despite its somewhat improvised character, wrote Kahler, the journal, the *Deutsche Blätter,* in which Mann published his encomium, possesses

a fine, courageous, and—something rare in general nowadays and especially among Germans—sure-footed (*instinktsicher*) moral attitude, equidistant from turncoatism (*Renegatentum*) and desertion from the German destiny and unthinking indignation at what is being done to the Germans today, such as we often encounter among honest, completely creditable, thoroughly anti-Nazi Germans. It is true, a great deal is being done to the Germans today. The irresponsibility and cluelessness (*Ahnungslosigkeit*) of the so-called liberators surpass all expectations. But we cannot and must not protest against it without being constantly aware of what the Germans have done themselves. *A qui le dis-je!* [17]

The French flourish signals the superior cultural standpoint from which *these* exiles are contemplating such dilemmas. To further suggest

[17] EF 105. "[. . .] eine schöne, tapfere und—was heute überhaupt und zumal unter Deutschen so rar ist—instinktsichere moralische Haltung, gleich weit entfernt von Renegatentum und Desertion aus dem deutschen Schicksal wie von jener unbekümmerten Empörung über das, was man den Deutschen heute antut, wie man sie selbst unter ganz unverdächtig rechtschaffenen, durch und durch antinazistischen Deutschen jetzt öfters antrifft. Es ist wahr, man tut den Deutschen heute sehr viel an, die Verantwortungs- und Ahnungslosigkeit der sogenannten Befreier geht über alle Erwartungen weit hinaus. Aber man kann und darf dagegen nicht protestieren, ohne dauernd dabei dessen bewußt zu bleiben, was die Deutschen selber angestellt haben. A qui le dis-je!" (BR.K 84–85).

something of Kahler's steadiness and solidity as a scholar of world history, Anna Kiel, the author of a comprehensive intellectual biography of Kahler, contrasts Mann's wobbly judgment on the value of Spengler's *The Decline of the West* with Kahler's clear and "annihilating" verdict, which judged the work "bizarre, pretentious, bloated and barren at the core."[18] There is a good deal of irony in this verdict, as none other than Hugo Hofmannsthal had compared the "telling expression" of reflections on the Austrian mentality in Kahler's first important production—*Das Geschlecht Habsburg* (Habsburg kindred; 1919)—to those of Spengler in *The Decline*.[19] Finally, to mark for the moment Kahler's relentless moral fervor, we have a cogent work by the intellectual historian Mark Greif titled *The Age of the Crisis of Man*.

Greif discusses the distress in mid-century America, including the Princeton circle, at the prospect of the loss of an indelible human substance.[20] To document the general dismay of the intellectual elite, Greif cites from *Man the Measure*: "'The idea of man, the counsel of a new humanism, are certainly the very last things to move the present world to a fundamental change' by themselves, wrote Erich Kahler, '[b]ut we may expect this idea to force itself upon men when the course of events' itself forces it."[21] His citation omits the conclusion to Kahler's sentence, probably owing to its unfashionable moral sentimentality; but to do so is to etiolate Kahler's deeply felt moral imagination. Greif's citation of Kahler omits the key event that might empower again the idea of a common humanity: it is, writes Kahler, the moment at which "the course of events *brings* [. . .] [*men to see*] [. . .] *that man needs goodness as he needs his daily bread.*"[22] "Goodness"? It is not a word that easily passes current today, it does not own a place in a prevailing moral

---

18   "unerhört, prätentiös, aufgebauscht und innerlich öde." Cited in Anna Kiel, *Erich Kahler, Ein "uomo universale" des zwanzigsten Jahrhunderts—seine Begegnungen mit bedeutenden Zeitgenossen: Vom Georgekreis, Max Weber bis Hermann Broch und Thomas Mann* (Bern: Peter Lang, 1989), 179f.

19   Lauer, "The Empire's Watermark," 65.

20   Reflecting on this demand, which was a generally stated problem at the time, the intellectual historian Martin Jay writes, "The idea of the *loss* of a common human substance [. . .] assumes that one knows what it was and when it was shared by everyone. Even during the Greek period, it was hard to pin down. Remember the famous anecdote: after Plato defined men as 'featherless bipeds,' Diogenes Laertius produced a plucked chicken and said, 'Behold, I've brought you a man.' The Academy apparently had to add 'with broad flat nails' to the definition. We have been trying to figure out what a common human substance might be ever since." Fair enough! Personal communication, March 12, 2021.

21   Mark Greif, The Age of the Crisis of Man: Thought and Fiction in America, 1933—1973 (Princeton, NJ: Princeton University Press, 2015), 22.

22   Kahler, *Man the Measure: A New Approach to History* (New York: George Braziller, 1956), 640; emphasis added.

vocabulary, but it is the thing—is it a *thing?*—that Kahler holds onto. It informs, for one, the representation of this crisis in his correspondence with Thomas Mann. Mann wrote: "I have not much faith—or even much faith in faith. I put more faith in goodness, which may exist without faith and may indeed be the product of *art*."[23] Kahler, too, will reach for an aesthetic lever: both are inheritors of German idealism, of Schiller's dictum, also conceived in response to the butchery of war—at that time the French Revolution—namely, "Man only plays when in the full meaning of the word he is a man, and *he is only completely a man when he plays*."[24] With play, we are to think, like Mann and Kahler, of that famously higher form of play—of art. (Mann was vexed again and again when American critics of his *Joseph* novels saw an only pontificated philosophy. For Mann, this was never true: these books were playful in a higher sense; they were designed to excite the play impulse in readers, where they might fully come to realize themselves in what has been called "the freedom of textuality, however meager and marginal that freedom may be."[25]) But to be the artist that Mann was, is not to be the acolyte of the aesthetic worldview a la Nietzsche, let us say—or as Mann did say, "We are no longer aesthetes enough as to fear affirming goodness, to be ashamed of such trivial notions and leading ideas as truth, freedom, justice.[26] Like Kahler, he took the loss of these principles to heart . . . certainly, at least, in the moment of uttering them.

---

23   A radio broadcast, "Thomas Mann's War," BBC Radio 4 FM, December 5, 2005, 0.15; emphasis added. The concept of "goodness" is *not* dead, nor has it lost all its value for political thinkers, as witness Paul Krugman's essay titled "Fall of the American Empire" (emphasis added):

His [Gunnar Myrdal's] belief that there was a core of decency—maybe even *goodness*—to America was eventually vindicated by the rise and success, incomplete as it was, of the civil rights movement.

But what does American *goodness*—all too often honored in the breach, but still real—have to do with American power, let alone world trade? The answer is that for 70 years, American *goodness* and American greatness went hand in hand. Our ideals, and the fact that other countries knew we held those ideals, made us a different kind of great power, one that inspired trust.

The essay goes on to rue the loss of this quality in American policy. Paul Krugman, "Fall of the American Empire," *The New York Times*, June 18, 2018, https://www.nytimes.com/2018/06/18/opinion/immigration-trump-children-american-empire.html.

24   Walter Kaufmann, *Hegel: A Reinterpretation* (Garden City, NY: Anchor Books, Doubleday, 1966), 29.

25   J. M. Coetzee, *Doubling the Point: Essays and Interviews,* ed. David Attwell (Cambridge, MA: Harvard University Press, 1992), 206.

26   "[W]ir [. . .] sind nicht mehr Ästheten genug, uns vor dem Bekenntnis zum Guten zu fürchten, uns so trivialer Begriffe und Leitbilder zu schämen wie

The empirical person Erich von Kahler—now Erich Kahler, having stripped away the syllable of his nobility—arrived in New York on November 3, 1938, and, two days later, on November 5, took the train to Princeton. Mann had vigorously encouraged him to move to Princeton: "What plans do you have? Or rather, what wishes? Naturally, I was thinking of you when I said that the better Europe would gradually be moving here to join 'us.' *Auf Wiedersehen.*"[27] And thereafter we have Mann's conclusion: "The happiest news I gathered was your growing resolution to come over here. Do so! What's the sense of staying now? And how fine it would be to live as neighbors."[28]

On that anticipated Saturday morning, Mann had himself driven to the Princeton Junction train station to meet Kahler; and, after a lengthy lunch, they talked for hours: they had not seen each other for months. Their friendship was actually two decades old: it had begun with a meeting on May 10, 1919, in Munich, at the home of Emil Preetorius.[29] Kahler had been invited to read aloud from the manuscript of his book *The Vocation of Science* (*Der Beruf der Wissenschaft*)—a polemic leveled against Max Weber's famous *Science as a Vocation* (*Die Wissenschaft als Beruf*) that criticized the specialization, remoteness from life, and abstruse impersonality of science. Kahler had another ideal in mind—a resolutely teleological pursuit of the knowledge of the detailed causal nets of empirical reality—a knowledge organic and irrational—of what today could be called "rhizomatic reality."[30] Mann, who was present, was impressed. He noted in his diary:

Wahrheit, Freiheit, Gerechtigkeit" (GW IX:710). Also in: *Nietzsches Philosophie im Lichte unserer Erfahrung, Vortrag am XIV. Kongress des Pen-Clubs in Zurich am 3. Juni 1947*, ed. David Marc Hoffmann (Basel: Schwabe, 2005), 40. The talk was famously delivered in English on April 29, 1947, at the Library of Congress. *Thomas Mann's Addresses Delivered at the Library of Congress, 1942–1949* (Washington, DC: Library of Congress, 1963), 69–103.

27   EF 19. "Welche Pläne haben Sie? Oder doch: welche Wünsche? Natürlich dachte ich an Sie, als ich sagte, das bessere Europa werde sich allmählich zu ‚uns' herüberziehen. Auf Wiedersehen!" (BR.K 17).

28   EF 21. "Das Glücklichste, was ich daraus entnahm, war Ihr sich festigender Entschluß, herüberzukommen. Thun sie das! Was wollen Sie noch drüben? Und wie hübsch wäre es, hier in Nachbarschaft zu leben" (BR.K 18).

29   Preetorius was to make a name for himself as the stage director of several epochal Wagner performances, but at that time (1920) he was an illustrator and producer of book decorations for Mann's books, among others.

30   Erich Kahler, *Der Beruf der Wissenschaft* (Berlin: Georg Bondi, 1920), 21–22. Cited in Lauer, "The Empire's Watermark," 67. For more on "rhizomatic reality," see Gilles Deleuze and Félix Guattari, *A Thousand Plateaus: Capitalism and Schizophrenia*, tr. Brian Massumi (Minneapolis: University of Minnesota Press, 1987), 4.

Severe and pained, in the tone of the George circle to which he is attached, recited, by the way, in a graceful delivery. Conversation with him about the Asian danger, the threatening chaos, the delusion of the Entente, the ghastly old man Clemenceau (who incidentally has slant-eyes and possibly a blood-right to promote the downfall of Western civilization). Agreement in disgust at Munich and the mixture, which in the Räte-Republik, namely, the first, took "shape" (Gestalt). I am very pleasantly touched by the personal and intellectual (geistig) nature of this perhaps 33-year-old. Possibility of a friendship? He might become a new [Ernst] Bertram, though he may not have his childlike affection, which, moreover, I cannot know.[31]

Their friendship would grow ever more intimate, especially, of course, in the years when they were Princeton neighbors.

---

[31] "Streng und schmerzvoll, im Tonfall des George-Kreises, dem er nahe steht, vorgetragen, übrigens mit anmutender Sprechweise. Gespräch mit ihm über die asiatische Gefahr, das drohende Chaos, die Verblendung der Entente, den schauderhaften Greis Clemenceau (der übrigens Schlitzaugen hat und möglicherweise ein Blutrecht darauf hat, dem Untergang der abendländischen Kultur Vorschub zu leisten.) Einverständnis im Ekel an München und der Mischung, die in der Räte-Republik, namentlich der ersten, 'Gestalt' wurde. Ich bin vom persönlichen und geistigen Wesen der etwa 33 jährigen überaus angenehm berührt. Möglichkeit einer Freundschaft? Er könnte ein neuer Bertram werden, wenn er auch wohl nicht dessen kindliche Anhänglichkeit besitzt, was ich übrigens nicht wissen kann." Thomas Mann Tagebücher 1918–1921, May 10, 1919 (Frankfurt am Main: S. Fischer Verlag, 1979), 233; also cited in Lauer, Die verspätete Revolution, 273–74. Hans Rudolf Vaget writes of the importance of the diaries that Mann kept during the postwar years: "Those [. . .] years also saw Mann's own slow and painful ideological 'conversion' from monarchist to republican." "Confession and Camouflage: The Diaries of Thomas Mann," The Journal of English and Germanic Philology 96 no. 4 (Oct. 1997): 570. Mann's 1922 speech, "Von deutscher Republik," has been widely regarded as the turning point in his political development. Whether such a view is in fact justified is the subject of an ongoing debate. For a skeptical view on the question of whether Mann, as artist, subscribed to any bedrock principle of political or ethical action, see Herbert Lehnert and Eva Wessel, Nihilismus der Menschenfreundlichkeit. Thomas Manns "Wandlung" und sein Essay "Goethe und Tolstoi," in Thomas-Mann-Studien, vol. 9 (Frankfurt am Main: Vittorio Klostermann, 1991). Finally, on "the Asian danger": It is clear that at least at this time—1919—both Mann and Kahler identified world civilization entirely with its European variant. Mann's embeddedness in this racialist sensibility calls for a full-scale treatment, which can be found in a luminous work by Professor Todd Kontje titled Thomas Mann's World: Empire, Race, and the Jewish Question (Ann Arbor: University of Michigan Press, 2011), a study of Mann as "a writer whose personal prejudices reflected those of the world around him." The actors in the world of conquest and conflict of 1938 have changed, but Mann's orientalist stereotypes have varied little.

Kahler left Mann's house that day, November 5, 1938, at 4:00 pm; after tea, Mann dined with his future son-in-law Giuseppe Borgese, who would marry Mann's youngest daughter, Elisabeth, in November of the following year. In the evening, Mann wrote a suggestive comment in his diary that bore on the day's contact with Kahler and Borgese. It reads, "Dispute about Fascism and *Menschheitsdämmerung*, exaggerated."[32]

The volume *Menschheitsdämmerung* (The dawn of humanity; 1919) was an epochal anthology of Expressionist poems whose utopian longings were seized on as supports for Kahler's dreamt-of "conservative revolution."[33] The latter called for the coherence and organicity of a *new*—the whole—man, in line with the Nietzschean ideal of a human culture based on "a new and improved *physis* [or: nature]." This increase is to be obtained via a philosophical renaturalization of an original *homo natura*—more pointedly, a scraping away of the accretions of a superficial, rationalistic, moralizing civilization.[34] That creation begins with an abrupt discrediting of the nineteenth-century bourgeois ethos. Already in 1911, eight years before *Menschheitsdämmerung*, Georg Simmel had perceived "a tragedy of culture, contending that the nineteenth century had piled up a 'stock of spiritual objectifications that reached to the sky,' and that such stocks could no longer be restored to living subjectivity."[35] It would be clear

---

[32] "Disput über Fascismus und Menschheitsdämmmerung, übertrieben" (T3 317).

[33] Lauer, *Die verspätete Revolution*, 267.

[34] See Nietzsche on "der Begriff der Kultur als einer neuen und verbesserten Physis," in *Unzeitgemässe Betrachtungen*, Zweites Stück (*Kritische Gesamtausgabe* III-1), 1.330/1.33. But the first task is "to translate man back into nature; to master the many vain and fanciful interpretations and secondary meanings which have been hitherto scribbled and daubed over that eternal basic text *homo natura*." *Beyond Good and Evil*, 230: https://babettebabichregardingnietzsche. blogspot.com/2016/. "Den Menschen nämlich zurückübersetzen in die Natur; über die vielen eitlen und schwärmerischen Deutungen und Nebensinne Herr werden, welche bisher über jenen ewigen Grundtext *homo natura* gekritzelt und gemalt wurden." *Jenseits von Gut und Böse*, "*Siebentes Haupstück* [sic]: *Unsere Tugenden*" (*Kritische Gesamtausgabe* VI-2), 175/5.169.

[35] Inner quote by Georg Simmel, *Der Begriff und die Tragödie der Kultur*, in Georg Simmel, *Das individuelle Gesetz* (Frankfurt am Main: Suhrkamp Verlag, 1987), 143. Outer quote by Lauer, "The Empire's Watermark," 63. "Simmel's concept of the 'tragedy of culture,' adds Martin Jay, "is not only an analysis of a particular period, the 19th century, but of culture in general. It could, of course, be historicized, as it was by Lukács, who claimed it would end with communism. Or it could be contrasted with an imagined period before the fall, a kind of organic society in which art and life were one. Kahler's nostalgia for an original *homo natura*, along with his lament for an Aristotelian notion of organic aesthetic form undermined by modernism [in works to come], expresses his adherence to this latter view. But Simmel would have rejected both alternatives." Personal communication, May 12, 2021.

from the above that Kahler, who was quick to identify the cultural precursors of fascism, would see the expressionist pathos as preparing the way, by a cruel irony, for the Nazi "revolution" and the super-reification of mass man. Siegfried Marck, a political philosopher and good acquaintance of Kahler and Mann, registered, precisely, the "fascist transmutation of a conservatively revolutionary 'myth of *origin*' into a progressivist 'myth of *anticipation*'"—a movement, in Erika Mann's phrase, "expansive and explosive [...] aggressive and bent urgently on action."[36] This botching of an ideal would have pained Kahler in more than one way: Kahler himself, in the view of Gerhard Lauer, wanted to be "the new man and poet, and to achieve this with the unconditionality and decisiveness that inspired the expressionist pathos at the time of World War I, an ethos that required 'full sacrifice of the person, sustained inwardness and great outward self-denial, and mortal exertion,' as Kahler himself expressed it."[37] The Nazis turned "inwardness" inside out, into spontaneous barbarism.

Mann's conversations with Kahler were important enough for Mann to leave occasionally detailed notations in his otherwise parsimonious diaries; I shall aim for a certain calendric completeness in recording their visits in Princeton, hoping that the historian-reader will find a chronicle, with commentary, interesting. On November 21, 1938, for example, Mann talked "with Kahler a lot about the fate of Switzerland, which is now getting the first of its threats. Of course, Switzerland is a relic of liberal times. The coming atomization and Europe's,—to which then the swollen Reich falls prey."[38] Mann's thought is truncated, but the topic is nonetheless visible, and it is one on which Kahler, if we can refer to his 1940 essay "Was soll werden?" (What is to become [of us]?), would have had a lot to say. On Switzerland's precious liberal democracy:

[36] Outer quote by Reinhard Mehring, "A Humanist Program in Exile: Thomas Mann in Philosophical Correspondence with His Contemporaries," in *Exile, Science, and Bildung*, 52. Inner quotes by Siegfried Marck, *Der Neohumanismus als politische Philosophie* (Zurich: Verlag der Aufbruch, 1938), n.p. For Erika Mann's comment, see Robert Galitz, "'A Family against a Dictatorship': Die Rundfunkstrategien der Familie Mann," in *Thomas Mann in Amerika*, ed. Ulrich Rauff and Ellen Strittmatter (Marbach am Neckar: Deutsche Schillergesellschaft, 2019), 45.

[37] Outer quote by Lauer, "The Empire's Watermark," 64; inner quote by Erich Kahler, "alle opfer der person, lange verhaltung nach innen und große enthaltsamkeit nach außen, moralische mühe," "Theater und Zeitgeist," *Jahrbuch für die Geistige Bewegung* 3 (1912): 101. A rich discussion of this passage is in Lauer, *Die verspätete Revolution*, 163.

[38] "Mit Kahler viel über das Schicksal der Schweiz, gegen die die ersten Bedrohungen fallen. Natürlich ist sie ein Relikt aus liberalistischen Zeiten. Die kommende Atomisierung und Europas,—der dann auch das geschwollene Reich verfällt" (T3 323).

Only one country in Europe can be compared to the United States in terms of the explicitness and unrestricted nature of [its] democracy: Switzerland. Only there one finds such a spontaneous unanimity of democratic sentiment; only there, the absence from the ground up of all class differences.[39]

Blessed are they who believe. One must recall that Mann and Kahler had lived productively, for the most part in peace and quiet prosperity, during the years of their exile in Switzerland—Kahler in Ascona and Zurich; Mann in Küsnacht—and Kahler can have been inclined to generalize from his relative contentment. One must stress "relative": foreign intellectuals in Swiss exile suffered countless constraints on their ability to publish or to earn money by their writings, and were never considered eligible for citizenship, i.e., truly welcome. Heinrich Rothmund, the Swiss chief of police, who is notorious for having been charged for decades with conceiving the idea of attaching a large letter "J" to the passport of every European Jew but who has since been exonerated, was nonetheless no friend of refugees fleeing from Nazi brutality. He is quoted as having said, in light of Mann's increasing anti-Nazi political activity, "We have absolutely no interest in the whereabouts of Herr Doktor Thomas Mann"—in effect, "We do not want him here."[40] Mann's letters from America, especially, are decisively ambivalent about his recently abandoned homeland, even while his sense of attachment—even "homesickness"—remains the major tone.[41]

Other words were missing from Mann's diary entry: they might well be intuited from their common hope of the benefit of the *union* of nations even under fascist rule. Kahler's later essay, cited above, speaks urgently of "the need for a mandatory supranational legal system, the plan of the United States of Europe, [which] is already widespread in many minds and has even penetrated into ministerial speeches."[42]

---

[39]   "Es gibt in Europa ein einziges Land, das sich an Eindeutigkeit und Unumschränktheit der Demokratie mit den Vereinigten Staaten vergleichen läßt: die Schweiz. Nur in ihr besteht eine solche spontane Einhelligkeit der demokratischen Gesinnung, nur in ihr fehlen von Grund auf alle ständischen Unterschiede." Kahler, "Was soll werden?" 313.

[40]   Hans-Albert Walter, *Deutsche Exilliteratur 1933–1950*, vol. 2, *Europäisches Appeasement und überseeische Asylpraxis* (Stuttgart: J.B. Metzlersche Verlagsbuchhandlung, 1984), 175.

[41]   Julia Schöll, *Joseph im Exil: Zur Identitätskonstruktion in Thomas Manns Exil-Tagebüchern und -Briefen sowie im Roman "Joseph und seine Brüder"* (Würzburg: Königshausen & Neumann, 2004), 35–48; 179–80.

[42]   "Die Notwendigkeit einer erstmalig zwingenden übernationalen Rechtsordnung, der Plan der Vereinigten Staaten von Europa, geht heute schon in vielen Gemütern um und ist sogar bis in Ministerreden gedrungen." "Was soll werden?" 302.

Within this unity of nations, there would ultimately arise a common impulse, even under the fascist knout, to cast off or let die the national government—and that would be an end to conflict among nations!

This idea, especially in its second iteration, seems extraordinary; it is all the more haunting to see it represented in *The New York Times* two days later, on November 23, 1938, in a midweek book review of Mann's *This Peace*, his scathing indictment of the Munich Agreement. The reviewer is Ralph Thompson, who paraphrases Mann's intuition of a "consoling effect" of the crisis:

> With the entire continent ruled by fascism, there would be at least a chance of establishing a United States of Europe, which in time might discard its original philosophy as idle or even useless. Jerome Frank raised this point in a book published last summer, and it is hardly as fantastic as it may sound. Mr. Mann explains why by declaring that "as fascism excludes peace, so peace excludes fascism."[43]

It would be interesting to capture Jerome Frank's original formulation of this idea in a book published in the summer of 1938: that book can only be his *Save America First: How to Make our Democracy Work*.[44] But Frank does not say that a triumphant totalitarian fascism will bring about a united Europe. At the same time, he is crystal clear—trenchant and insistent—on the point that only European integration could save the continent from a perpetual, lethal economic competition—that is to say: from perpetual war. His words are worth quoting in this context at some length.

> That struggle in each European country today may be considered as a phase of the fight for continental integration. It may be that that fight cannot be won under industrialized "Capitalism," because each of the Capitalist groups in each separate nation has

43 Ralph Thompson, "Books of the Times," November 3, 1938, https://timesmachine.nytimes.com/timesmachine/1938/11/23/98211874.pdf.

44 Jerome New Frank, *Save America First: How to Make Our Democracy Work* (New York and London: Harper and Brothers, 1938). Further references to this work will be assigned a page number in parenthesis. Frank (thus Wikipedia [July 21, 2021, at 05:58 UTC], which is highly informative in this instance) was a Chicago-educated "American legal philosopher and author who played a leading role in the legal realism movement." In addition to serving in such advanced capacities as chairman of the Securities and Exchange Commission in 1937 and thereafter as a United States circuit judge of the United States Court of Appeals for the Second Circuit, he was the author of redoubtable works of legal philosophy.

a vested interest in its separate national set-up, and the resistance of each such group to European unification is therefore undeniably violent; perhaps, therefore, only Communism will make this integration possible. But European continental integration, whether under one or another system, is today the fundamental issue. We in America must not confuse the European issue. We must see that the striving for indispensable unity underlies the contest between Fascism and Communism in European countries.

(28–29)

The Communists say that it was the presence of Capitalism that caused the difficulties of Italy and Germany. The Fascists say that the cause was the presence of political democracy. Analysis seems to show that the basic cause was neither the presence of Capitalism nor of political democracy—but the absence of continental integration.

Fascism in any European country is a desperate program of the economically powerful to save the situation and to retain much of their own power while maintaining the profit system. [. . .] Faced with that misery [of economic privation] and the danger it involves of the destruction of their own privileges, the economic rulers in each European country have sought to avert, or are flirting with the idea of averting, that destruction by a political dictatorship conducted primarily in their interest.

(29–30)

For so long as European countries remain separate entities, their living standards must inevitably be degraded, because those standards are based on too narrow a foundation of resources. It is that underlying factor that presages doom and breeds the despair which, in turn, fosters the growth of Communism and thus provokes Fascism.

(35)

Fascism is a desperate effort to seize absolute power in order to command the crew of a sinking ship. The hole in the European ship, which is making it sink, was made by a collision with the implacable fact that an unintegrated Europe is in a condition of economic anarchy and that no one of the several European nations can today approach self-sufficiency.

(35)

There [in Europe], a group obsession—the devotion to the perpetuation of separate small national states—is bringing about a condition in which the profit system cannot operate. There is a fatal contradiction between that valued institution and the equally valued institution of the small independent national state. We are now witnessing the consequences of that contradiction. In an effort to avoid those consequences Germany and Italy abandoned democracy. Such abandonment was not too difficult in Germany, for she had remained predominantly feudal well into the nineteenth century. And Bismarck had accustomed that country to a kind of dictatorship not entirely different from Hitler's, so that dictatorship has long been a part of the German mores.

(36–37)

The last sentence, in particular, coincides with a point Mann would make repeatedly in his public speeches on behalf of democracy. On the other hand, on the topic of America's being urged, wrongfully in Frank's view, to declare war on Nazi Germany—a view not yet fully publicly advanced by Mann—Frank writes, "*There might be some point in America's fighting or threatening to fight to unify Europe; such a consummation might be worth sacrifices on our part for it would probably ensure future peace in Europe.*" But here he departs radically from Mann's late Anglophile preferences: "*In such an enterprise, however, England would not be our friend or ally but our enemy. She does not want peace in Europe by means of European integration; that is a price she has always presumed to pay*" (162).[45]

Frank's antipathy to England's anti-democratic character and to any notion of bonding with England in a war against Germany comes as no surprise. Earlier, Frank had declared England's colonialist policies to be nothing less than proto-fascism in action: "Their treatment of the Irish, for at least *a hundred years*, throughout the nineteenth century and in the twentieth century until recently, was only slightly (if at all) better than Germany's treatment of the Jews *for the past five years*" (156–57). Frank then cites the famously atrocious refusal of the British to allow their navy to ship food to Ireland, knowing full well that to do so meant starving some Irish to death; and he cites reports of horrible tortures and hangings inflicted on Egyptian villagers by irritated, exercised British officers (427). It needs to be added, however, that by early 1940 Frank had abandoned all his liberal, isolationist assumptions. "It is to [. . .] [his] credit that [. . .] he came to see the impossibility of isolating

---

[45]   For Mann's gratitude to England for its resistance to the Nazis, see his essay "This War," tr. Eric Sutton, in *Order of the Day, Political Essays and Speeches of Two Decades* (New York: Knopf, 1942), 186–227.

America from the events in Europe. Unlike many other liberals of his day, he was able to [. . .] recognize the threat which Hitler presented to the institutions and traditions of Western democracy."[46]

In a diary entry in Sweden on September 5, 1939, following the German invasion of Poland, Mann will return to the view of a triumphant fascism *ultimately* enabling an integrated Europe by citing a less radical variation of the idea. It is a citation from what appears to be a conversation with none less than H. G. Wells: "One must hope that the war lasts a long time so that the necessary social changes can occur— changes that lead to a European federalism and a liberal collectivism."[47] It is bemusing to consider whether, after decades of immeasurable suffering, the European Union today might be regarded as the dialectical fulfillment of such a possibility. It has proved precarious. The noble idea of a European confederation achieves a grotesque completeness— with serious political thinking returning as farce—in Mann's diary report on November 16, 1939:

> Almost sick from the morning on from an interview with Papen [Franz von Papen, former vice-chancellor under Hitler], in which he proclaimed the European Confederation as Germany's war aim! Commonwealth! Nazi Commonwealth! Every time one would have thought that so much shameless stupidity, stupid shamelessness were not possible.[48]

Mann's conversations with Kahler do not falter in their apparent intensity and the degree to which they engage him. On December 21, 1938, he discussed with Kahler the newest book of Ernst Jünger—*Auf den Marmorklippen* (On the Marble Cliffs)—which, Mann writes, "is bound to be a painful [*arge*] entertainment."[49] This phrase may be an echo of Kahler's grim view: Kahler's idea might very well have been as

---

46 Walter E. Volkomer, *The Passionate Liberal: The Political and Legal Ideas of Jerome Frank* (The Hague: Martinus Nijhoff, 1970), 205.

47 "Man muß wünschen, daß der Krieg lange dauert, damit die nötigen sozialen Veränderungen sich vollziehen können, die zum europ. Foederalismus und einem liberalen Kollektivismus führen" (T3 465).

48 "Fast krank von morgens an von einem Interview Papens, worin er als Deutschlands Kriegsziel die europäische Confoederation proklamiert!! Commonwealth! Nazi-Commonwealth! Jedesmal hätte man so viel schamlose Dummheit, dumme Schamlosigkeit nicht für möglich gehalten" (T3 501).

49 "Kahler über das neueste Buch von E. Jünger, das eine arge Unterhaltung sein muß" (T3 335).

radical then, in Mann's living room, as it was years later in Kahler's essay "The Germans," in which he considers *Auf den Marmorklippen* part of the extreme guilt Jünger bears—"the heaviest responsibility for preparing German youth for the Nazi state."[50] On New Year's Day 1939, Mann and Kahler talked "a lot of politics and history" over champagne, invoking "Heine, Nietzsche, Napoleon, Bismarck, the Germans, and the clearing out of the mask of reactionary politics (*die Reaktion*) and the most rancid moral attitude. A botching (*Verhunzung*) of history."[51] Three days later they again dined together in advance of "an animated philosophical conversation" ("Angeregtes philosophisches Gespräch" [T3 344]). A week later, on January 9, 1939, Mann recorded an "evening [spent with] Kahler, reading the lecture [on Wagner's *Ring*] aloud to him [. . .] to the extent that I've written it, which even so lasted more than an hour. Discussion. The pedagogical aspect noted with approval. The omission of Marx tactically right. The Christian dimension as a defensive barrier. The conclusion still tricky."[52] The dates suggest a heightening of their intimacy and undeniable need for one another as conversational partners: in the following months and years there would be a great many such evenings.

Kahler was there for Mann; Mann trusted his advice. On January 19, 1939, Mann had been "unsettled and distracted by a question circulated by the journal *Common Sense*, asking for a response to an article by Bertrand Russell that counseled America's neutrality in the perhaps coming war. [. . .] After dinner," Mann notes, "[With] Kahler, at my request, to discuss the Russell question. It is the wrong question, not one I may answer."[53] Russell was then teaching at City College in New York: the article in question concerned "The Case for American Neutrality."

The public intellectual Selden Rodman had organized a poll of the opinions of a number of prominent intellectuals; Mann replied that he

50   Erich Kahler, *The Germans*, ed. Robert and Rita Kimber (Princeton, NJ: Princeton University Press, 1974), 290.
51   "Nachher Kahler, Champagne. Viel Politik und Geschichte. Heine, Nietzsche, Napoléon, Bismarck, die Deutschen und das Aufräumen in der Maske der Reaktion u. des ranzigsten Gemütes. Verhunzung der Geschichte" (T3 343).
52   "Abends Kahler. Vorlesung vor ihm des Vortrags [über Wagners *Ring*] soweit ich ihn geschrieben, was schon mehr als eine Stunde dauerte. Diskussion. Das Pädagogische beifällig bemerkt. Die Auslassung Marxens taktisch richtig. Das Christliche als Schutzwehr. Der Schluß noch heikel" (T3 345).
53   " [. . .] Zerstreut und abgelenkt durch eine Rundfrage von *Common Sense* über Artikel B. Russels [*sic*], der Amerika Neutralität im vielleicht nahen Kriege rät. [. . .] Nach dem Abendessen auf meinen Wunsch Kahler, zur Besprechung der Russel-Frage. Sie ist falsch gestellt und für mich nicht zu beantworten" (T3 349).

was unable to express his views, since as a noncitizen he was reluctant to intervene in the political affairs of his host country. But he then did compose a response—"laboriously," "scrupulously, pénible[ment]"— and, the following day, "tossed it off in a rage," angered by Russell's main thesis, namely, "the advisability of American neutrality in the war which, as many believe, is inevitable."[54] Mann's reply reads:

In the first paragraph of his essay, Mr. Russell warns the political left against believing that the war, when it comes, will be anything like a holy war. He says that it will be a war like any other, a war for imperialist and economic purposes. I do not quite agree with him. The word "holy" is not just a word of palliation but a terrifying word whose vengeful sense mocks human affirmation or negation; and the "sanctity" of this war, were it to come, would lie in its objective character as a catastrophe, the logical, moral consequence of the unbearable shamefulness that Europe has made itself guilty of during the last decades in acting—*and tolerating* [such action]—against spirit, morality, and humanity. That an epoch that makes every better person spiritually sick and denies to the famished moral craving even the least refreshment; that an epoch so dominated by falsehood, wickedness, and the unbelievable toleration of evil would end in a bloodbath such as the world has not yet seen—[all] that would have a horrible *rightness*; it would be gratifying for the spirit that insists on its rights, deeper even than all the creaturely horror with which such an incalculably terrible court of judgment would fill us all.

To summon this war, to incite it, to put upon ourselves any responsibility for the devastation it would bring; Heaven forbid each one of us from such a thing. On the contrary, all credit to him who, when evil comes, can say to himself that he has done his best to avert it and has made every effort to control the rise of the powers and to clarify their true nature, which, because he has let them grow large, will one day force the world to war. This day, however, seems rather remote, for the full insight into the moral as well as the physical threat to the order of the world emanating

---

54   "[. . .] Arbeit an der Replik, skrupulös, pénibel. [. . .] Die Antwort an Russell zornig hingeworfen." "[in re] seine Haupt- und Schluß-These, nämlich der Ratsamkeit amerikanischer Neutralität in dem, wie viele glauben, unvermeidlichen Kriege"(T3 357, 895).

from those powers has not yet matured and will probably be withheld from the people in the future.[55]

Mann's (clairvoyant) views were fiercely attacked; but only a few months later, Russell abandoned his pacifist stance. In the weeks following, Mann recorded a potent observation by the philosopher Max Horkheimer in the notable *Zeitschrift für Sozialforschung* in New York. Horkheimer had assumed ("rightly," thus Mann) that he, Mann, did not feel altogether easy with the philosophical-political message that had been "put into his custody." Horkheimer, as Mann notes, "speaks of the transparent coloring (*Lasurfarbe*) of irony, which the experienced reader still detects in my political compositions."[56] But while this judgment might apply decisively to Mann's earlier *Reflections*

---

[55] "Mr. Russell warnt im ersten Paragraphen seines Aufsatzes die politische Linke, zu glauben, daß der Krieg, wenn er kommt, irgend etwas wie ein Heiliger Krieg sein werde. Er werde, sagt er, ein Krieg wie jeder andere, ein Krieg um imperialistischer und ökonomischer Ziele willen sein. Ich bin nicht ganz seiner Ansicht. Das Wort 'heilig' ist nicht nur ein Wort der Beschönigung, sondern ein schreckensvolles Wort, dessen rächender Sinn menschlicher Bejahung oder Verneinung spottet; und die 'Heiligkeit' dieses Krieges, wenn er käme, läge objektiv in seinem Charakter als einer Katastrophe, welche die logisch-moralische Folge der unerträglichen Schändlichkeiten wäre, deren Europa sich während der letzten Jahrzehnte handelnd *und duldend* gegen Geist, Moral und Menschheit schuldig gemacht hat. Daß eine Epoche, die jeden besseren Menschen gemütskrank macht und dem lechzenden moralischen Bedürfnis auch das kleinste Labsal verweigert; daß eine dermaßen von Lüge, Niedertracht und unmöglicher Duldung des Bösen beherrschte Epoche in ein Blutbad ausginge, wie die Welt es noch nicht gesehen hat, das hätte seine entsetzliche *Richtigkeit*, es läge darin für den auf seinem Rechte bestehenden Geist eine Genugtuung, tiefer noch, als alles kreatürliche Grauen, mit dem ein so unabsehbar schreckliches Strafgericht uns alle erfüllen würde.
"Diesen Krieg herbeizurufen, zu ihm aufzureizen, irgendwelche Verantwortung für die Verheerungen, die er bringen würde, auf uns zu laden, davor bewahre der Himmel einen jeden von uns. Wohl vielmehr jedem, der, wenn das Unheil hereinbricht, sich sagen kann, daß er sein Bestes getan hat, es abzuwenden und zwar, indem er nach seinen Kräften bemüht war, dem Aufkommen der Mächte zu steuern und über ihr wahres Wesen aufzuklären, die, da man sie hat groß werden lassen, die Welt wohl eines Tages zum Kriege zwingen werden. Dieser Tag aber scheint noch ziemlich fern, weil nämlich die volle Einsicht in die moralische sowohl wie physische Bedrohung, die von jenen Mächten auf die Ordnung der Welt ausgeht, noch nirgends herangereift ist und den Völkern auch wohl künftig vorenthalten wird" (T3 895–96).

[56] "Horkheimer [. . .] nimmt mit Recht an, daß ich mich bei der zugesprochenen philosophisch-politischen Botschaft nicht wohl fühle. Spricht von der Lasurfarbe der Ironie, die der Erfahrene noch über meinen politischen Kompositionen entdeckt" (T3 361–62).

of a Nonpolitical Man—and to unnamed essays thereafter—it hardly applies to his enraged rebuttal to Russell's pacifism.

Perpetually in demand by the needs of others and foremost by his own artistic superego, which craved to finish his Goethe novel, Mann nonetheless took the time to listen to Kahler's reading of Kahler's own work—and was quick with his praise. On February 1, 1939, after dinner at the Kahlers with Erich and his talented and cultivated mother—the artist and amateur classical scholar Antoinette von Kahler—Kahler read aloud his essay "The Moral Unity of the World," intended for an American magazine, which Mann judged "good, apt, and useful" ("gut, richtig und nützlich"; D 318, T3 355). Regrettably, Kahler's text was never published, nor was it found in his surviving papers.

It might be pertinent at this juncture to recall that on Kahler's arrival in Princeton in late 1938, he was severely strapped financially. Everything he owned in Germany had been confiscated by the Nazis. This situation had a profound effect on his mode of production as a writer. He was no longer an independent scholar, as he had been in the 1920s, writing from his villa in Wolfrathshausen and living on inherited wealth. He was now a journalist and itinerant academic battling for his life. If during his pre-exilic—by contrast—paradisiacal freedom as a writer he published articles now and again, the quantity of such pieces in the following four decades jumped fourfold.

Mann was not shy of showing off to his company of powerful admirers his learned though penurious friend and the very accomplished Antoinette (T3 359). On February 11, 1939, a Saturday evening, the Manns hosted an elegant "soirée" at home. The guests—a select company in formal dress—will tell us which persons Mann was especially happy to honor: the "Flexners"—Abraham Flexner, the intellectual eminence behind the Bamberger family's funding of the Institute for Advanced Study in Princeton, quite particularly Einstein's patron, and thereafter director of the institute between 1930 and 1939; the "Gauss"—meaning, Dean Gauss, Mann's patron at the university, and his wife; "Lowe"—H. T. Lowe-Porter, Mann's translator, together, very likely, with her husband, the distinguished paleographer resident at the institute; and then, unmissably, the "Kahlers." Kahler was a standing guest at the Manns' dinner parties, as when—looking ahead to January 17, 1940—he once more joined Mann's good acquaintances: the Lowe-Porters; Dean Gauss of Princeton and his wife; and the Shenstones. Alan Shenstone, a professor of physics at Princeton, vigorously supported Mann's political views—Mann thought him a very good man—and his wife Molly, a dear friend of Katia Mann, was also helpful to Mann in matters of translation and enunciation (T4 9).

Kahler was again invited to the Manns on the evening of February 14, 1939, for a meeting of minds (Mann's oldest son, Klaus, was also present) on the topic of the (dim) possibility of a novel about "National Socialism." Mann's comments in his diaries, whenever Kahler was at hand, are detailed the way conversations with others at Princeton are not. The discussion concluded with the impossibility of bringing art to fascism—this grotesque degradation of life, a "lifeless abomination."

> Kahler came after dinner. Klaus gave a reading from his émigré novel [*Der Vulkan. Roman unter Emigranten* (1939)]. Aesthetic and political discussion. The impossibility of a satirical novel (*Dead Souls*). The phenomenon of National Socialism's being undeserving of the artist's skill. Failure or despair or renunciation of the word, the feebleness of denunciation. Have reality and art ever before been so utterly incompatible? Art not applicable to "life." The deadliness of Nazism, the paralysis it spreads.[57]
>
> (D 319)

The "Goethe novel," on which Mann was working—a partly satirical work nonetheless embedding a grand reality—casts the alternative into the teeth of this impossibility. And how rewarding it was for Mann once again, in front of Kahler and Mann's wife and children—Katia, Erika, Golo, and Medi [Elisabeth]—to read aloud, in emphatic, near ecstatic italic, "the almost thirty recently written pages of the seventh chapter— the Goethe monologue—of *Lotte in Weimar*," whose "charm and esteem" ("Ansehen und Reiz"), he was to record, had increased as a result (T3 363).

Dinners with Kahler invariably concluded with conversations about German literature, history, and politics. Kahler was crucial to Mann's maintaining his prized "Germanness"—the feeling of being a representative of the German language at its national height, and the intellectual life conducted through it and embedded in it. Typically, on March 6, 1939, we read of Mann's visit to the Kahlers (in enthusiastic italic!) for dinner: "Champagne afterwards and drinking to one another's well-being. Kahler read from [Friedrich] Gundolf's *Literary History in Verse* [a spoof, still in manuscript], a gift to F. K. [Fine Kahler, Erich's estranged wife]—an intimate knowing play with language and Germanness. [We spoke] about [Stefan] George"—the latter a pregnant topic. As a young man Kahler was close to George yet sought and

---

57 "Nach dem Abendessen Kahler. Vorlesung Klaus aus seinem Emigrationsroman. Ästhetische und politische Diskussion. Unmöglichkeit des satirischen Romans ('Tote Seelen'). Das Phänomen 'Nat. Sozialismus' der künstlerischen Kraft nicht würdig. Versagen oder Verzagen oder Entsagen des Wortes, Mattheit des Schimpfs. War es je, daß Wirklichkeit und Kunst so völlig inadäquate Sphären wurden? Kunst nicht anwendbar auf das 'Leben.' Lebloser Greuel, Ohnmacht verbreitend" (T3 361).

maintained his independence. Mann speaks of "resistance" on his own part, as he conjures Hofmannsthal, a poetic counterweight to George.[58] When Kahler is mentioned in these diaries, his name *almost always* appears in italic—a distinction reserved for him alone among the many hundreds of persons found there.

On the very evening following Mann's return from a strenuous March-April 1939 cross-country lecture trip, Kahler (once again in enthusiastic italic!) was his guest, as if Mann could hardly wait to be with him again and discuss an urgent topic of the moment: what Mann calls the dark side of Roosevelt's critical message to Hitler and Mussolini on April 14, 1939—following Italy's invasion of Albania—asking their readiness to sign a nonaggression pact with some thirty nations. Mann had taken note of its "dark side" in conversations a few days earlier in Washington: "A memorable document, but two-edged. A calculated move for reasons of domestic policy? Is it not plain that Hitler could not be a member of a peaceful world?"[59] Mann is continually aware of the war dynamic of fascism, its vile entelechy: "But how will they survive peace?"[60]

I would like to continue to proceed calendrically, in the manner of a chronicle: in this manner, something of the tempo and concrete flavor of their meetings can be conveyed in a way that a single, generalizing picture cannot. But this matter might also prove skeletal, with too little conversational meat on the bones of the bare facts of their meetings. Yet even these "flavors"—hints or even absent mentions—should heighten the sense of how very often they were together and how deeply they needed their friendship, and so I have continued this chronicle as an Appendix I. It is there for the reader who does not want to miss *anything* of the Mann-Kahler friendship! But several mentions are finally too interesting to relegate there, as follows:

On July 8, 1940, Mann notes from California, where he has been spending the summer, that he has written an "extensive, detailed" ("ausführlich") letter to Kahler. It is a poignant letter, full of the evidence of intimate trust: "I feel the need to say how much we wish that we had you here together with us during this period of agonizing and numbing expectation. It is painful and constricting that we should be so far apart now of all times." It takes up the pressing political concerns of the

[58]   "Champagner nach Tisch und Lebenswohl getrunken. Kahler las aus Gundolfs Vers- Literaturgeschichte vor. [. . .] Vertrautes Spiel mit Sprache und Deutschtum. Über George. Abwehr meinerseits. (Hofmannsthal)" (T3 369).

[59]   "Denkwürdiges Dokument, aber zweischneidig. Innenpolitischer Schachzug? Ist es klar, daß Hitler nicht Mitglied einer Friedenswelt sein kann?" (D 326; T3 392).

[60]   "Aber wie wollen sie [die faschistischen Länder] Frieden ertragen?" (D 327; T3 407).

moment, "a ghastly situation": the Nazi war victories, England's uncertain capacity for resistance. Mann doubts whether even his hitherto dependable access to "a kind of personal serenity" can relieve the feeling of being trapped in a defenseless horror: hence, surely, this *cri de coeur* to his friend.[61] June 6, 1940: "Dinner with Kahler [among others] [. . .]. Kahler all too admiring of Hitler. [Mann:] Furious!"[62] The course of true friendship never did run smooth. After a long conversation between them some years earlier, Mann noted in his journal, "Kahler's objective recognition of the positive [dimension] of what is happening in Germany (what cannot be done) goes dangerously far."[63] As an historian of life forces, Kahler was prepared to lend meaning impartially to every eruption, thinking that none would end altogether badly given the ineluctably progressive thrust of human history. One could worry, along with Mann, just how much personal and moral pain Kahler was prepared to endure and to grant to "Hitler" as a premium in exchange for the perception of Hitler's historical significance. In this sense, the Kahler Circle would verge on a victimary circle.[64] George Steiner has put this

---

61 "Ich habe das Bedürfnis [. . .] Ihnen zu sagen, wie sehr wir wünschten, Sie hier zu haben, damit wir diese Zeit quälender und lähmender Erwartung zusammen verbringen könnten. Es ist schmerzlich und beeinträchtigend, daß man gerade jetzt so weit auseinander ist. [. . .] Die Lage ist furchtbar. [. . .] Ich habe immer daran geglaubt, daß eine gewisse heitere Bestimmung des Persönlich-Individuellen sich auch gegen das düsterste Äußere durchsetzt. [. . .] Aber jetzt fühle ich mich oft heillos in die Enge getrieben" (T4 114; EF 31; BR.K 26).

62 "Abendessen mit [. . .] Kahler. [. . .] Kahler allzu bewunderungsvoll über Hitler. Zornig" (T4 92).

63 "Zum Abendessen E. v. *Kahler*, der klug und sympathisch war wie immer, aber in seinem objektiven Anerkennen des Positiven, was in Deutschland geschehe (nicht getan werde) gefährlich weit geht" (September 28, 1935). Thomas Mann, *Tagebücher 1935–1936*, ed. Peter de Mendelssohn (Frankfurt am Main: S. Fischer Verlag, 1978), 180.

64 "The victimary circle" is a concept employed by Fernando Bermejo-Rubio to interpret Kafka's story *The Metamorphosis*. In its light, the "hero's" physical metamorphosis into a "monstrous vermin" is not a real event but a delusion inspired by other people's view of him. Once assailed by (many) others' low opinion, one agrees to find it reasonable and begins to conform to it, which in turn "proves" the charge that one is vermin indeed and justifies the power of one's persecutor. See "Does Gregor Samsa Crawl over the Ceiling and Walls? Intra-narrative Fiction in Kafka's 'Die Verwandlung,'" *Monatshefte* 105, no. 2 (2013): 278–314. Wouldn't Mann fear that his Jewish friends in exile might be especially vulnerable? One reads in *Circumfession*, an autobiographical text published by Jacques Derrida in 1991, that "whether they expelled me from school, or threw me into prison, I always thought the other must have good reason to accuse me." Cited in John Gray, "Deconstructing Jackie," a review of Peter Salmon, *An Event, Perhaps: A Biography of Jacques Derrida* (London: Verso, 2020), https://www.newstatesman.com/an-event-perhaps-biography-jacques-derrida-review.

conundrum incisively, noting, with concern, Kahler's "almost ontological optimism, the classic strength of his faith in man," which may have blinded him to an urgent question. "The barbarism of our time [. . .] arose in the very heartland of high civilization." Might there be "a powerful element in fact within civilization, that not only failed to oppose barbarism but helped produce it? Do the habits of mental abstraction, of fictional conceptualization, which liberal humanism placed at the center of its educational process [*Bildung*] in some way incapacitate men's more immediate political reflexes?" The necessary goal, as Thomas Mann perceived with special emphasis, would be a "politics of civilized life."[65]

Martin Jay has also commented trenchantly on Mann's fury at Kahler's expression of sympathy for aspects of Nazism: "It shows the difference between a genuine conservative and a conservative revolutionary. Perhaps this is why Kahler could combine his meta-narrative of civilizational decline with optimism about the future. You need an apocalypse to push out the rotten culture that is dying in order to make way for its replacement."[66]

As an interlude in this angry matter:—Mann, who has written to Kahler, receives a letter from his friend on July 24, 1940, that he judges "beautiful" (*schön*): it is Kahler's letter from Woodstock, New York, dated July 20, expressing his gratitude for Mann's display of warmth and intimacy (T4 121). It is good to quote; it makes up the heart of our thesis of the importance and intensity of their friendship and their shared purposes.

> Your news was eagerly awaited, and your letter, however freighted it was, was comforting and warming in its affirmation of human intimacy. I don't need to tell you how awful it is for *me* to be apart from you for so long. What is left to us in this gruesome world other than the few people to whom one is attached and together with whom it is easier to carry the burden one has to carry! I am moved to hear you speak in a way I am not used to hearing from you: I was always happy to let you lead me to brighter vistas; I was so grateful for your faith, and I often enough blamed myself for my skepticism, which I could not keep secret. Underneath, I *never* believed in an Allied victory ever since

---

[65]   George Steiner, "A Note in Tribute to Erich Kahler," *Salmagundi* 10/11 (Fall 1969–Winter 1970): 193–94.

[66]   Martin Jay, "Commentary," personal communication, May 12, 2021. For more on Kahler's apocalyptic thinking, see Introduction, footnote 18, *supra*.

Munich, yes, since Spain, since Baldwin, and Blum, and even more so ever since the first days of Chamberlain and Daladier; and it seems to me in no way illogical the way things have come about. I felt too strongly the way the wind was blowing, I was too convinced of the depth of the transformation which we are going through. When I look back now, everything I have ever done seems to me only an attempt to save, to preserve, to transport what was dear to us, to help this transformation, through intellectual-spiritual control, achieve the goal that in one or another way it must come to. It was a childish undertaking, because upheavals of such dimensions necessarily take the sort of elemental path that sets the masses of earth and filth in motion.

Forgive me for speaking like this, although I am aware that your hundredfold efforts outside and inside your poetic work went in the same direction. But we must admit: it doesn't help; yet I believe one thing in spite of and beyond everything, that it will not have been for nothing—one day, beyond ourselves. We could not keep anything from humanity. There was not enough time for preparation and education, there was not enough human space for the development of the impetus for goodness. The necessity of circumstances and drives is faster and more powerful.

Oddly enough—I wonder myself about it—I am not quite as pessimistic about this country as you, although I also recognize the danger as enormous. But I can still feel fresh forces of resistance here, and their primitiveness and torpor can benefit both good and bad. In any case, it is worth every last effort to recruit, to wake up, to make people aware of what is at stake: we have no other choice. We shouldn't and may not give up as long as we still possess a measure of life.[67]

---

[67] "Lieber und verehrter Freund: Ihre Nachrichten waren schon sehnlich erwartet, und Ihr Brief, wie belastet er auch klingt, war doch tröstlich und erwärmend durch die Bekräftigung menschlicher Nähe. Ich brauche Ihnen nicht zu sagen, wie arg *mir* ist, in dieser Zeit so lang von Ihnen getrennt zu sein. Was bleibt einem noch in dieser grausigen Welt als die wenigen Menschen, an denen man hängt und mit denen gemeinsam man doch leichter trägt, was getragen werden muß! Es ergreift mich, Sie so reden zu hören, wie ich es nicht von Ihnen gewohnt bin: so gerne hab ich mich ja immer von Ihnen mitnehmen lassen in lichtere Ausblicke, so dankbar war ich für ihren Glauben, und oft genug habe ich mich angeklagt wegen meiner Skepsis, die ich nicht zum Schweigen bringen konnte! Im Untergrunde habe ich *nie*, seit München, ja seit Spanien, seit Baldwin und Blum schon und erst recht seit den ersten Tagen von Chamberlain und Daladier, an einen Sieg der Alliierten geglaubt, und es erscheint mir nicht anders als folgerichtig, so wie es gekommen ist. Zu sehr hab ich die Windrichtung gespürt,

But it will be good to conclude this part of the chronicle with the evening of March 17, 1941, Mann's last night in Princeton, which he spent with Kahler in Princeton's "French Restaurant," surely Lahiere's on Witherspoon Street. Lahiere's continued to serve guests of the university for another sixty-nine years (T4 235). The friends said their goodbyes and went "home." Weeks later, on April 1, 1941, in California, Mann wrote a letter to Agnes Meyer containing a dispositive word about his friendship with Erich Kahler. His pen heavy with a sense of obligation to her, Mann wrote, "Next to our saying goodbye to you, saying goodbye to our friend Kahler [. . .] was the saddest, the most wistful (*wehmütigste*)."[68]

Postscript

To understand Kahler better, and something of the asymmetry of his relationship with Mann, I will cite a powerful letter from Kahler to Mann soon after Mann had decamped to Pacific Palisades. Here Kahler speaks of the "animal" passion with which intellectuals of his ilk pursue

---

zu sehr war ich überzeugt von dem Tiefgang der Umwandlung, in der wir begriffen sind. Wenn ich jetzt zurückschaue, so erscheint mir alles, was ich je unternommen habe, nur als ein Versuch zu retten, zu bewahren, überzuführen, was uns teuer war, dazu beizutragen, daß diese Umwandlung durch eine geistige Beherrschung zu dem Ziele gelangt, das sie so oder so erreichen muß. Es war ein kindliches Unterfangen, denn Umwälzungen von solcher Dimension gehn notwendig den elementaren Weg, der die Erdmassen und die Dreckmassen in Bewegung setzt. Verzeihen Sie, daß ich so rede, wiewohl ich mir dessen bewusst bin, dass Ihre hundertfältigen Bemühungen außerhalb wie auch innerhalb Ihres dichterischen Werks den gleichen Sinn verfolgten. Aber es hilft ja nichts, wir müssen es uns eingestehn, und das eine glaube ich ja trotz allem und über alles hinaus, daß es dennoch nicht für nichts gewesen sein wird, einmal, jenseits unsrer selbst. Nur ersparen konnten wir der Menschheit nichts. Da war nicht Zeit genug für Vorbereitung und Erziehung, da war nicht menschlicher Raum genug für die Entfaltung des Impetus zum Guten. Die Not der Umstände und der Triebe ist schneller und gewaltiger.

"Merkwürdigerweise—ich wundere mich selbst darüber—bin ich für hier nicht ganz so pessimistisch wie Sie, wenn ich auch die Gefahr als riesengroß erkenne. Aber ich spüre hier noch frische Kräfte des Widerstandes, und ihre Primitivität und Dumpfheit kann ebenso dem Guten wie dem Bösen zugutekommen. Es ist jedenfalls unsere letzte Anstrengung wert, hier zu werben zu wecken, bewußt zu machen, um was es geht, und es bleibt uns ja auch nichts andres übrig. Aufgeben sollen und dürfen wir es ja nicht, solang uns noch eine Spanne zum Leben bleibt" (BR.K 28–29). Freer translation at EF 33.

[68] "Nach dem Abschied von Ihnen war der von unserem Freunde Kahler [. . .] der wehmütigste" (BR.M 260).

their work. "Anyone who has ever been really obsessed with a many-layered project understands that craving to get to work, and to do nothing else! The feeling is comparable only to physical thirst. [. . .] And he knows also the animal fury that flares uncontrollably against anything that detains him from work."[69] That degree of passionate investment can also bite back when "the work" is not received and read with the same excitement.

In spring 1941, Kahler lectured each week at the New School for Social Research in New York, which was hospitable to a number of German-Jewish émigré intellectuals, including the sociologist Peter Berger, the psychologist Max Wertheimer, and the philosophers Hannah Arendt and Leo Strauss.[70] In a letter to Mann, who had recently removed to Pacific Palisades, Kahler speaks of a "weekly 'juggling act' [. . .] forty English pages of storming through world history. [. . .] Incidentally, I have even managed in this way to draft an outline of my long-planned history of man," the book published in 1943 as Kahler's opus *Man the Measure*.[71] The book would come equipped with the exalted recommendations of his friends Thomas Mann and Albert Einstein. Mann wrote on the front cover: "Of all the minds at work today, his is one of the cleverest, finest, and richest. This work, a composition broad and towering as a mountain range, evidences once more the magnificent propensity of this mind for the comprehensive and the universal. It is" (as we have heard) "no more and no less than the novel of humanity." Einstein wrote, "This is the work of a man who has searched passionately for the reasons of the breakdown of values and ways of life which we are witnessing. I will not feel that I have finished this book before having pondered every line in it."[72] Hermann Broch contributed a lengthy review, praising its excavation of a basic human nature, although in line with his own philosophical concerns, he regretted the

---

[69] EF 71. "[. . .] jene animalische Wut [. . .]. Wer je von einer weitschichtigen Arbeitsidee wirklich bedrängt gewesen ist, der weiß und versteht jenes Gefühl, das nur dem physischen Durst vergleichbar ist. [. . .] Und der kennt auch jene animalische Wut, die gegen alles Abhaltende unhemmbar aufschießt" (BR.K 57).

[70] The New School for Social Research, "Our History," https://www.newschool. edu/nssr/history/.

[71] EF 47. Erich Kahler, *Man the Measure: A New Approach to History* (New York: George Braziller, 1956). [. . .] "meine wöchentliche 'Gaukelei'[. . .] 40 englische Seiten Raserei durch die Weltgeschichte [. . .] und nebenbei hab ich sogar einen Abriß meiner lang geplanten 'Geschichte des Menschen' beisammen [. . .] (BR.K 38).

[72] *Man the Measure*, inside the front jacket.

absence of an "epistemological" grounding.[73] (Broch had written earlier of *his* great aim: to produce "the epistemological novel [. . .] i.e., the novel which would refer psychological motivation to its epistemological basis, just as it has been the task of philosophy to free itself from psychologism").[74]

But to Kahler's despair, the book was neither particularly well nor badly received—it was received, by his account, with a shrug. And then comes a great, a signal confession:

> I have had the misfortune (though I am also at fault because of my slowness) to have my principal books come out in exile. I am everywhere an unwanted foreigner, without authentic authorization by a native land—alas, I never had any such unequivocal native land. I have fallen between two stools, not only with respect to countries and groups, but also with respect to the categories in which people are accustomed to classifying products of the mind. And so, I do not meet with any ready apperception. The intellectual senses necessary to perceive even the problems that concern me don't seem to exist—those problems seem to lie either below or at the threshold of stimulation. No wonder that so far this book is suffering the same fate here as *Der deutsche Charakter* did in Switzerland. As yet, the major newspapers and magazines in New York, Boston, and Washington have made no comment at all, and in the reviews that have appeared I detect a good deal of anxiously embarrassed, vague, lukewarm, empty praise, which I don't care about at all, but not a single really concerned examination, not a single coming to grips with the *subject*, which alone might bring my work back into the general consciousness and achieve for it some real reverberation. Characteristic of this attitude is a remark by the *New York Times* critic (Orville Prescott), whom somebody asked about my book: "We are frightened by this book, we are simply out of our depth." The only review so far that really

---

[73]   Hermann Broch, *Philosophische Schriften 1: Kritik, Kommentierte Werkausgabe Hermann Broch*, ed. Paul Michael Lützeler (Frankfurt am Main: Suhrkamp, 1974–81), 10/1: 299, 310.

[74]   " [. . .] *'erkenntnistheoretische Roman,'* [. . .] d.h. der Roman, in dem hinter die psychologische Motivation auf erkenntnistheoretische Grundhaltungen [. . .] zurückgegangen wird, genau so wie es die Aufgabe der Philosophie gewesen ist, sich vom Psychologismus frei zu machen." Hermann Broch, *Briefe, Gesammelte Werke* (Zurich: Rhein-Verlag, 1957), VIII: 23.

gave me pleasure was a vicious attack in the *Daily Mirror*, which scented a "fellow traveler" in me.[75]

Reading this letter, one is inclined to return to *Man the Measure*—for the profit of rereading the eye-catching conclusion to Kahler's discussion of Goethe's *Faust*. There Kahler writes: "It is not surprising that the essential work of Goethe remained alien to his contemporaries, as he himself often remarked with bitterness. It was met with shy reverence on the part of the public, who were only attracted by the urbanity of his genius that maintained the contact with his contemporaries through poems for various occasions, through lyrical utterances and experiments in all the more popular forms of writing."[76] Kahler did not possess such means to maintain the contact with *his* contemporaries; but like Goethe, in this respect, he was insufficiently valued during his lifetime, with the exception of a circle—the Circle—of cognoscenti.

It is noteworthy that Kahler speaks of his work as an answer to a set of *problems* (surely dealing with the loss of a common human substance); and his book, aiming to restore individual human agency to the center of history, must be understood in light of its intention. Kahler's intellectual dialogist Hermann Broch writes similarly of his masterwork *The Death of Virgil*: rather than being a novel, it is something "engendered

---

75 EF 72–73. "Ich hatte das Unglück (—freilich nicht ohne eigene Schuld meiner Langsamkeit—) mit meinen wesentlichen Büchern im Exil herauszukommen, überall ein unerwünschter Fremdling ohne ursprüngliche Autorisation durch ein Heimatland.—ich hatte ja leider überhaupt kein solches eindeutiges [*sic*] Heimatland. Ich bin aber nicht nur zwischen den Ländern und Gruppen, sondern auch zwischen den Rubriken, in die man geistige Produkte einzuordnen gewohnt ist, und so treffe ich auf keinerlei vorbereitete Apperzeption. Die geistigen Sinne scheinen nicht vorhanden, um auch nur meine Problematik aufzunehmen—sie scheint unterhalb oder oberhalb der Reizschwelle. Kein Wunder also, daß es mir mit meinem Buche hier bisher so ergeht wie mit dem 'Deutschen Charakter' in der Schweiz. Die großen Zeitungen und Zeitschriften in New York, Boston, Washington haben sich überhaupt noch nicht geäußert, und in dem, was vorliegt, erfahre ich viel verlegen-ängstliche, flaue, vage Loberei, an der mir nichts liegt, habe nicht eine einzige wirklich beteiligte Auseinandersetzung, nicht ein einziges Eingehen auf die *Sache*, das allein meine Arbeit in das allgemeine Bewußtsein einreihen und ihr eine eigentliche Resonanz verschaffen könnte. Charakteristisch für diese Haltung ist eine Äußerung eines Kritikers der New York Times (Orville Prescott), den jemand über mein Buch gefragt hat: We are frightened by this book, we are simply out of our depth." Die einzige Äußerung, die mich bisher wirklich gefreut hat, war eine Anpöbelung im Daily Mirror, der in mir einen "fellow traveler" gewittert hat" (BR.K 58).

76 *Man the Measure*, 502–3.

by necessity out of its constellation of problems."[77] In the next chapter, we shall be exploring several of these problems, which turn on the most fundamental concern for the endangered human being, following the "loss of the Absolute . . . [which] alone can produce a valid, life-commanding *value*." Kahler's description of Broch's ultimate concern is at once a description of his own: a matter of rescuing "this compelling value, which sustains the world and life of men; of rescuing of this value, which is at one with the rescuing of the Absolute—it is on this which the fate of the human depends."[78]

In the interest of probity, it must be pointed out that Kahler's book, as Gerhard Lauer and Martin Jay, among others, have written, "has not really held up." Jay continues, informatively:

> its current influence is minimal. A quick survey of contemporary discussions of the philosophy of history fails to reveal much resonance of Kahler's "new approach to history." If anything, it is seen as symptomatic of an overblown "crisis of man" rhetoric that belabors familiar points about the dangers of collectivism and the erosion of individuality in the inflated rhetorical style fashionable during the war and its aftermath (as Mark Greif shows in *The Age of the Crisis of Man*). Its narrative of civilizational decline is unreflectively Eurocentric and filled with the pathos of a humanist elite schooled in the values of *Bildung* and alarmed by cultural forces it cannot fully comprehend. It draws on a venerable tradition of lamenting the on-going "crisis" of Western culture, a plaint whose historical origins in the 18th century are identified by Reinhart Koselleck in *Critique and Crisis*. [. . .] This is not to deny that the rise of fascism can justifiably be seen as a moment of great menace for many of the values we still hold dear [. . .] , just that Kahler's approach is too cosmic to make much sense of it. As Eric Bentley recognized in a trenchant review in *The Kenyon Review* when the book appeared, *Man the Measure* "schematize(s)

---

77 "als etwas, das in Notwendigkeit aus seiner Problemkonstellation entstanden
ist." *Materialien zu Hermann Broch "Der Tod des Vergil,"* ed. Paul Michael Lützeler (Frankfurt am Main: Suhrkamp, 1976), 224, cited in translation by Kathleen Komar in "'The Death of Vergil': Broch's Reading of Vergil's 'Aeneid,'" *Comparative Literature Studies* 21, no. 3 (Fall 1984): 269.

78 "[. . .] die Erkenntnis vom *Schwund des Absoluten*, zugleich aber auch die Erkenntnis, daß allein ein Absolutes einen gültigen, lebensgebietenden Wert schaffen kann. Um diesen zwingenden, die Menschenwelt und das Menschenleben zusammenhaltenden Wert geht es; von der Rettung dieses Wertes, die eins ist mit der Rettung des Absoluten hängt das Schicksal des Humanen ab." Erich Kahler, *Die Philosophie von Hermann Broch* (Tübingen: J.C.B. Mohr, 1962), 7.

the history of Western man too crudely and compactly" and its "thinking about the present and future is pious aspiration and no more."[79]

Kahler's hopes do bear a more than troubling affinity with Martin Heidegger's notorious pronouncement: "Only a god [Kahler: "goodness"] can save us."[80] Paul Michael Lützeler, an expert scholar of the Princeton enclosure at One Evelyn Place, the home of Kahler and Broch, judges the friendship between Mann and Kahler as genuine, "although it is also obvious that Kahler acknowledged Mann's superiority. What Mann liked about him was the limitless admiration that is, for example, documented in Kahler's essay on *Doktor Faustus*." Lützeler's judgment as to the staying power of the Mann-Kahler friendship is surely correct: it is owed to Kahler's unbridled appreciation of Mann—yes, his "limitless admiration." Add to this, though, Kahler's greater command of intellectual history. We are now well aware of their after-dinner conversations in Princeton often lasting quite late into the night, with Kahler (implicitly) dictating a variety of Mann's "positions" on the world-historical events of the day. Mann did evidence a genuine affection for him, doing everything *not* to turn him away: aside from their meetings in person, he wrote to Kahler when he (Mann) was away from Princeton. He would find it worth noting in his diary, written late at night just before going to bed, that he had received a letter from Kahler or had even written to him (T4 143–44). There was a glimmer of human warmth in Mann's few friendships—and indeed, for Kahler, unique on the East Coast, much more than a glimmer. Lützeler continues: "Kahler was intensely politically engaged. That comes through in his correspondence with Hermann Broch as well. After the Second World War, they planned to write a book together on democracy. Kahler wrote letters to American presidents about the atomic bomb and other threats. It is true, there was mutual respect, and Thomas Mann could learn from Kahler (as he did from many other philosophers of his time), and yet Kahler's admiration for Mann was greater than the other

79 Martin Jay, "Commentary," personal communication, May 12, 2021. References are to Reinhart Koselleck, *Critique and Crisis: Enlightenment and the Pathogenesis of Modern Society* (Cambridge, MA: MIT Press, 2000); and Eric Russell Bentley, a review of *Man the Measure. A New Approach to History* by Erich Kahler and *The Condition of Man* by Lewis Mumford. *The Kenyon Review* 7, no. 1 (Winter 1945), 143–49.

80 Martin Heidegger said, "Nur noch ein Gott kann uns retten" in an interview with Rudolf Augstein and Georg Wolff on September 23, 1966, subsequently printed in *Der Spiegel* 30 (May 1976): 193–219.

way around." If Mann was grateful for Kahler's support, Kahler thrived on the affection and support Mann could spare him: Kahler was the needier one. One cannot forget his letter to Mann on January 5, 1944, which we have just read, recounting the dispiriting, threadbare American reception of his work (EF 72–73). "Still," Lützeler concludes, with finality, "they profited intellectually from each other—a good basis for a friendship."[81]

---

[81]   Personal communication, February 5, 1920.

Three Hermann Broch in Princeton

Broch led an exilic, nomadic, and diasporic existence, and his writings are filled with the motifs of the peregrinus, *of farewell and a hoped-for arrival, of "Abschied" and "Heimkehr."*

—Paul Michael Lützeler

The Death of Virgil, *as wide as the sea in its "tritonic, immeasurable reality."*

—Hermann Broch

Hermann Broch (1886–1951) was a philosopher, essayist, novelist, and poet of great distinction. Since his death, it has not been unusual to hear him praised as the German poet-author who had few rivals, in the first half of the twentieth century, for "thinking through the problems of modernity and, in particular, modern literature—more particularly: the modern novel—in so various and comprehensive a fashion."[1] Broch, an Austrian Jew, developed his critique in the 1930s in response to the political violence around him, which he would soon experience on his own body. The problem of literary form captivated him especially during his work on his masterpiece *The Death of Virgil* in the years 1937–45, several of which he spent in Princeton as Mann's intellectual confidant.[2] Broch's rejection of "the novel" is inspired by a deep-seated *libido sciendi* to get to the foundations of real knowledge capable of effecting political change: it discredits a so-called traditional, chiefly nineteenth-century manner of telling stories—its representation of the surfaces of an all-too familiar, bourgeois world—and, hence, the putative

---

[1] Richard Brinkmann, "Romanform und Werttheorie bei Hermann Broch," in *Hermann Broch: Perspektiven der Forschung*, ed. Manfred Durzak (Munich: Wilhelm Fink, 1972), 35.

[2] Hermann Broch, *The Death of Virgil*, tr. Jean Starr Untermeyer (New York: Random House, 1972) [originally, Pantheon, 1945]).

claim of the realist novel to produce real knowledge, let alone heighten the sense of the urgency of political action. Broch's *Death of Virgil*, which Broch did not consider a novel, intends, by its elevation of lyric and philosophical reflection, to constitute a dialectical *pendant* to the novel.[3] The fact that we can appreciate Broch's achievement is owed, in good part, to the editorial ministrations of Broch's friend and landlord Erich Kahler, who, like Max Brod for Kafka, brought Broch's thought to light by composing a book-length study of his philosophy and editing and introducing, among other abandoned papers, Broch's poems, which Broch kept "veiled in a certain modesty."[4] Kahler's *The Philosophy of Hermann Broch* proposes a table of Broch's interests and abilities ranging beyond literature and aesthetics and addressing value theory, epistemology, mathematics and logic, psychology, law, and crowd psychology. Broch struggled to bring the products of these fields of thought into a single complex—inspired, as Kahler wrote, by an overriding "concern for the endangered human condition" while suffering "the martyrdom of one who strives to hold these entangled autonomies together"—and fails![5] That failure is essentially owed not to a subjective shortcoming but to the objective fact of a human world disintegrated and become unintelligible. Broch's efforts were known and valued by such capable personalities as Robert Musil; Elias Canetti, whose work Broch furthered; and not to mention Broch's good friend Hannah Arendt; as well as Giuseppe Antonio Borgese and Thomas Mann. Many scholars of German literature judge Broch's fiction comparable in distinction with the works of the established triad Kafka, Musil, and Mann.

Broch was born to a wealthy Jewish family in Vienna on November 1, 1886. He mastered the economics of textile manufacture, helped to manage his parents' factory, and only years later, after selling the factory, began a university course in mathematics and philosophy. He was forty before devoting himself fully to thinking and writing about literature and political philosophy and composing stories and novels.

---

3   "[D]er Vergil ist kein Roman [. . .]." "[. . .] [Das Buch] war nicht mehr das Sterben des Vergil, es wurde die Imagination des eigenen Sterbens." *Hermann Broch, Briefe 3 (1945–1951)*, in Hermann Broch, *Kommentierte Werkausgabe*, ed. Paul Michael Lützeler (Frankfurt am Main: Suhrkamp, 1981), 13/3: 26–27, 65.
4   "[S]o hat er seine Gedichte noch mit einer besonderen Reserve umgeben [. . .] immer in eine eigentümliche Schamhaftigkeit gehüllt." Erich Kahler, "Einleitung," in *Gedichte [von Hermann Broch]*, ed. Erich Kahler (Zurich: Rhein-Verlag, 1953), 46.
5   "[. . .] [die] Sorge um den gefährdeten menschlichen Zustand [. . .] das Martyrium des Menschen, der [. . .] [diese] entwickelten Autonomien zusammenhalten will." Erich Kahler, *Die Philosophie von Hermann Broch* (Tübingen: J.C.B. Mohr, 1962), 2.

As told by Eileen Simpson, the first wife of the poet John Berryman and a frequent visitor to the Kahler Circle,

> Broch's secular road to Damascus [. . .] occurred in Vienna, on the route he traveled every morning in a chauffeur-driven car to the textile factory of which he was the director. He was forty years old at the time and had taken it for granted [. . .] that he would live his life as a businessman, though a businessman who spent his evenings discussing philosophy and literature with intellectuals at the Café Central. On this particular day, which had begun like any other day, he felt a sudden compulsion to tell the driver to stop, to turn back. He never again returned to the factory, and thereafter devoted his life to writing.[6]

I note this colorful account, which is much less a tribute to the truth than evidence of Broch's buoyant personality, for he would have made up this story for Eileen Simpson, whom he met at the home of Erich Kahler. As the story has circulated, it asks for a root-and-branch correction, provided here by Broch's expert editor and biographer, Paul Michael Lützeler. Broch often joked about his "sudden conversion" in biblical proportions from industrialist to novelist. (A rival account has the conversion occurring at a Wagner opera.) In fact, until ca. 1914, such factory directors had their villas close by. Together with his wife and young son, Broch lived near his spinning and weaving factory in Teesdorf; ergo, no chauffeur was necessary or on hand to bring him from Vienna to Teesdorf "every morning." Moreover, it was not a "sudden compulsion" that prompted Broch to tell the apocryphal chauffeur to return home. He had been thinking about selling the factory for some seven years; and, indeed, once it had been sold, he continued for another two years to advise the new owner, who remained a friend.

To return, on a less civil note: after the Nazi annexation of Austria, Broch endured a bleak period of incarceration (he feared he would be beheaded!). Once freed, he made haste to immigrate by way of Scotland to the United States in 1938, afflicted now by a sense of the "superfluousness of aesthetic and even academic-intellectual (*geisteswissenschaftliche*) production" in coping with the terrors of the time.[7] But the claim of an experience of the threat of death took

---

6   Eileen Simpson, *Poets in Their Youth: A Memoir* (New York: Farrar, Strauss and Giroux, 1990), 100–101.
7   "Überflüßigkeit ästhetischer und sogar geisteswissenschaftlicher Produktion." Hermann Broch, Letter to (his wife) Anne Marie Meier-Graefe Broch (August 15, 1938), *Hermann Broch, Briefe 2 (1938–1945)*, in Broch, *Kommentierte Werkausgabe*, ed. Lützeler, 13/2:14.

precedence: it forced, by his own admission, the writing of *The Death of Virgil.* "It was a condition that demanded ever more compellingly the preparation for death." Once more: "It was no longer Virgil's dying, it became the imagination of my own dying."[8] New York and Princeton were the first stations of his cross: his time in America, although fiercely creative intellectually, was marked by penury and illness. Broch's initial experience of emigration was accompanied—as Lützeler writes—by a resurgence of psychic energies: "Broch developed a feverish activity as novelist, political theorist, organizer of aid for refugees, and active participant in projects bearing on exile."[9] But all this had to be done with no secure means of support and under continual stress. In the last year of his life, Broch was appointed honorary lecturer in modern German literature at Yale University—unlike Mann's appointment at Princeton, it came without a salary and with no obligation to teach. After years of precarious health, Broch died in New Haven on May 30, 1951. He had continued to make many friends and had numerous correspondents, who admired his intellectual power and his courteous and engaging personality— among them, his several lovers, whom he maintained simultaneously.

Broch composed his first major work, *Die Schlafwandler* (*The Sleepwalkers*), between 1928 and 1932—a trilogy of novels, each one centered on the life of a semi-conscious personality illustrating the ethical decay of his era—a hesitant Prussian officer, ca. 1888; a restless Luxembourger bookkeeper, ca. 1903; and an Alsatian war profiteer and murderer, ca. 1918. That the lead figure of the second novel, *Esch oder die Anarchie* (Esch or anarchy), should be a bookkeeper might be surprising, but the third volume contains Broch's dictum that "the two great rational ways of understanding in modernity are the language of science in mathematics and the language of money in bookkeeping,"[10] a point that we shall be taking up in chapter 4, "Goethe and the Circle." This emphasis can be traced to Broch's early tenure as the chief director of a very large family-owned factory, subsequently confiscated by the Nazis.

---

8   "Doch jedenfalls war es ein Zustand, der mich zwingender und zwingender zu Todesvorbereitung, zu sozusagen privater Todesvorbereitung nötigte." *Broch, Briefe* 13/3: 65.

9   Paul Michael Lützeler, "Einleitung: 'Optimische Verzweiflung': Thomas Mann und Hermann Broch im Exil," *Freundschaft im Exil: Thomas Mann und Hermann Broch*, ed. Paul Michael Lützeler (Frankfurt am Main: Vittorio Klostermann, 2004), 13. This introduction is the best single piece of writing on the relation of Broch and Mann I have seen.

10   "Die beiden großen rationalen Verständigungsmittel der Moderne [sind] die Sprache der Wissenschaft in der Mathematik und die Sprache des Geldes in der Buchhaltung." Hermann Broch, *Die Schlafwandler: Eine Romantrilogie* (Frankfurt am Main: Suhrkamp Taschenbuch, 1994), 537–38.

In a letter to Erich Kahler, his best friend in Princeton, Broch rather charmingly declares that as a result of having dictated the letter, he has lapsed "atavistically" into his "lovely business German."[11] Kahler, on the other hand—recall that his family name was "von Kahler"—began his literary career as part of a cultured élite free to pursue his personal *Bildung* at a good *Gymnasium* and university, and thereafter, in Kahler's case, as a sometime member of the Circle of the "Dichterfürst," "the poet-king," Stefan George. Decades later, in Princeton, as we now know, Kahler would become the center of a circle of his own.

On Broch's first encounter with Kahler on October 10, 1938, the day after Broch's arrival in New York, "contact was established instantly"— thus Kahler—"and soon developed into a lifelong friendship."[12] The grounds for such harmony were manifest. Despite the difference in their formal education, they shared an early social maturity in Vienna as the sons of prosperous Jewish businessmen. For many years, both were financially independent writers of poems and essays (and, in Broch's case, novels) bearing on the crisis of the age: the disintegration of the values that had seemed prima facie to define the human being—in Kahler's triad, self-consciousness, an historical awareness, and a general feeling for humanity; in Broch's view, a (now-vanishing) ethical substance. Kahler was inclined, in the Princeton years, to imagine a positive development, an intensification of the human being arising even out of the fascist inferno. (This progressivist notion appalled Thomas Mann.) Broch was attuned, rather, to the ever-present potential for barbarism, grown dangerous under the condition of a pathology of the masses. But their shared intellectual concerns outnumbered their differences. Both knew that cure lay elsewhere than in a heaping-up of scientific (even "scientific-humanistic") pieces of knowledge, as were being accumulated in the specialized disciplines of the universities. Hope lay only in a global will to cooperation, bent on establishing a comity of nations and a program of inalienable "human rights" as an ethical absolute.[13]

On the evening of his meeting with Kahler, Broch visited Albert Einstein in Princeton "to thank him for vouching for him in the matter

---

11   "[. . .] atavistisch ins geliebte Kaufmannsdeutsch." Hermann Broch, letter to Erich Kahler, July 1, 1940, in Hermann Broch, *Briefe an Erich Kahler (1940–1951)*, ed. Paul Michael Lützeler (Berlin: De Gruyter, 2010), 4.

12   "Der Kontakt hat blitzartig eingeschlagen und wurde sehr bald zu einer Lebensfreundschaft"; cited in Paul Michal Lützeler, *Hermann Broch: Eine Biographie* (Frankfurt am Main: Suhrkamp, 1985), 243. In describing Broch's meeting with Kahler, Lützeler quotes from *Hermann Broch-Daniel Brody, Briefwechsel 1930–1951*, ed. Bertold Hack and Marietta Kleiss (Frankfurt am Main: Buchhändler-Vereinigung, 1971), 392A.

13   This passage is informed by Lützeler's exemplary "Einleitung des Herausgebers: 'Libru [lieber Bruder], guter Alter,'" in Broch, *Briefe an Kahler*, vii–xx.

of the visa."[14] A month earlier, Broch had sent Einstein a surpassingly
eloquent letter of thanks for his support in this difficult matter.[15] In later
years Broch would describe Einstein as the "greatest [*großartigste*]
human being whom I have ever met."[16] They would become good
friends, an event entirely predictable in light of their shared ethical and
political concerns.

Mann's first encounter in Princeton with Broch ("from Vienna"), on
October 13, 1938—Broch having been invited for tea—was a less
affectionate affair; Mann describes his guest merely as "extremely
tired." Of course, he too was well acquainted with Broch; the year
before, on August 5, 1937, he had read Broch's "Völkerbund-
Resolution"—his speculative program aimed at resuscitating a league
of nations with humanistic aims—finding it "well-intentioned, well-
meaning . . . but thick, opaque."[17] This sort of judgment did not bode
well for the possibility of a lifelong friendship, and yet a considerable
intimacy and respect did grow up between them. Their affinity was
long latent in Broch: he had been enthusiastic about much of Mann's
work from early days. In 1913 he published an essay on Mann's *Death
in Venice*, writing of its "lofty perfection"—although his judgment of
Tonio Kröger could not have been further from Kafka's: Kafka took the
story to heart; Broch found it unsalvageably mediocre. Still, many years
later—in 1944—Broch would be writing very respectfully to Mann:

> I should like to seal my exit from literature, as once I did my entry
> into it, with an essay on Thomas Mann [*sic*], showing that the
> evolution which lies between *Death in Venice* and *Joseph* is nothing
> less than the development of the *Zeitgeist* and its potentialities for
> artistic expression. As far as I can recall, as far back as 1912, I
> correctly divined in *Death in Venice* the renunciation of bourgeois
> expression and therefore of the novel itself. And although you
> have retained the novel form [in what was to become *Doctor
> Faustus*], it is clear to me that you have put on a magnificent and
> inimitable display of farewell fireworks. What is more, they are
> already being aimed into new territory. I need not say with what
> suspense I am looking forward to your *Faust*.

14   Paul Michael Lützeler, *Hermann Broch—A Biography*, trans. Janice Furness
     (London: Quartet, 1987), 175.
15   Hermann Broch, letter to Albert Einstein, September 4, 1938, *Broch, Briefe 2*,
     13/2: 26–27.
16   "[E]r ist ja doch das großartigste menschliche Wesen, dem ich je begegnet bin."
     Hermann Broch, letter to Else Spitzer, February 24, 1945, ibid., 13/2: 437.
17   "Wohlgedacht, wohlgesinnt, aber dickflüssig, undurchsichtig, unübersetzbar"
     (T3 86).

Broch goes on to explain: "Since the world has become overpowering to man, the possibility of literary expression has also come to an end. [. . .] The boundary of expression has just been crossed."[18] Broch's first important "reading experience" of *Death in Venice*—as Lützeler notes—continued to have an effect a quarter century later on *The Death of Virgil*: "The consciously articulated architectonics and the musical structure, the thematics of death and the recourse to ancient myths, the motif of love and the sense of the end of times—indeed even such details as the figure of the psychopomp [the conductor of souls to the afterworld] and the death barque—are present in both works."[19]

Broch's visit to Mann in Princeton soon after Broch's arrival from England was by no means their first face-to-face meeting: Broch had collared Mann at a reading from the *Joseph* novel—the topic: "Jacob's Wedding"—that Mann held in Vienna on October 21, 1932, hoping to get him to recommend *The Sleepwalkers* to the American Book of the Month Club. "Apart from this intermezzo," Broch wrote to his publisher Daniel Brody, "Mann's reading was really full of charm, of that dry grace thoroughly peculiar to this man; and I was thoroughly enchanted by the story he read—by the Protestant dignity with which he had fashioned oriental lasciviousness."[20] The degree of their intimacy increased bit by bit. Mann's diary for March 25, 1934, records "Hermann Broch to tea" (D 204); Lützeler intuits that the conversation turned on Mann's *Young Joseph*, during which Broch proposed writing a review, although he never did.[21] On July 3, the two met in Zurich, this time to

---

18   (EF 92–93). "[Ich] möchte [. . .] meinen Austritt aus der Literatur wie einstens meinen Eintritt mit einem Aufsatz über Thomas Mann besiegeln, zeigend, dass die Entwicklung, die zwischen dem 'Tod in Venedig' und dem 'Joseph' liegt, nichts anderes als die des Zeitgeistes und seiner künstlerischen Ausdrucksformen selber ist. Soweit ich mich erinnere, habe ich 1912 schon die Abkehr von der bürgerlichen Expression und also auch vom Roman ganz richtig im 'Tod in Venedig' erraten, und wenn Sie auch die Romanform beibehalten haben, es ist mir doch klar, daß Sie ihr ein großartiges und unnachahmliches Schlußfeuerwerk bereitet haben u. z. eines, das bereits in Neuland abgebrannt wird. Mit welcher Spannung ich da dem 'Faust' entgegensehe, brauche ich nicht eigens zu sagen. [. . .] Da die Welt für den Menschen übermächtig geworden ist, hat ihr auch seine dichterische Ausdrucksmöglichkeit erliegen müsse [. . .] denn die Ausdrucksgrenze ist erst jetzt überschritten" (BR.K 74–75).
19   Lützeler, *Freundschaft*, 10.
20   "Von diesem Intermezzo abgesehen war sein Vortrag wirklich voller Scharm, von jener darren Grazie, die diesem Menschen durchaus eigentümlich ist, und ich war von der vorgelesenen Geschichte (Hochzeit Jaacobs aus dem Roman), von der protestantischen Würde, mit der hier orientalische Geilheit gemacht wird, restlos entzückt." *Freundschaft im Exil: Thomas Mann und Hermann Broch*, ed. Paul Michael Lützeler (Frankfurt am Main: Vittorio Klostermann, 2004), 53.
21   Lützeler, *Freundschaft*, 12.

discuss the initial plan of the "Völkerbund-Resolution," which was forever a chief predilection of Broch's. On July 21, 1936, "After tea [Mann] wrote to Broch"—I set down this bare notation chiefly to suggest their increasing intimacy in a time of mutual emigration.[22] Some months later, on the morning of December 30, 1936, Mann composed his famous reply to the Dean of the Faculty of the University of Bonn, who had withdrawn Mann's honorary degree following the loss of his German citizenship; but Mann still found it worthwhile to note in his diary that he had also "read aloud [to Hans Reisiger] a long letter from Hermann Broch, typical of the situation, dealing, again, with a plan for reconstituting a league of nations."[23] In the summer of 1937, Mann did care enough about Broch's "Völkerbund-Resolution" to consider publishing it in his journal *Mass und Wert* (Measure and Value)[24]—but finally chose not to; recall that he found it dense. Broch, as we know especially from a glance at "The City of Man," was forever engaged in a fundamental, philosophically grounded project for a supranational agency to regulate the tribalism of separate states.[25]

In the months before their meeting in Princeton, Broch was often on Mann's mind. Broch was desperate to escape Europe; as noted, he had been briefly imprisoned by Austrian Nazi police before managing to escape to the United States via Scotland and England. Along with Einstein, Mann helped him to obtain a visa. Mann's diary, composed on May 6, 1938, at the Bedford Hotel in New York, notes that he had "afterward received some ladies regarding an affidavit for Hermann Broch in Vienna."[26] The matter was one of securing a solid income for

---

[22] Ibid., 260. The otherwise exhaustively complete register of Mann's letters makes no mention of this letter. How odd! *Die Briefe Thomas Manns: Regesten und Register*, vol. 2, *Die Briefe von 1934 bis 1943*, ed. Hans Bürgin and Hans-Otto Mayer (Frankfurt am Main: S. Fischer Verlag, 1980).

[23] D 264. "[. . .] einen langen Brief Herm. Brochs zur Verlesung gebracht, für die Situation charakteristisch und den Plan einer neuen Konstituierung des Völkerbundes behandelnd." *Thomas Mann, Tagebücher 1935–1936*, ed. Peter de Mendelssohn (Frankfurt am Main: S. Fischer Verlag, 1978), 415.

[24] "Zu den Essays," *Die Entropie des Menschen: Studien zum Werk Hermann Brochs* (Würzburg: Königshausen & Neumann, 2000), 100.

[25] "*The City of Man* is a militant appeal outlining the principles and values of democracy; warning against the lethal threat posed by Nazi-fascism; and calling for the unconditional defense of these principles and values in their ideal embodiment: a unity of all nations under one world government." Chapter 3, *The Mind in Exile: Thomas Mann in Princeton* (Princeton, NJ: Princeton University Press, 2022). The program was published as *The City of Man, A Declaration on World Democracy by Fifteen Authors, Issued by G. A. Borgese, Lewis Mumford, Thomas Mann, Erich Kahler, Hermann Broch, et al.* (New York: The Viking Press, 1940).

[26] D 299. "Danach Damen empfangen wegen Afidavit für Broch in Wien" (T3 219).

Broch as the condition of immigration, which never amounted to a sinecure (D 379). Thereafter, Broch was obliged to live from hand(out) to mouth—or, as he put it, somewhat flowery—"like the lilies of the field."[27] Broch's relation to Einstein, Mann's neighbor, was the more cordial one and also full of mutual respect. It had to become the more active and substantial relation in the decade following Mann's departure from Princeton. For Broch, in his unsettled circumstances, having Einstein as a friend was a comfort and a bit of exceptional luck. Their intimacy had developed through a variety of letters earlier that year. Some dealt with Broch's wish to enlist Einstein for the "Völkerbund-Resolution"; like Mann, Einstein found the paper obscurely speculative, though he obviously valued the nobility of the intention. The following year, Broch conceived a plan for establishing a research center for the "phenomena of mass hysteria" at the Institute for Advanced Study, where Einstein was the star resident. The center would be based on Broch's "Proposal for the Establishment of a Research Institute for Political Psychology and the Study of the Phenomena of Mass Hysteria," an idea that was already latent in the "Völkerbund-Resolution."[28] Einstein read the proposal and found the idea interesting: "Your working hypothesis, which is meant to serve as the leading theme for elucidating this important and timely subject, strikes me as promising"; but Einstein rejected the idea of an entire research center with many independent hands at work.[29] In a subsequent letter on July 15, 1939, Broch thanks Einstein for his positive reception of his "essay on the psychology of the masses"—a subject matter that would occupy Broch until the day of his death. The law of Broch's production is a permanent "in progress," requiring the incessant addition or subtraction of material, a rethinking of first principles, a revision of what was to be kept on, and so forth. A longish passage from this letter to Einstein shows this law at work and something of the tone in which the Princeton humanists spoke to one another: "Allow me, now," Broch addresses Einstein,

to present you, so to speak out of a pedantry of conscience, with a supplement that has proven to be necessary [. . .]. It has turned

---

27   "[I]ch lebe seitdem wie die Lilie auf dem Felde." Hermann Broch, letter to H. F. Broch de Rothermann, July 1, 1939, in *Broch, Briefe 2*, 13/2: 93.

28   Hermann Broch, *Massenwahntheorie: Beiträge zu einer Psychologie der Politik, Broch, Kommentierte Werkausgabe*, ed. Lützeler, 12:42.

29   "Ich habe Ihre originelle Schrift mit viel Interesse gelesen. Ihre psychologische Arbeitshypothese, die als Leitmotiv zur Aufklärung des wichtigen und aktuellen Gegenstandes dienen soll, erscheint mir aussichtsreich." Letter from Einstein to Broch, June 23, 1939; cited in Lützeler, *Hermann Broch: Eine Biographie*, 272.

out [. . .] that I have oversimplified too much the schema
organizing a theory of value (*das werttheoretische Schema*) on which
my sketch is based and which constitutes an abbreviation of a
rather extensive investigation into the foundations of a theory of
value, and that this [sketch] gave rise to the view that I had
wanted to derive the concept of value—in a way based on
Kierkegaard—exclusively from the phenomenon of anxiety; this
was not my intention, because anxiety is merely a second-category
phenomenon where values are concerned, and so I have expanded
and clarified the introduction to Section II of my composition
(*Elaborate*).[30]

Lützeler notes that this supplement is lost (!).[31]

My point is that this fragment from Broch's correspondence with
Einstein should suggest the freedom and harmony of their relation.
Consider, too, the fact that Einstein invited the homeless Broch to live in
his house from August 15 through September 15, 1939, while Einstein
was on vacation. And on the occasion of Broch's being granted
citizenship, years later, on January 17, 1944, Einstein served as witness.

These friendly and respectful relations among members of the Kahler
Circle should be understood, meanwhile, as something exceptional
among American emigrants. Broch was given the opportunity early on
to be critical of Mann's behavior during Mann's exile in America. A
letter Broch wrote in August 1939 to his translator Ralph Manheim
begins, "You are absolutely right if Thomas Mann's political activity
seems inadequate to you." Here, we have an immediate indication of
one of the dire elements of exile, touching the fortunate Mann as well as
the more desperate ones. (In his notorious letter to Walter von Molo at
the end of the war on "Why I Am Not Returning to Germany," Mann
reminded his countryman of the costs: "the cardiac asthma of exile, the
uprooting, the nervous terrors of homelessness" (*das Herzasthma des
Exils, die Entwurzelung, die nervösen Schrecken der Heimatlosigkeit*" [GW

---

30   "Gestatten Sie noch, daß ich nun, sozusagen aus Gewissenspedanterie [. . .]
Ihnen eine Ergänzung vorlege, die sich nach Ausschickung des Textes als
notwendig erwiesen hat: [. . .] es hat sich nämlich herausgestellt, daß ich das
werttheoretische Schema, auf dem meine Skizze basiert und daß eine
Abbreviatur einer ziemlich ausgedehnten Untersuchung über werttheoretische
Grundlagen ist, allzu weit simplifiziert hatte und daß hiedurch die Meinung
entstanden ist, ich wolle den Wertbegriff—in gewisser Anlehnung an
Kierkegaard—ausschließlich aus dem Angstphänomen ableiten: dies war nicht
meine Absicht, denn die Angst ist im Wertgeschehen bloß ein Phänomen zweiter
Kategorie, und so habe ich die Einleitung zum Abschnitt II meines Elaborates
[. . .] erweitert und verdeutlicht. *Briefe 2*, 13/2:103.
31   Ibid., 104.

XII: 955]). The ordeal of exile is again vivid in this summary of Adorno's account of the harms inflicted on every emigrant: "the incomprehensible foreign environment, the expropriation of language, the loss of historical dimension, isolation, distrust, the poisoning of human relationships among the emigrants, the overemphasis on the private."[32] It is the quarrels among the emigrants that here in Manheim's letter casts a shadow.

One might cite a corroborating, rather sinister diary entry from Mann: "Borgese is right about the detrimental effect of the European intellectuals landing here, of the germs they bring" (T4 161–62).[33] The thought tallied with an impression he had of an evening at the home of Rolf Nürnberg, a trusted friend, along with Kurt Goetz, a playwright: "Partly amusing, but this emigrant-incest, this living in a past epoch, driven to memories on the basis of preserved documents that one has grown out of, is by no means the right thing and altogether detrimental. The high point [not unsurprisingly—SC] was Goetz's white setter Athenia" (T4 153).

To return to Broch's probity: to his credit, he makes an only very measured use of this opportunity to condemn the behavior of a fellow exile. He writes about Mann:

Nothing is really achieved in praising democratic institutions; for many, however, it is balm to hear such a thing. But there is a lot to note:

---

32 Erhard Bahr, "Exil als 'beschädigtes Leben,' Thomas Mann und sein Roman, *Joseph, der Ernährer*," in *Exilerfahrung und Konstruktionen von Identität 1933–1945*, ed. Hans Otto Horch et al. (Berlin: De Gruyter, 2013), 245–46. This is Bahr's summary of Theodor Adorno's reflections on "the damaged life" of the emigrant in the latter's celebrated *Minima Moralia: Reflexionen aus dem beschädigten Leben* (Frankfurt am Main: Bibliothek Suhrkamp, 1976), 41.

33 What, then, are these alleged microbes? Mann and Borgese are dealing with the "dubious side" of this emigration of Germans, Frenchmen, and Italians. Their objections are thinly sketched out: "vanity and cheap psychology. Before long the French will urge food assistance for France, that is, for Hitler." One might try to develop an answer by consulting this very diatribe in Allan Bloom's *The Closing of the American Mind* (New York: Simon and Schuster, 1987), which laments the intellectual imports of the chiefly German-Jewish émigrés: psychoanalysis, collectivism, historical relativism. But, then again, it is hard to imagine Mann, as a lover of "Freud and the Future," objecting to this first term; or Mann and Borgese, as democratic socialists of "The City of Man," objecting to the second; and both, of course, were hell-bent on curing the third by invoking a humanistic Absolute. Lützeler takes Bloom to task in rejecting his diagnosis; see his "Visionaries in Exile: Broch's Cooperation with G. A. Borgese and Hannah Arendt," in *Hermann Broch: Visionary in Exile. The 2001 Yale Symposium*, ed. Paul Michael Lützeler (Rochester, NY: Boydell & Brewer, Camden House, 2003), 67.

1. Mann is concerned basically solely with maintaining human dignity and freedom, in short, with a humanity that has so far prospered for better or worse under the protection of democracy; and if the subsidy of "worse" comes from the capitalist system, there is still a considerable portion of "better" remaining, the origin of which is to be found in morality;

2. In the Bible there are the twelve great and twelve small prophets; and outside the Bible there is the class of the smallest prophets, perhaps about twenty-four, who are the poets; for what defines the poet is a certain feeling of timelessness with which he listens backwards and forwards; and by virtue of this feeling, Mann knows that everything that is to come, whether fascism or revolution, will inevitably carry the seed of a cultural chaos;

3. From a purely personal point of view, what comes out of Mann's words is the fear of losing his work; he wants to prevent the fire in the Alexandrian library and must therefore be conservative.[34]

One might wonder whether Broch has in mind the fact that Mann did witness (though from afar) the burning of his books by Nazi students in 1933.

Broch and Mann will work together—the North German Protestant and the Viennese Jew—for they could not fail to respect one another's

----

[34] "Sie haben vollkommen recht, wenn Ihnen die politische Tätigkeit Thomas Manns als inadäquat scheint. Mit der Lobpreisung der demokratischen Einrichtungen ist wahrhaft nichts getan; für viele allerdings ist es Balsam, solches zu hören. Doch es ist einiges dazu festzuhalten: (1) es geht Mann im Grunde bloß um die Aufrechterhaltung der menschlichen Würde und Freiheit, kurzum eine Humanität, welche bisher unter dem Schutze der Demokratie schlecht und recht gediehen ist, und möge auch der Zuschuß des 'schlecht' vom kapitalistischen System herstammen, es bleibt immerhin noch eine beträchtliche Portion 'recht' übrig, deren Herkunft im Moralischen zu suchen ist; (2) in der Bibel gibt es die 12 großen und die 12 kleinen Propheten, und außerhalb der Bibel gibt es die Klasse der kleinsten Propheten, vielleicht etwa 24 Stück, welche die Dichter sind; denn was den Dichter ausmacht, das ist ein gewisses Zeitlosigkeits-Gefühl, mit dem er nach vor- und rückwärts hört, und kraft dieses Gefühls weiß Mann, daß alles, was kommen wird, ob nun Faschismus oder Revolution, notgedrungen den Keim in sich trägt, das Kulturchaos zu entfesseln. (3) rein persönlich betrachtet, spricht also aus Mann die Angst um den Verlust seines Werkes; er will den Brand der alexandrinischen Bibliothek hintanhalten und muß daher konservativ sein." Allerdings, mit der Lobpreisung des demokratisch-parlamentarischen Instrumentes wird die Freiheit nicht zu retten sein." Hermann Broch, Letter to Ralph Manheim (August 3, 1939), *Briefe 2*, 13/2: 123.

intellect and moral drive; but the main portion of their fraternal affections go to others—in Princeton, chiefly, to Erich Kahler! Mann's great friends—Bruno Frank, Alfred Neumann, and Bruno Walter— lived in California: living among them was the boon of the bourn, the goal of Mann's forever vivid plan to leave the dignified wintry East for the intermittent, sunlit pleasures of Los Angeles. True, his attachment to Kahler remained considerable, if we recall the letter written shortly after his arrival at Pacific Palisades: "For we often speak of you among ourselves, since we have the habit of comparing everyone here with whom we are on a friendly footing with you and saying, 'But Kahler was better!'"[35] Meanwhile, the very great thrust of brotherly affection goes to the friendship of Kahler and Broch: they supported one another intellectually, morally, and pragmatically in a never-failing, exemplary manner.

We return to Broch's wanderings: after a late summer 1939 at Einstein's house at 112 Mercer Street, Broch moved into a tiny, cramped room in the house of another friend, Jadwiga Judd, on 11 Alexander Street, where he stayed until the end of the year. Now that Broch was in Princeton, however, he and Mann could see a good deal of each other. With Broch living within walking distance of Mann's villa, it was an easy matter for Mann to invite Broch to lunch, as on October 8, along with Dr. Martin Gumpert—a Berlin doctor and writer and friend of the family—together with Mann's daughter, Elisabeth ("Medi"). For many years, Broch and the much younger Medi had liked each other very much: Medi admired the mind and talent of this statuesque acquaintance of her father. Broch's *Sleepwalkers*, she declared, was a favorite book. After lunch that day, they talked politics, agreeing, especially, on the impossibility of negotiating a genuine peace with Hitler (T3 484).

Some weeks later, together with the composer Roger Sessions, Broch was honored, surely, as one of the main witnesses to Elisabeth's marriage on November 23, 1939, to Giuseppe Antonio Borgese, whom we have met as the very vital, energetic, and accomplished scholar and enemy of fascism. Mann, Borgese, Broch, and (indirectly) Kahler would be signal contributors to "The City of Man" conference in May 1940. Hans Rudolf Vaget has given a vivid account of the formal wedding dinner at Mann's home. Broch is at the table, watching his young admirer being given away and being startled, along with his host, by the dramatic appearance of Mann's other son-in-law, Erika's titular husband, W. H. Auden:

---

[35]   EF 49. "Es ist nämlich öfters die Rede von Ihnen unter uns, da wir die Gewohnheiten haben, jedem, mit dem wir grad Freundschaft halten, mit Ihnen zu vergleichen und sie sagen: 'Kahler war doch besser!'" (BR.K 40).

The high point of this stylish celebration was marked by W. H. Auden, the brother-in-law of the bride, who did not fail to take the opportunity to appear among the company and arrived with a grand gesture. Auden had written a demanding and allusive epithalamium—eight stanzas and 128 lines long—especially for the occasion. He had had it printed, with a dedication to the bride and groom, and now, at the wedding dinner, recited it himself.

(VA 273–74)

It includes the lines:

Yet the seed becomes the tree;
Happier savants may decide
That this quiet wedding of
A Borgese and a Mann
Planted human unity;
Hostile kingdoms of the truth.
Fighting fragments of content,
Here were reconciled by love,
Modern policy begun
On this day.[36]

The "hostile kingdoms of the truth" are very likely the opposing religions. It is moot whether Thomas Mann understood the cryptic English in which "unity" is couched; Broch would have had the better access.

Mann's diaries go on to mention memorable evenings at home with Broch. In what follows—once again, as in the case of Mann and Kahler—I shall present the full calendric evidence of their meetings. By doing so, I hope to convey the immediate flavor of these meetings, along with their contribution to the intellectual universe of Mann and Broch and, by extension, to that of the Circle in toto. All in all, Mann and Broch met some twenty times during Mann's stay in Princeton.

Many of these meetings were centered on their reading to one another from their latest work. On October 20, 1939, Mann invited Broch to dinner, who "afterwards in the library read aloud portions of his Virgil novel (*The Death of Virgil*)." Mann commented: "A subtle poetry of a deep soul (*Tiefseelen-Dichtung*) as it casts off life, certainly

---

[36]   W. H. Auden, "Epithalamion" (For Giuseppe Antonio Borgese and Elizabeth Mann, Nov. 23, 1939), https://archive.org/stream/in.ernet.dli.2015.215337/ 2015.215337.The-Collected_djvu.txt. For a fine discussion of this poem, see Susannah Young-Ah Gottlieb, "'With Conscious Artifice:' Auden's Defense of Marriage," *Diacritics* 35, no. 4 (Winter 2005): 33.

remarkable."[37] He was less enthusiastic after he had read the entire manuscript. A diary notation for February 5, 1941, reads: "Occupied with manuscripts. Broch's *Virgil*, a stream of noble ennui, breathless, without pauses, unarticulated, one craves a Book II. But there are beautiful [passages] and a feeling for the danger and constriction of the human condition."[38] It may be helpful to remind ourselves that the scope of this vast lyrical novel is restricted to the last eighteen hours of Virgil's life. Among the obsessions he and his author share is a dark view of their own times, marked by a disintegration of values. They are moments of cultural transition that forever occupied Broch, as par excellence in *The Sleepwalkers* trilogy. A comment by his friend Hannah Arendt goes to the heart of this obsession: "Every crisis, every turning of the times, is at once a beginning and an end. As such, it harbors, in Broch's words, a threefold: the 'Nicht-mehr (No longer)' of the past; the 'Noch-nicht (Not-yet)' of the future; and the [properly untranslatable] 'Doch-schon (Indeed-already)' of the present."[39] These "ecstasies" of temporality are value-laden: the fortunes of the Roman Empire, like Broch's own time, suffered a debasement of civic values; the anxiety and terror of the moment; and the hope for another, a finer dispensation (Broch represents Virgil as a "Vor-Prophet," the precursor of a new prophet).[40] Broch

---

37 "Zu diesem *Broch*, der nachher in der Bibliothek aus seinem Vergil-Roman vorlas. Subtile Tief-seelen-Dichtung, das Leben abstreifend, sicher bemerkenswert" (T3 491).

38 "Beschäftigung mit Manuskripten. Brochs Vergil, pausen- und atemloser Strom von noble ennui, ungegliedert, man lechzt nach einem römisch II. Aber Schönheiten und Sinn für das beklemmend u. gefährlich Menschliche" (T4 219).

39 "Jede Krise, jede Wende der Zeiten ist Anfang und Ende zugleich. Als solche birgt sie, in den Worten Brochs, ein Dreifaches in sich: das 'Nicht-mehr' der Vergangenheit, das 'Noch-nicht' der Zukunft und das 'Doch-schon' der Gegenwart." Hannah Arendt, "Hermann Broch und der moderne Roman," in Durzak (ed.), 25. For the friendship between Broch and Arendt, see *Hannah Arendt-Hermann Broch: Briefwechsel 1946 bis 1951*, ed. Paul Michael Lützeler (Frankfurt am Main: Jüdischer Verlag, 1996).

40 Kathleen L. Komar writes informatively: "Broch selected his historical material—the last day of Vergil s life, Vergil's desire to burn the *Aeneid*, his debates with Augustus—specifically to reflect the political climate and the political pressures on the poet of the 1930s and 40s. In a letter to Kurt Wolff in 1943, Broch suggests that 'Vergil lived in a time which can be compared with our own in many ways, in a time which was filled with blood, horror, and death . . .' (See p. 216 of *Materialien zu Hermann Broch 'Der Tod des Vergil,'* ed. Paul Michael Lützeler [Frankfurt am Main: Suhrkamp, 1976] for the original German. Translation mine [KK]). And in his letter to Hermann Weigand (*Materialien*, p. 234), he [Broch] again cites parallels between the 1st century B.C. and Europe of the 1930s, parallels such as wide-spread war, dictatorship, decay of old religious forms, and even compulsory emigrations." "*The Death of Vergil*, Broch's Reading of Vergil's *Aeneid*," 267n18.

never took his eye off this threefold—a stimulus to a never-ending meditation. The scholar Kathleen Komar emphasizes this point: "Broch saw himself very much in the position of the dying Vergil—operating at the very borders of the possible, approaching the edges of transcendence [. . .]. The sense of 'not yet' and 'yet still' [sic] of the moment of transition to some finer state runs throughout Broch's *Death of Vergil* as Broch felt it ran through Vergil's own writings, life, and death."[41] The sum of Broch's meditations on this critical moment amounts to a quasi system, although Kahler offers this caveat: "What, today, we might recognize as his system, did not arise from the outset as an intention and a claim to a closed systematicity. It developed gradually through the incorporation of ever wider domains and problems; in a word, it is not deliberately constructed but grew up involuntarily in the flow of contemplation, itself a process."[42] We might well be reminded of Thomas Mann's account of how *The Magic Mountain* also assumed its systematically symbolic form apart from the intention of the author, as an autotelic process: "It is possible for a work to have its own will and purpose, perhaps a far more ambitious one than the author's—and it is *good* that this should be so. For the ambition should not be a personal one; it must not come *before* the work itself. The work must bring it forth and compel the task to completion. Thus, I feel, all great works were written."[43]

It is timely here to raise the question of correspondences between the major works of Mann and Broch: I broached this question earlier on, mentioning the lasting effect on *The Death of Virgil* of Broch's first reading of Mann's *Death in Venice*. But here we must be content with the bare outline of an answer. Scholars have pointed out the overriding motif of time and temporal consciousness in *The Magic Mountain* and in

---

41   Ibid., 258.
42   "Daher ist, was wir heute als sein System erkennen mögen, nicht von vornherein aus Absicht und Anspruch auf geschlossene Systematik entstanden, es hat sich allmählich durch den Einschluß immer weiterer Gebiete und Probleme ausgebildet, es ist, kurz gesagt, nicht willentlich errichtet, sondern unwillkürlich im Fluß der Betrachtung, und selbst ein Prozeß, erwachsen." Kahler, *Die Philosophie von Hermann Broch*, 6.
43   Thomas Mann, "The Making of 'The Magic Mountain,'" tr. H. T. Lowe-Porter, *The Atlantic Monthly* (January 1953): 42–43. "Ein Werk hat unter Umständen seinen eigenen Ehrgeiz, der den des Autors weit übertreffen mag, und das ist gut so. Denn der Ehrgeiz darf nicht ein Ehrgeiz der Person sein, er darf nicht vor dem Werk stehen, sondern dieses muß ihn aus sich hervorbringen und dazu zwingen. So, glaube ich, sind die großen Werke entstanden, und nicht aus einem Ehrgeiz, der sich von vorneherein vorgesetzt, ein großes Werk zu schaffen." "Einführung in den 'Zauberberg'"; Für Studenten der Universität Princeton" (GW XI: 607–8).

The Death of Virgil. Timm Collmann, for one, stresses the importance of lived time in *The Death of Virgil*—a problem—"mysterious and threatening"—that Virgil must "solve." "Hans Castorp's meditations on the riddle of 'time' in Mann's *The Magic Mountain*," Collmann adds, "are well known: 'Yes, time is a puzzling thing; there is something about it that is hard to explain!' And there are Castorp's long reflections on his experiences of time, which begin with the words 'What is time? A secret—insubstantial and all powerful.'" Equally—and this is the crux—Broch's Virgil asks the same "penetrating question: 'What was the mysterious feature of time?'"[44]

A second note on a marginal consanguinity of their novelistic work is the presence in Broch's novels of a Mann-inspired leitmotif technique. Broch had the "musical structure" of *Death in Venice* in mind while composing *The Death of Virgil.*[45] Before then, there are traces of the modality of the leitmotif in *The Sleepwalkers*, but unlike Mann's scrupulous and systematic application of the technique, "absolutely characteristic of his narrative manner," Broch's use of the device here is random.[46]

This *Death of Virgil*—Broch's masterpiece—is a metaphysically charged, lyrical vision embedding details of the life—and death—of the poet Publius Vergilius Maro: his work—the *Georgics*, the *Eclogues*, the *Aeneid*; his contemporaries, chiefly Octavian Caesar Augustus, his dialogist; and their milieu—a disintegrating Roman Empire. It is, by scholarly consent, a selective, idiosyncratic use of what is known of the real poet (henceforth, "Virgil" is Broch's). The work is also subjective in involving a reflection on the life and personality of the author Broch. Virgil is very ill; he will die at the end. Broch was often in poor health while composing the novel. Virgil is dissatisfied with his *Aeneid*; it celebrates Imperial Rome at the cost of ignoring the (vile) life he has glimpsed in the cities: he imagines burning the book. How often did Broch contemplate burning *The Death of Virgil*? We have the well-known view of the Germanist Erich Heller: "In the very year the novel appeared, Broch confessed to 'a deep revulsion' from literature as such—'the domain of vanity and mendacity.' [. . .] He [Virgil] commands

44 *The Magic Mountain*, tr. John E. Woods (New York: Knopf, 1995), 139, 339.
"Ja, die Zeit ist ein rätselhaftes Ding, es hat eine schwer klarzustellende Bewandtnis mit ihr!" "Was ist die Zeit? Ein Geheimnis—wesenlos und allmächtig." *Der Zauberberg* (Berlin und Darmstadt: S. Fischer Verlag, 1956), 130, 316. All the above citations are given (in German) in Timm Collmann, *Zeit und Geschichte in Hermann Brochs Roman "Der Tod des Vergil"* (Bonn: Bouvier, 1967), 7.
45 Lützeler, *Freundschaft*, 10.
46 Gerald Harlass, "Das Kunstmittel des Leitmotivs: Bemerkungen zur motivischen Arbeit bei Thomas Mann und Hermann Broch," *Welt und Wort* 15 (1960), 269.

the manuscript of the *Aeneid* to be destroyed [. . .] because it is poetry and not 'knowledge.'"[47]

In the novel, we read, very early on, Virgil's plaint: "Only at the edge of his fields had he walked, only at the edge of his life had he lived. He had become a rover, fleeing death, seeking death, seeking work, fleeing work, a lover and yet at the same time a harassed one, an errant through the passions of the inner life and the passions of the world, a lodger in his own life."[48] Broch was famously "harassed" by the several women who imagined him as their faithful lover. A "lodger in his own life"? He was literally a lodger—but in another man's life; as we know, he occupied the mansard in the Princeton house of Erich Kahler for a good deal of the time he spent writing this book. Broch's pessimism about the value of literature—it might be opposed by political action, by individual and social ethical transformation—is the crucial thrust of this work.

Broch began his *Virgil* in 1937; he would continue to write it in times of great strain—literally, while incarcerated, then in flight from Nazi Europe, then in exile in America, often penniless, unsure of his powers and the value of his book, which, during its composition, was often disliked by readers. The work would finally be published in 1945 in German and, simultaneously, in English; Jean Starr Untermeyer, the translator, contributed greatly to the English version.

After Mann's notation on the fragment of *Virgil* that he had read, he spoke with Broch, on October 24, 1939, on an institutional matter of the sort that greatly concerned Broch, "the question of the Guild" (T3 492). A certain Hubertus Prinz zu Löwenstein, who had immigrated to America, had founded the American Guild for German Cultural Freedom with the intention of fostering a German culture in exile by enlisting needy, cultivated émigrés. The important educator Robert M. Hutchins of the University of Chicago was among its officers. Together with his assistant Volkmar von Zühlsdorff, Löwenstein also founded the German Academy of Arts and Sciences in Exile. The roster of its members was formidable, including, besides Mann and Broch, none less than Freud, Heinrich Mann, Stefan Zweig, Arnold Zweig, Franz Werfel, and Alfred Döblin.[49]

---

47   Erich Heller, "Hitler in a Very Small Town," *The New York Times*, January 25, 1987.
48   *Death of Virgil*, 13. "[B]loß am Rande seiner Felder war er geschritten, bloß am Rande seines Lebens hatte er gelebt; er war zu einem Ruhelosen geworden, den Tod fliehend, den Tod suchend, das Werk suchend, das Werk fliehend, ein Liebender und dabei doch ein Gehetzter, ein Irrender durch die Leidenschaften des Innen und Außen, ein Gast seines Lebens." *Der Tod des Vergil* (Frankfurt am Main: Suhrkamp, 1976), 13.
49   Lützeler, *Broch: A Biography*, 176–77.

Broch was forever active in encouraging the formation of committees for major initiatives to advance his concerns—*and* those of his fellow emigrants. In the letter to Kahler mentioned earlier, in which Broch alludes to his ancient lovely "business German," he speaks of his efforts to establish an organization ("Immigrants Loyalty League") to protect Hitler's exiles from internment should America enter the war against Germany. With few exceptions, the Europeans escaped this fate, as the Japanese did not, owing, it is surmised, to the pressure of important voices (including Mann's and Einstein's) exerted on the State Department, not otherwise distinguished by its generosity toward immigrants.[50]

It is important to note that with few exceptions, Mann did by and large support Broch's eleemosynary undertakings. "By and large" is a necessary qualification, for the two were not fundamentally of one mind, although both registered this difference as a stimulant. That difference is especially vivid in their political writings. Here, Lützeler makes the necessary discrimination: Mann's statements addressed the given historical situation; Broch sought to analyze long-term developments and to discuss the fundamental questions—the crises— of the era. If Mann respected the range of Broch's intellect, he also rued its impracticality in the short term.[51] We have this concrete example. In a letter to Broch on August 9, 1938, Mann expressed his enthusiasm for the proposal sent to him—an "Appeal to the Conscience of the World." But in its lofty academic diction, however deep and smart, it would not have the effect that Broch surely wanted: it needed the character of a manifesto! It would have to be conceived, not as a scholarly monograph, but as a summons, apt to enlist the engagement of others![52]

Shortly after the October meeting with Broch, when they discussed the question of the Guild, Mann dictated a letter of recommendation for a Guggenheim Fellowship,[53] which he cited *to Broch* as

striking strong, deep, tremulous tones, noting the recent reading [of the *Virgil* novel], which gave me a first rough picture of the work, whose completion needs to be assured. A more suitable object for Guggenheim's patronage is hard to imagine. I made

---

50   The extremity in the predicament of the German and Italian émigrés was never quite comparable to that of the Japanese, who were interned, not as resident aliens, but as American citizens of Japanese descent. A similar fate was never considered by our government for Americans with German or Italian backgrounds.

51   Lützeler, *Freundschaft*, 29.

52   *Die Briefe Thomas Manns: Regesten und Register*, vol. 2, 170–71.

53   Ibid., 495, 843–44.

that clear and that I must never again be asked for an appraisal if this one does not receive respectful consideration.[54]

The appraisal did get the respectful consideration Mann and no doubt Broch hoped for: it was successful in allowing Broch to continue his work in Princeton on the novel (which he did not call a novel), as well as on crowd psychology.[55] On November 17, 1939, an important occasion, Mann invited Broch to lunch along with Borgese and Professor Siegfried Marck—a political philosopher who, like Borgese, taught at the University of Chicago; Marck came to Princeton especially for this meeting. Marck had commented cogently on Mann's early political writing, especially in a 1938-volume titled *Neo-Humanism as Political Philosophy*, which represented Mann as a philosophically grounded thinker and dialectician—a description with which Mann did not agree.[56] It is interesting in light of the different temper of Mann's and Broch's political writings that in a subsequent letter to Marck, Mann would write, "You must not forget that my political digressions are not composed like your writing, from the point of view of absolute philosophy, but rather represent a kind of *haut* propaganda and possess a polemical-pedagogical character."[57] The purpose of inviting Marck to

---

[54]   "Eben habe ich mein Gutachten an die Guggenheim Foundation diktiert und starke, tiefe, tremolierende Töne angeschlagen, auch der Vorlesung von neulich gedacht, die mir von dem Werk, dessen Fertigstellung es zu sichern gilt, ein erstes ungefähres Bild gegeben hat. Ein passenderes Objekt für das Guggenheim'sche Mäzenatentum ist ja kaum vorzustellen. Ich habe das zu verstehen gegeben, und man könnte mich eigentlich nie wieder um ein Gutachten angehen, wenn man sich um dieses nicht scherte." *Thomas Mann Briefe 1937–1947*, ed. Erika Mann (Frankfurt am Main: S. Fischer Verlag, 1963), 117.

[55]   His findings on the madness of crowds would be published only decades later in editions supervised by Kahler and Lützeler.

[56]   Siegfried Marck, *Der Neohumanismus als politische Philosophie* (Zurich: Verlag der Aufbruch, 1938). The intellectual exchange between Mann and Marck is discussed by Reinhard Mehring in "A Humanist Program in Exile: Thomas Mann in Philosophical Correspondence with his Contemporaries," in *Exile, Science and Bildung, The Contested Legacies of German Émigré Intellectuals*, ed. David Kettler and Gerhard Lauer (New York: Palgrave Macmillan, 2005), 52.

[57]   "Sie dürfen nicht vergessen, daß meine politischen Exkurse nicht, wie Ihre Schriften, unter dem Gesichtspunkt absoluter Philosophie verfaßt sind, sondern daß sie eine Art von höherer Propaganda darstellen und einen polemisch-pädagogischen Charakter haben." Thomas Mann, Letter to Siegfried Marck (September 19, 1941), *Thomas Mann Briefe*, 208. Cited in Mehring, "A Humanist Program in Exile," 53.

the present meeting was to discuss "the plan of a collective volume as a propaedeutic for a restored Western world (*Abendland*)." Their project was soon subsumed by the plan of a manifesto that would be published as the remarkable *The City of Man* (T3 502).

Throughout these months, and despite the differences in genre, Mann valued Broch as a political philosopher as well as, typically, an auditor: on November 28, 1939, for example, Mann read to Broch, together with Kahler, a revision of Mann's essay on "The Problem of Freedom," a version of which he had read on receiving an honorary doctorate from Rutgers University earlier that year. At the end of 1939, Mann sent Broch a copy of *Lotte in Weimar* with a dedication "declaring his faith" in the recipient. Broch acknowledged the gift with heartfelt appreciation in a letter to Mann sent from New York on January 16, 1940, and added some smart reflections on *Lotte*. He detects in the novel a threefold instance of the motif of farewell, which he reads allegorically as a testament to their present compulsory "bidding farewell to humanity" in presumably once-loved parts of the world. On the other hand, the work, in its perfection and the fact of its realization in a time of grief and exile, becomes a warrant of hope for the "continuance of humanity."[58] When it would come to Mann's recommending the publication of *The Death of Virgil*, he employs the same trope of thought—namely, that it is wonderful that a work of such luster might be accomplished, after all, in a time of grief and exile.

On March 12, 1940, Broch introduced Mann to the painter Rudolf von Ripper, a brave soldier of fortune and capable painter: Broch and von Ripper were good friends and remained on the best of terms as long as Broch lived. (T4 12). Ripper drew a brilliant portrait of Broch, which appeared in 1940 in the "Exiled Writers Issue" of *The Saturday Review of Literature*, alongside a short piece by Broch titled "Ethical Duty." The essay treats the function of the intellectual in the United States and is absolutely cogent today.[59] This ethical duty arises precisely *because* the United States, unlike England, has a written constitution, with many of its drawbacks:

a certain inflexibility of the tradition, reducing the political will of the nation [. . .] so that in the end nothing remains but a certain

---

58 "vertrauensbekundend"; "eines Abschiednehmens von der Humanität"; "einer Gewährleistung der Menschlichkeit und ihres Fortbestandes." Hermann Broch, from a letter to Thomas Mann (January 16, 1940), *Freundschaft im Exil*, 102.

59 Hermann Broch, "Ethical Duty," *The Saturday Review of Literature*, October 19, 1940, 8, accompanied by a striking portrait by Rudolf von Ripper.

sense of duty to defend the constitutional rights. The founding of
the constitution takes on an almost magical aspect—a virtuous
purification and absolution for all possible future political sins
[. . .] which permits all those who follow to free themselves from
all political responsibility, turning it over to the professional
politician.

And what is the politician's resource? The party machinery, which is
scarcely hospitable to the aims of idealistic intellectuals—to be precise,
democratic-socialist-minded intellectuals. What is to be done? Broch
answers: Despite the hardships, foster among intellectuals a sense of
ethical-political duty!

The American intellectual could until now afford to remain in his
ivory tower, but today, when democracy is in danger, it wants
more than ever the stratum of the spirit [presumably *Geist*,
intellect] which transcends all classes: the fluctuating hierarchy of
the select. This lofty aim of democracy in establishing the balance
of social order is threatened, and therefore the intellectual is
urgently called to his ethical duty.[60]

A few days after their meeting with von Ripper, Mann and Broch
spent the evening of March 16 in conversation—we may assume that
the matter had the customary weight, leavened afterwards by their
listening together—Mann literally enraptured—to Toscanini conducting
Strauss's *Till Eulenspiegel* (T4 45). Some months later, on May 22, both
Kahler and Broch were at Mann's, where Broch once again read aloud
from *The Death of Virgil* and Mann noted: "Vivid internal pictorial
quality. Re-creation (*Rückschöpfung*) to the logos. Strange music."
Thereafter, they spoke, as we might recall, about moods of anguish,
given "the universal prevalence of evil, with no way out and no refuge
for the mind."[61]
When Broch was finally ready to have his manuscript published in
1945, after countless revisions, Mann was asked, along with other
notables, to support the project. As we know, Mann was of at least two

---

[60]   Ibid.
[61]   "Vorlesung Brochs aus seinem Vergil-Roman. Innere Bildhaftigkeit,
    Rückschöpfung bis zum logos. Merkwürdige Musik. Anschließendes Gespräch
    über die Anfälle von Angst vor dem Universellwerden des Bösen, ohne Ausweg
    und Refugium für den Geist" (T4 80).

minds about the entire enterprise but would celebrate it in somewhat anodyne fashion soon after its publication:

> I was extraordinarily pleased to hear that Hermann Broch's prose-poem *The Death of Virgil* is appearing simultaneously in the original version and in the English translation (by Jean Starr Untermeyer), whose devoted loyalty I am aware of. As one who was permitted to read the work in manuscript, I have no doubt that it belongs among the highest achievements of German literature, but above all for being one of the most essential, most novel works of our time—a boldly conceived, original, and astonishing creation, whose magic is bound to captivate everyone who falls under its spell. German literature in exile may be proud that it is able to give the world a poetic work of such stature.[62]

In response to a letter to Einstein that year in which Broch speaks about the inexpressibility of genuine knowing, Einstein replied:

> Dear Hermann Broch, I am fascinated by your *Virgil* and am constantly defending myself against it. The book clearly shows me what I fled from when I committed myself heart and soul to science. I was aware of it beforehand, if not so clearly (this escape from the I and from We into the It); what you said about intuition in your letter speaks from my heart [here, *Seele*, soul]. The logical form exhausts the essence of knowing as little as meter, the essence of poetry, and the teaching of rhythm and chord progression, the essence of music. The essential remains

---

[62] "Es war mir eine außerordentliche Freude, zu hören, daß Hermann Brochs Prosagedicht "Der Tod des Vergil" gleichzeitig in der Originalfassung und in der englischen Übertragung (durch Jean Starr Untermeyer), um deren hingebungsvoller Treue ich weiß, erscheint. Für mich, dem gestattet war, das Werk im Manuskript zu lesen, besteht kein Zweifel, daß es zu den höchsten Leistungen deutschen Schrifttums gehört, vor allem aber, daß es eines des wesentlichsten, neuartigsten Werke unserer Zeit ist—eine kühn konzipierte, originelle und erstaunliche Schöpfung, deren Magie jeden gefangen nehmen muß, der in ihren Bannkreis gerät. Das deutsche Schrifttum im Exil darf stolz darauf sein, daß es der Welt ein dichterisches Werk solchen Ranges zu geben vermag." "Über Hermann Brochs 'Der Tod des Vergil'" (GW XIII: 449).

mysterious and will always remain so: it can only be felt but not grasped.

Kind regards to all of you from your Albert Einstein.[63]

* * *

We possess these last mentions of Broch during Mann's stay in Princeton. They spoke and conferred together at the seminar convened to produce a significant declaration—"The City of Man." Mann's diary reads "Atlantic City, Saturday, May 25, 1940" and registers immediately his "exhaustion from participating in the [previous day's] group sessions (*Sitzungen*)," which he nonetheless finds "not uninteresting and not useless." The next morning, following the first discussion, Mann spoke, "making an impression not so much for what was said [as for the expressiveness of his conviction] and, as an exception, produced applause."[64] Thereafter, he and Broch went for a walk and had lunch together. The following day, Mann was again with Broch and Borgese in the Pullman car on the way back to Princeton (T4 83). Borgese was depressed, no doubt by an anticipation of the futility of their work, despite its fervor and high-mindedness. A week later, on May 31, Mann and Broch shared lunch—just the two of them—dealing with the worrisome question of a suspected attempt by the US government to intern German "aliens." They then repaired to Kahler's house for coffee and, certainly, more of this discussion (T4 87). On June 6, 1940, Mann's sixty-fifth birthday, he received a telegram in English signed by both

63   "Lieber Hermann Broch, Ich bin fasziniert von Ihrem Vergil und wehre mich beständig gegen ihn. Es zeigt mir das Buch deutlich, vor was ich geflohen bin, als ich mich mit Haut und Haar der Wissenschaft verschrieb; es war mir schon vorher bewußt, wenn auch nicht so deutlich ['Flucht vom Ich und vom Wir in das Es'], was Sie, in Ihrem Brief über das Intuitive gesagt haben, ist mir aus der Seele gesprochen. Die logische Form erschöpft nämlich das Wesen des Erkennens so wenig wie das Versmaß das Wesen der Poesie oder die Lehre vom Rhythmus und Akkordfolge das Wesen der Musik. Das Wesentliche bleibt mysteriös und wird es immer bleiben, kann nur erfühlt, aber nicht erfaßt werden. Herzliche Grüße an Sie alle von Ihrem Albert Einstein." Letter to Hermann Broch (n.d. [1945]), *Briefe* 13/3: 18–19.
64   "Erschöpfung durch die Teilnahme an den Sitzungen, den ganzen Vormittag und nachmittags von ½ 4,—die ich nicht uninteressant, auch nicht nutzlos nennen will"; [...] und hielt, mit ganzem Einsatz, meine Ansprache, die Eindruck machte, nicht so sehr durch das Was, und ausnahmsweise Beifall auslöste." "K. und ich machten mit Broch einige Schritte hinaus und lunchten mit ihm" (T4 81–82).

Broch and Kahler: "Your world may remain / all our wishes." If the sense is obscure, the affectionate intention is not.

Despite the disparity in achievement and recognition between the older Mann and his devoted companions—and discounting Mann's occasional hints of ill temper (on one late occasion on meeting Broch at Yale, there blew around him—thus Broch—the "magic cloak of cheerlessness")—they remained "friends in exile."[65] When the Manns made their final departure from Princeton to California on March 18, 1941, Broch sat with them in their compartment on the train from Princeton to Pennsylvania Station. And thereafter, Mann continued to write to Broch from his villa in Pacific Palisades, and even to meet him in New York on Mann's infrequent return visits.

Once, in appreciation of Mann's hospitality and encouragement during his Princeton stay, Broch gave him a gift of a recording of a Beethoven piano concerto, which Mann mentioned greatly enjoying (T4 97–98). Let this enjoyment be a light kiss planted on the brow of this martyr of humanistic thought—an act of love, with inverted sign, much attenuated, like Virgil's gift of the *Aeneid* to Octavian Caesar Augustus.

---

65   "der Zaubermantel der Ungemütlichkeit." Lützeler, *Freundschaft*, 14.

Four Goethe and the Circle

Everyone in the Circle admired Johann Wolfgang von Goethe: in their speeches and publications they were quick to cite or allude to him. He was a vital part of what Mann called their "moral blood structure." In a famous anti-Nazi speech delivered at the Albert Hall in London in 1933, Einstein celebrated the creative power of individual liberty and invoked Goethe as one who thrived on it:

> I am glad that you have given me the opportunity of expressing to you here my deep sense of gratitude as a man, as a good European, and as a Jew. [. . .] We are concerned not merely with the technical problem of securing and maintaining peace, but also with the important task of education and enlightenment. Without such freedom there would have been no Shakespeare, no Goethe, no Newton, no Faraday, no Pasteur, and no Lister.[1]

In a rich essay, the historian of science Gerald Holton shows how Einstein's *Weltbild* (world-picture, a term prominent in the writings of the entire Kahler Circle) was conditioned throughout by—or, as he prefers, "in resonance with"—his reading of Goethe.[2] Einstein's association with Goethe goes back to his high school essay on *Götz von Berlichingen*, Goethe's first work, a play about a very independent, belligerent knight whose loyalty is to no one other than himself, the emperor Maximilian, and God. Here, Holton is calling attention to one cultural root—heroes of an independent character also abound in the novels of the German Romantics—shaping Einstein's

---

[1] http://www.openculture.com/2013/04/albert_einstein_on_individual_
     liberty_without_which_there_would_be_no_shakespeare_no_goethe_no_
     newton_.html.
[2] Gerald Holton, "Einstein and the Cultural Roots of Modern Science," *Daedalus*
     127, no. 1 (Winter 1998): 1–44.

own rebellious nature; but in this paradox, it is precisely Einstein's devotion to a traditional German culture that shapes his intellectual character—his determination to seek wholeness and unity among natural phenomena. In a letter to Marcel Grossman, Einstein wrote what Holton calls his "chief preoccupation in science for the rest of his life," viz. "To recognize the unity of a complex of appearances which [...] seem to be separate things."[3] Think of Faust's craving to see the elements that weave together in Nature's "Inmost." One of Goethe's maxims, from *Maxims and Reflections*, reads: "To escape the endless profusion, fragmentation, and complication of modern science and recover the element of simplicity, we must always ask ourselves: What approach would Plato have taken to a nature which is both simple in essence and manifold in appearance?"[4] Einstein, it is reported, often quoted snippets of *Faust* while in conversation with peers;[5] it is moving and appropriate that his ashes were consigned to the wind accompanied by the last lines—Goethe's—on the death of Schiller:

He gleams like some departing meteor bright,
Combining, with his own, eternal light.[6]

The Goethean view of wholeness was an ideological football; it was not long in coming to Einstein, since it had been established as an integral piece of "the Germanic ideology" decades earlier, and one that never died. There was a critique of university science coming from the Right, one prong of the allegedly conservative reaction against modernism—against democracy, industrialization, urbanization— witness Julius Langbehn, whose "Weltbild" resonates with Einstein's to

---

3   Ibid., 23.
4   *The Essential Goethe*, ed. Matthew Bell (Princeton, NJ: Princeton University Press, 2016), 1006. "Um sich aus der grenzenlosen Vielfachheit, Zerstückelung und Verwickelung der modernen Naturlehre wieder ins Einfache zu retten, muß man sich immer die Frage vorlegen: Wie würde sich Plato gegen die Natur, wie sie uns jetzt in ihrer größeren Mannigfaltigkeit, bei aller gründlichen Einheit, erscheinen mag, benommen haben?" https://freeditorial.com. J.W. v. Goethe, "Maximen und Reflexionen," no. 134.
5   Jürgen Neffe, *Einstein—A Biography*, tr. Shelley Frisch (Baltimore, MD: Johns Hopkins University Press, 2005), 372.
6   "Er glänzt uns vor, wie ein Komet entschwindend,/ Unendlich Licht mit seinem Licht verbindend." "Epilog zu Schillers Glocke." http://www.zeno.org/ Literatur/M/Goethe,+Johann+Wolfgang/Gedichte/(Gedichte.+Nachlese)/ Epilog+zu+Schillers+Glocke.

the degree that he builds on Goethe. Here, I cite Fritz Stern's study of German cultural pessimism titled *The Politics of Cultural Despair*:

He [Langbehn] allowed the possibility of science, provided it would turn into an *intuitive, mystical endeavor*: "Only a science of laws, a science of the spirit [*Geist*] can really be called a science and that kind of science stands close to art." The inductive method, Langbehn averred, could never lead to an understanding of what he alternately dubbed *Geist des Ganzen* or *Tektonik der Natur*; only after the structure had been intuitively grasped could the facts acquire meaning. As a positive example of this "science" he cited Goethe's theory of colors and asserted that its total wrongness was preferable to, say, Darwin's "partial truths."[7]

Without suggesting in the least that Einstein had Langbehn in mind when he professed his "themata" (thus Holton) —his leading ideas of wholeness, simplicity, and symmetry in advance of the gathering of empirical data—the originating intuition of Einstein's procedure is well characterized as one of the *"Geist des Ganzen"* or *"Tektonik der Natur."*

Hermann Broch repeats Langbehn's claim from the Left, in speaking of the fortunes of art and science within his major concern: the fate of literature in what was until recently our century—the twentieth. Writing on Broch's sense of the task of a literature responsive to "art and science,"[8] the Germanist E. W. Herd observes, "It is significant that Broch has at times been interpreted as a mystic, at other times as a rationalist constructor of algebraic novels," or, as the poet Nathaniel Tarn puts it, one who would "open the algebraic eyes of paradise."[9] "If," writes Broch, "literature has a task—and it is precisely the case since Goethe—it lies in bringing to light the evidential *mystical* remainder," meaning, the higher irrationality in experience, the metaphysical intuition.[10] These concerns, along with the philosophy of

---

7   Emphasis added. Fritz Stern, *The Politics of Cultural Despair: A Study in the Rise of the Germanic Ideology* (Berkeley, CA: University of California Press, 1974), 125.

8   E. W. Herd, "Hermann Broch on Goethe's View of the Artist's Task," *PEGS* 29 no. 1 (1960): 36. I am following several of Herd's suggestions of cogent texts by Broch.

9   Ibid., 36. Translations of Broch are mine throughout. Nathaniel Tarn, "Poems: Nathaniel Tarn," "Old Savage/Young City," *Dialectical Anthropology* 11, no. 2/4 (1986): 301.

10   Emphasis added. "Wenn es eine Aufgabe des Dichterischen gibt, und seit Goethe gibt es eben diese, so liegt sie in der Hebung jenes beweisenden mystischen Restes." Hermann Broch, *Briefe 1 (1913–1938)*, *Kommentierte Werkausgabe* (Frankfurt am Main: Suhrkamp, 1981), 13/1: 186.

history, thus Broch, are no longer addressed in the (human) sciences. Here, Goethe serves Broch's *Weltbild* as the vital *terminus ante quem* for literature's quandary and a unique example of its solution.

Broch's invocation of Goethe in formulating the task of the artist is based on a pained recognition of the splitting of parts in the world and in the self. This awareness is dominant in Goethe, leading to "the problem of creating a new synthesis of the part-selves." Broch's letter to one Herbert Bergmüller—who, in 1935, in the *Frankfurter Zeitung*, had published a "großes Feuilleton" on Broch—speaks of the splitting of the ego:

> And there it seems to me that you find yourself in a most dubious split, in a tearing apart of reason, emotion, drives, in an inner splitting of personality that, to be sure, is probably necessary for the poet, since otherwise he could never think dramatically. Goethe's life, too, was one specifically split. But this is at the same time his greatest danger; for the work of art, poetry, is successful only when the poet succeeds in collecting his self again in his work and bringing it to a unity, for which Goethe again is a good example.[11]

According to Broch, the century following Goethe's *Wilhelm Meister's Journeyman Years* and *Faust* suffered the loss of a universalist science and a universalist literature—a defect that Goethe intuited. Broch develops his claim.

It is certainly possible, indeed, probable that Goethe had foreseen this development [i.e., the loss of a universal knowledge]. Otherwise, it would be impossible to explain why he—the contemporary of Kant, Fichte, and Schelling; the friend of Schiller, a Kantian—could find no way to relate to Kant's philosophy; and it would be otherwise impossible to explain why Goethe, whose

---

11   "Und da will mir nun scheinen, das Sie sich in einer höchst bedenklichen Spaltung befinden, in einer Auseinanderreißung des Verstandesmäßigen, des Gefühlsmäßigen, des Triebmäßigen, in einer inneren Personzersplitterung, die zwar für den Dichter wahrscheinlich unerläßlich ist, da er sonst niemals dramatisch denken könnte—auch Goethes Leben war ein spezifisch aufgespaltenes—, die aber gleichzeitig seine höchste Gefahr ist; denn das Kunstwerk, die Dichtung, gelingt nur, wenn es dem Dichter gelingt, im Werk seine Person wieder zu sammeln und zur Einheit zu bringen, wofür wieder Goethe als Beispiel anzuführen ist." *Briefe 1 (1913–1938), Kommentierte Werkausgabe,* 13/1: 365. Cited in Peter Bruce Waldeck, *The Split Self from Goethe to Broch* (Lewisburg, PA: Bucknell University Press, 1979), 157–58.

scientific interests were truly universal, could almost *hate* the science of specialists (*Fachwissenschaftlichkeit*). *These are negations that have been sufficiently exploited by the most varied of worldviews: every vagueness seeks to build its Goetheanum in the shadow of the great one.* This rejecter of speculative theology became a "great pagan"; the poet was branded a despiser of rigorous knowledge, a strangely roaring *Weltkind* for whom the only thing that mattered was a vague concept of "life"; and his rejection of Kant's philosophy brought him the distinction of being one of the first positivists. And because he termed himself a dilettante, every amateur summoned him as "compurgator," a sworn witness. What a gross and ever-persistent blasphemy! For it was clearer to no one more than to Goethe how deeply literature (*das Dichterische*) is anchored in the problem of knowledge; no one opted for literature with a greater sense of responsibility. His dilettantism was that of a man who, unsatisfied by specialist science, strives to achieve the universality of all knowledge: it [this dilettantism] is the great and serious responsibility of a man bent on *knowing*, since he burst the precincts of rational knowledge and, outstripping them, began to look for something that can be supplied neither by the speculative epistemology of theology nor philosophy nor by the so-called *real* knowledge of exact science. It was the knowledge and the well-founded skepticism of the *responsible* man, who thus anticipated what would become a fact a hundred years later; and it was the knowledge of the actual goal of his *voluntas sciendi*, directed to *the mystical remainder* that lies in all experience—to that higher reality that overshadows all external "positive" reality, to that truly metaphysical knowledge—which, to raise up, became the genuine and essential but also super-bourgeois task of Goethe's poetry.[12]

---

[12]   Latin and emphasis supplied. "Es ist durchaus möglich, ja wahrscheinlich, dass Goethe diese Entwicklung vorausgeahnt hat. Anders wäre es nicht zu erklären, dass er, der Zeitgenosse Kants, Fichtes, Schellings, er, der Freund des Kantianers Schiller, keinerlei Verhältnis zur Kantschen Philosophie hatte finden können, anders wäre es nicht erklärlich, dass er, dessen wissenschaftliche Interessen wahrlich universal zu nennen sind, doch beinahe mit Hass die Fachwissenschaftlichkeit betrachten konnte. Es sind dies Negationen, die von den verschiedensten Weltanschauungen zur Genüge ausgeschrotet worden sind: jede Verschwommenheit sucht ihr Goetheanum im Schatten des Großen zu errichten. Der Ablehner der spekulativen Theologie wurde zum 'großen Heiden,' der Dichter wurde zum Verächter der strengen Erkenntnis gestempelt, zu einem seltsam brausenden 'Weltkind,' dem bloß ein vager Begriff 'Leben' etwas galt, und seine Ablehnung der Kantschen Philosophie trug ihm den Titel eines ersten Positivisten ein. Und weil er sich Dilettant nannte, hat jeder

For Broch, the modern writer's inescapable task, again invoking Goethe, is to embrace the whole of human experience in the unity of the work, "mirroring," in Broch's special idiom, "the cosmogony of the world in items selected from the vocabulary of reality (*in der Auswahl der Realitätsvokabeln die Kosmogonie der Welt zu spiegeln*)."[13] The form of that work to come—the new work of totality—is the "polyhistoric novel." The repeated return to Goethe is a reminder of an exemplary achievement: Goethe was the last to accomplish the writer's task of "totalization." It would not have been possible, and it will not be possible in the future, except through a devoted cognitive and imaginative effort.

Goethe took on this task. He wanted it to be understood as religious; and this at a time when Christian religiousness was a good deal livelier than today. For him, it was closely related to the concept of *Bildung* (education, self-formation). [. . .] *Bildung* has the task of selecting out the polyhistorical cognitive capital (*Wissensgut*) of the age, of organizing it in accordance with the highest value, of making it ethically fruitful, as it were, and thus constructing, for the person to whom the education is conveyed, the being that he is—what he should be: a personality. And again, it is a testimony to Goethe's forward-looking genius that the religious element had to fade even more; that one hundred years

---

Dilettantismus ihn zum Eideshelfer angerufen. Welch ungeheuerliche und ewig noch fortgesetzte Blasphemie! denn niemandem war es klarer als Goethe, wie sehr das Dichterische im Erkenntnisproblem verankert ist, niemand hat die Entscheidung für das Dichterische mit größerer Verantwortlichkeit getroffen. Sein Dilettantismus war der des Menschen, der in keiner Fachwissenschaft Genüge findet und der die Universalität alles Wissensgutes zu erreichen trachtet, und es ist die gewaltige und ernste Verantwortlichkeit des Wissenden, da er die rationalen Erkenntnisgebiete sprengend und sie überflügelnd, nach etwas zu suchen anhob, das weder von der spekulativen Erkenntnistheorie der Theologie oder der Philosophie, noch von der sozusagen realen Erkenntnis der exakten Wissenschaft geliefert werden kann: es war das Wissen und die fundierte Skepsis des Verantwortlichen, der damit das vorwegnahm, was hundert Jahre später zur Tatsache wurde, und es war das Wissen um das eigentliche Ziel seines Erkenntniswillens, gerichtet auf den mystischen Rest, der in aller Erfahrung steckt, auf jene höhere Realität, die alle äußere positivistische Realität überschattet, auf jene wahrhaft metaphysische Erkenntnis, die zu heben die eigentliche und wesenhafte, aber auch überbürgerliche Aufgabe der Goetheschen Dichtung geworden ist." *Schriften zur Literatur I, Kritik, 9/1, Kommentierte Werkausgabe,* 9/1: 85–86. Cited in Herd, "Hermann Broch on Goethe's View," 29.

13   *Schriften zur Literatur I, Kritik, 9/1, Kommentierte Werkausgabe,* 9/1: 85. Cited in Herd, "Hermann Broch on Goethe's View," 36.

had to pass before literature might assume, had to assume, the Goethean legacy. The modern novel has become polyhistorical. Its elements of the vocabulary of reality (*Realitätsvokabeln*) are the great world views of the time.[14]

Broch alludes to "the great naturalistic worldviews of the French novel, of Dostoyevsky's great psychological (*psychisch*) worldview. [. . .] But the task of the Goethean-polyhistorical novel is still broader [. . .] and the approaches to achieving this task can be seen everywhere." Broch continues:

Certainly, much in the modern novel can no longer be termed Goethean. Only the structure and the task are Goethean. [. . .] But as remote as some of these attempts may be from the spiritual sphere of Goethe, or from an attitude such as that sought by Thomas Mann [*presumably, the ironical love and dissolution of tradition*], a common goal (*Wertziel*—literally, target-value) is visible for all these efforts, and this is no more and no less than the new goal of the novel [. . .]. And even if the path is marked by the name of Goethe, the path that leads to this goal need not be Goethean—every genius that approximates him is in a deeper sense Goethean [. . .].[15]

---

14   "Goethe hat diese Aufgabe auf sich genommen. Es war ihm die Aufgabe, in der er das Religiöse verstanden haben wollte, und dies in einer Zeit, in der das christlich Religiöse noch von einer ganz anderen Lebendigkeit war als heute. Es war ihm mit dem Begriff der Bildung eng verschwistert. [. . .] Bildung in diesem Sinne aber hat auch die Aufgabe, das polyhistorische Wissensgut der jeweiligen Zeit auszuwählen, es unter die Leitung des obersten Wertes zu stellen, es gewissermaßen ethisch fruchtbar zu machen und damit den Menschen, dem die Bildung übermittelt wird, als das aufzubauen, was er ist, was er sein soll: Persönlichkeit. Und wieder ist es ein Zeugnis für das vorausschauende Genie Goethes, daß das Religiöse erst noch weiter verblassen musste, daß hundert Jahre vergehen mussten, ehe die Dichtung das Goethesche Erbe antreten durfte, antreten musste. Der moderne Roman ist polyhistorisch geworden. Seine Realitätsvokabeln sind die großen Weltbilder der Zeit. Wir haben anfangs von den großen naturalistischen Weltbildern des französischen Romans gesprochen, von dem großen psychischen Weltbild Dostojewskijs. Die Aufgabe des Goetheisch-polyhistorischen Romans ist noch weiter gefasst, und die Ansätze zur Erfüllung dieser Aufgabe sind allenthalben zu sehen. *Schriften zur Literatur I, Theorie,* 9/2: 115–16.

15   "Sicherlich kann vieles im modernen Roman nicht mehr als Goetheisch bezeichnet werden. Goetheisch ist bloß die Struktur und die Aufgabe. [. . .] Aber so weit sich auch manche dieser Versuche von der geistigen Sphäre entfernen mögen, die die Sphäre Goethes war, oder von einer Haltung, wie sie von Thomas

Goethe's achievement guides Broch's conception of the only validity
that literature can claim: achieving the task of a totality of the knowledge
of its time.

> If literature has any justification, [as] a timelessness of artistic
> creation, then it lies in [its producing] a totality of knowledge. For
> the totality of an understanding of the world, such as the work of
> art strives for—at least in Goethe's sense—compresses all
> knowledge of the infinite development of mankind into a single
> simultaneous act of cognition.[16]

Broch is alluding to Goethe's own words, as reported in a productive
essay by the philosopher Charles Hendel, titled "Goethe's *Faust* and
Philosophy": "True, a poet is always inclined somewhat to be an
Epicurean, for he is interested in the present moment, but as Goethe
often said, the poet seeks to 'lend eternity to the moment,' and it is that
making of an experience eternal that is the poet's essential joy."[17] Broch
finally elaborates:

> Eternity must be included in a single existence, in a single work of
> art and its totality; and the closer the work of art advances to the
> limit of totality, the more durable it proves to be. In this highest
> sense, the artist creates not only for the entertainment and
> instruction of his audience, but he works solely on the formation
> of his own existence. It is education as Goethe understood it, as he
> opposed it to philosophy and the sciences. It is that hard and strict
> task of knowledge that accompanied him all his life, compelling
> him, with always unsatisfied hunger, to take up and in the true
> sense of the word transform all the manifestations of life in
> himself. And it is that totality of existence that pushed him to
> completely new forms of expression and which laid the foundation

---

Mann angestrebt wird, es ist für alle diese Bemühungen ein gemeinsames Ziel
sichtbar, und dieses ist nicht mehr und nicht weniger als das neue Wertziel des
Romans. [. . .] Und wenn es auch durch den Namen Goethes gekennzeichnet ist,
so braucht der Weg, der zu ihm führt, kein Goetheischer zu sein,—jedes Genie,
das ihm nahekommt, ist in einem tieferen Sinne Goetheisch." Ibid., 116.

[16]   "Wenn es eine Existenzberechtigung der Literatur gibt, eine Überzeitlichkeit
des künstlerischen Schaffens, so liegt sie in solcher Totalität des Erkennens.
Denn die Totalität einer Welterfassung, wie sie das Kunstwerk, zumindest
das im Goetheschen Sinne, anstrebt, drängt alles Wissen der unendlichen
Menschheitsentwicklung in einen einzigen simultanen Erkenntnisakt
zusammen." *Schriften zur Literatur I, Kritik,* 9/1: 86.

[17]   Charles Hendel, "Goethe's *Faust* and Philosophy," *Philosophy and
Phenomenological Research* 10, no. 2 (December 1949): 162.

stone of the new literature (*Dichtung*), the new novel, in *Wilhelm Meister's Journeyman Years or The Renunciants*. But it is also the totality of form that is adequate to it, that is, the complete mastery of all aesthetic means of expression, subordinate to the universality of content, in the way that *Faust* exploded all forms of the theatrical.[18]

In his *Man the Measure*, Erich Kahler adds other lights to Broch's perception of Goethe's split self; he then opposes Goethe to Thomas Mann, whom we shall soon be addressing. Here is Kahler on Goethe:

Goethe was the first to mirror split worlds ["the sphere of individual everyday life" and "the scene that the poet uses for his background"]. His thoughts and images move in a sphere that [. . .] belongs [. . .] to a very much enriched and erudite culture. In his effort to establish a comprehensive connection between the various contents of his world, there is a conscious strain created by the tension he feels between [. . .] the exigencies of individual life and the vital questions of human existence and of nature. [. . .] Here, for the first time, the problem of civilization emerges, the conflict of the individual with his cultural world. Goethe's [. . .] entire lifework can only be understood as a tremendous effort to master human instincts and passions and to integrate them in the cultural order of man, to create harmony not only between the overpowering contents of culture itself but also between human urges and the demands of a highly developed society. Goethe was concerned with equilibrium, with human, artistic and

---

18   "[I]n einem einzigen Dasein, in einem einzigen Kunstwerk und seiner Totalität soll die Ewigkeit eingeschlossen werden, und je näher das Kunstwerk an die Grenze der Totalität vorstößt, desto zeitüberdauernder erweist es sich. Der Künstler in diesem höchsten Sinn schafft nicht nur zur Unterhaltung und Belehrung seines Publikums, sondern er wirkt einzig und allein an der Bildung seines eigenen Daseins. Es ist die Bildung, wie Goethe sie verstanden hat, wie er sie der Philosophie und den Wissenschaften entgegengehalten hat, es ist jene harte und strenge Aufgabe der Erkenntnis, die ihn sein ganzes Leben begleitete, ihn zwingend, mit stets ungestilltem Hunger alle Lebenserscheinungen in sich aufzunehmen und im wahren Sinne des Wortes umzubilden. Und es ist jene Totalität des Daseins, die ihn zu ganz neuen Ausdrucksformen drängte, und die in den *Wanderjahren* den Grundstein der neuen Dichtung, des neuen Romans, legte, aber es ist auch die ihr adäquate Totalität der Form, d.h. die völlige Beherrschung sämtlicher ästhetischer Ausdrucksmittel, untergeordnet der Universalität des Inhalts, wie sie im *Faust* alle Formen des Theatralischen sprengte." *Schriften zur Literatur I, Kritik*, 9/1: 86.

cosmic order. [. . .] In "Tasso," "Iphigenie," and in "The Elective Affinities," elemental urges and relations are subordinated to the law of form, of measure, of cultural harmony represented by educated society, by humanity, by sublimated morality. The educated individual of modern times is subject to the law of self-control and renunciation. [. . .] And the cosmic drama of *Faust*—the first to treat the theme of man's transcendence, of the daring, modern Prometheus, the secularized human mind that tries to dominate the universe by knowledge—this great drama takes place on another, purely spiritual plane; the sphere of wonted everyday life is left behind.[19]

Kahler begins the task of measuring Goethe against Mann with an epochal survey of literary-intellectual trends.

In the representative literary production at the end of the nineteenth century, the individual I is no longer the bearer of action but the passive object of impersonal powers and currents [. . .]. From this time on, in the literature of the twentieth century, the loss of substance, the dissolution and the transcendence of individual life is accelerated. More and more, personal destinies and relations become the mere occasion, the mere material for the presentation of social, cultural or metaphysical needs. The path the bourgeois century has taken becomes especially clear when we compare the basic features of the work of Thomas Mann with the fundamental ideas of Goethe, to whom he has an inner relationship. For he too is concerned with affirming and saving human form that is guaranteed by civilization. But while Goethe still attempts to build up the human form from within, from the harmony of human substance and elements, and to force the powers and contents of personality, society, and nature into one cosmos, the twentieth-century writer is no longer capable of mastering such a task.[20]

The last claim of Kahler's is very interesting as prompting, almost word-for-word, Mann's denial. In a famous sentence Mann wrote to the learned Yale Germanist Hermann Weigand, Mann declared:

---

[19]   Erich Kahler, *Man the Measure: A New Approach to History* (New York: George Braziller, 1956), 501–3.

[20]   Ibid., 507.

Even in these times it is possible for a man to construct out of his life and work a culture, a small cosmos, in which everything is interrelated, which, despite all diversity, forms a complete personal whole, which stands more or less on an equal footing with the great life-syntheses of earlier ages.[21]

He was entitled to think that his own achievement had met this standard, and everything he accomplished at Princeton belonged to it. Kahler continues:

Thomas Mann's fundamental aim is, as it were, the negative of Goethe's. He stakes off the human form from without, from the periphery. In his work, he traverses various border-regions, the spheres of physical and psychic forces that are more powerful than the individual and that endanger personality: the degeneration of a family ("Buddenbrooks"), disease ("The Magic Mountain"), crime ("Felix Krull"), erotic enchantment ("Death in Venice"), the play with psychic powers ("Mario and the Magician"), the impersonality of modern government ("Royal Highness"), the hypertrophy of genius ("The Beloved Returns"), the mythical chaos and the totemistic and animal dregs in the depths of the soul ("Joseph and His Brothers"), the disruption of the organism ("The Transposed Heads"). And herein the writer himself is often deluged and swept along by the power of the forces he has conjured. The subconscious currents in the ego, with all their flotsam and jetsam, break forth with greater strength than he is prepared to admit. They can only be controlled by the flexible irony characteristic of his style, by the continual motion of going beyond, leveling down, keeping all the all-too-serious threats within bounds.[22]

[21]   Letter from Thomas Mann to Hermann Weigand, April 29, 1952, in *The Letters of Thomas Mann, 1889–1955*, tr. Richard and Clara Winston (New York: Knopf, 1970), 642. "Auch heute ist es möglich, aus seinem Leben und Werk eine Kultur, einen kleinen Kosmos zu machen, indem alles sich aufeinander bezieht, der bei aller Diversität ein geschlossenes persönliches Ganzes bildet, und mit dem man vor den großen Lebenssynthesen früherer Epochen einigermaßen besteht." Cited in Thomas Klugkist, *Sehnsuchtskosmogonie: Thomas Manns "Doktor Faustus" im Umkreis seiner Schopenhauer-, Nietzsche- und Wagner-Rezeption* (Würzburg: Königshausen & Neumann, 2000), 423.
[22]   Kahler, *Man the Measure*, 508.

Certainly, there is science in Mann's approach, this "staking off the human form from without, from the periphery." A friend of Kahler, Walter Kaufmann, a professor of philosophy at Princeton, who some years later frequented the same Princeton café as Kahler although not necessarily at the same time or table, also wanted his readers to accept Goethe's skepticism "as basically right about science"—namely, it can thrive even with false hypotheses.[23] These remarks constitute Kaufmann's plaidoyer for the circle's refusal of an objectivist science. Also citing Goethe's anti-Newtonian theory of colors, Kaufmann writes, "It does not matter for our purposes"—an intellectual history of "the mind"—"who was right."[24] Nonetheless, despite one's feeling that this criterion does matter, "Goethe," continues Kaufmann, "contributed a great deal to the discovery of the mind."[25] In doing so, it was in despite of mathematics, which Goethe famously disparaged. If Kahler heard this argument years before its publication by Kaufmann—the cliché of a good, affect-laden science, a staple of the "conservative revolution," of which he was at one time an adherent—he would have affirmed it

---

[23]   Under the heading "Some Cafés and Coffee Houses," in a memoir of his tenure at the Institute for Advanced Study in Princeton, the late mathematician Carl Clifton Faith wrote:

> In later years (1968) [. . .] I gravitated to the newly opened PJ's Pancake restaurant, and at least one other mathematician, Solomon Bochner, gravitated with me. Other habitués were Walter Kaufmann, Louis Fischer, and Erich Kahler, who wrote *The Disinherited Mind*.

The author of this work is not in fact Erich Kahler but the late Erich Heller. Faith might be thinking of Kahler's *Disintegration of Form in the Arts* (New York: George Braziller, 1968), which was based on lectures delivered at Princeton University in spring, 1967. Carl Clifton Faith, *Rings and Things and a Fine Array of Twentieth Century Associative Algebra* (Providence, RI: American Mathematical Society, 2004), 354.

Although—according to Faith—Kahler and Kaufmann used to frequent the same coffeehouse (the correct name of the "café" is PJ's Pancake *House*), one cannot know whether they actually shared a table or, like father and son, as in Kafka's *Das Urteil*, merely dined there at the same time, viz. "das Mittagessen nahmen sie gleichzeitig in einem Speisehaus ein." When I told Rob Tempio (executive editor of the Princeton University Press) about the meeting of Kahler and Kaufmann and my idea about a book on the Kahler Circle, he was quick to suggest the title, modeled on Sarah Bakewell's excellent *At the Existentialist Café: Freedom, Being, and Apricot Cocktails* (New York: The Other Press, 2016)— namely, *At PJ's Pancake House: Nature, Extremity, and Flapjacks.*

[24]   Walter Kaufmann, *Discovering the Mind*, vol. 1: *Goethe, Kant, and Hegel* (New Brunswick, NJ: Transaction, 1991 [originally published in 1980 by McGraw-Hill]), 35.

[25]   Ibid., 46.

while insisting that it be edited in conformity with such statements of it by his friend Einstein as

The most beautiful thing we can experience is the mysterious.[26] It is the fundamental emotion which stands at the cradle of true art and science. Whoever does not know it and can no longer wonder, no longer marvel, is as good as dead and his eyes are dimmed [. . .].[27] To know that what is impenetrable to us really exists, manifesting itself as the highest wisdom and the most radiant beauty, which our dull faculties can comprehend only in their most primitive forms—this knowledge, this feeling is at the center of true religiosity.[28]

Here is a final word on Kaufmann's very approving discussion of Goethe's exceptional science. It follows an animus against Goethe's abstruse arch-romantic rivals: "What Goethe ranked above everything in science as in poetry, was 'Anschauung,' a word that combines the senses of seeing and contemplating—a contemplation that arises, legitimately, only from concrete visual apprehension."[29] We have this nice paraphrase by Charles Hendel: "'The lesson of (modern) empiricism,' [. . . Hegel] said in his *Logic*, 'is that man must see for

---

26   "Das schönste und tiefste Gefühl, das wir erleben können, ist die Erfahrung des Geiheimnisvollen." The "mysterious" (*das Geheimnisvolle*) is often translated tendentiously as the "mystical." On one website, a slight variant of this sentence is rendered as "The most beautiful and profound feeling that we can experience (*erleben*) is the experience (*Erfahrung*) of the *mystical*" (emphasis added). Here is the culpable website: http://www.dober.de/reli-rallye/einstein. html. This falsification is productively exposed on "ZITATFORSCHUNG: FALSCHZITATE mit Belegen und Kommentaren," https://falschzitate. blogspot.com/2017/12/das-tiefste-und-erhabenste-gefuhl.html?m=0.

27   Albert Einstein, *Ideas and Opinions*, ed. Carl Seelig and trans. Sonja Bargmann (New York: Bonanza Books, 1954), 11.

28   "Das schönste, was wir erleben können, ist das Geheimnisvolle. Es ist das Grundgefühl, das an der Wiege von wahrer Kunst und Wissenschaft steht. Wer es nicht kennt und sich nicht mehr wundern, nicht mehr staunen kann, der ist sozusagen tot und sein Auge erloschen. [. . .] Das Wissen um die Existenz des für uns Undurchdringlichen, der Manifestationen tiefster Vernunft und leuchtendster Schönheit, die unserer Vernunft nur in ihren primitivsten Formen zugänglich sind, dies Wissen und Fühlen macht wahre Religiosität aus." Albert Einstein, *Mein Weltbild* (Amsterdam: Querido Verlag, 1934), 16. The translation of the concluding sentence of this passage is provided in David Rowe and Robert Schulmann, *Einstein on Politics: His Private Thoughts and Public Stands on Nationalism* (Princeton, NJ: Princeton University Press, 2007), 229–30.

29   Kaufmann, *Discovering the Mind*, 47.

himself and feel that he is present in every fact of knowledge which he has to accept.' Certainly that was Goethe's way—to see for himself and to be present with everything that may be known and to place his own valuation upon each moment of existence."[30] The discoveries made by such "Anschauung," continues Kaufmann, have contributed greatly to the discovery of the mind, as "the hankering for certainty and the model of mathematics" have not; in fact the latter "have been extremely harmful."[31] Before one gets on one's rationalist high horse, Kaufmann would have us know that Goethe was not "an apostle of feeling" in the sense of justifying "a plea of incomprehensibility [. . . but he] felt that understanding cannot dispense with feeling." Kaufmann's appreciation of the marriage of science and feeling, like that of Broch's, arises from a deep place in his work: it is the long-standing plaidoyer that cites Nietzsche's wish for a new, full human type, the "musiktreibender Sokrates" (a musical Socrates). This is the fully human type that the German "conservative revolution" of the first decades of the twentieth century sought to conjure—and whose literary and philosophical supports Kahler, as we have stressed, helped to provide. The "new man" anchors the "Goethaneums" that both humanists Kaufmann and Kahler construct and to which Broch—and, with provisos, Mann and Einstein, contributed.

The Goethe of the Circle figures interestingly in the historical judgment made by Broch that we noted in the preceding chapter: "The two great rational ways of making things intelligible (*Verständigungsmittel*) in modernity are the language of science in mathematics and the language of money in *bookkeeping*" (emphasis added).[32] What are the special sources, one might ask, from which Broch draws his judgment? One such source must once again be this very Goethe—his novel *Wilhelm Meister's Apprenticeship*—for, in book 1, chapter 10, Wilhelm's friend Werner praises double-entry bookkeeping as "among the finest inventions of the human mind (*eine der schönsten Erfindungen des menschlichen Geistes*)."[33]

Now, one must add that this sentence is not an assured positive aesthetic judgment that can be attributed to Goethe. In evoking Werner's

---

[30]   Hendel, "Goethe's *Faust* and Philosophy," 161.

[31]   Kaufmann, *Discovering the Mind*, 48.

[32]   Hermann Broch, *Die Schlafwandler: Eine Romantrilogie* (Frankfurt am Main: Suhrkamp Taschenbuch, 1994), 537–38.

[33]   https://www.gutenberg.org/files/36483/36483-h/36483-h.htm; https://www.gutenberg.org/ebooks/2335. In this, Goethe's second novel, the bureaucrat Albert, the antipode to the poetic visionary Werther in *The Sufferings of Young Werther*, reappears, figuratively, as the type of the businessman that Wilhelm is unable to transcend. Terry Eagleton observes, "Wilhelm Meister

passion for balancing the books, can Goethe have been writing only ironically? Mirrors upon mirrors: the arch-romantic Novalis (whom Kaufmann so disliked) saw *Wilhelm Meister* as dominated by its worldly prose, its unpoetic character, lacking all "nature and *mysticism*" (*Mystizism*), merely "a poetized bourgeois and domestic story (*eine poëtisierte bürgerliche und häusliche Geschichte*)." Years later, in another polemic against the *Lehrjahre*, Novalis saw its "true principle [. . .] [as] the economic (*Die Oeconomische Natur ist die Wahre*)." At the same time, he calls the book a "farce (*Hinten wird alles Farçe*)."[34]

Broch is taken with the concept of bookkeeping, as we might recall from the preceding chapter, deploying it to confer unity on his novel *Esch oder die Anarchie* (Esch the Anarchist, 1929), the second volume of his grand trilogy *Die Schlafwandler* (The Sleepwalkers). The important idea of *ethical* bookkeeping surfaces both as a topic and a narrative practice. August Esch, the eponymous hero, is a bookkeeper who gets fired after realizing that his boss has been cooking the books. A hero of conscience—though a lamed one—Esch is maddened by his discovery but cannot manage to report the crime. He leaves.

In the course of his wanderings, Esch visits a variety show, where an inarticulate woman, said to be Hungarian, has a man throw knives at her; her virtual martyrdom makes a deep impression on him. Next, Esch visits a political rally, which leads to a trumped-up charge against a friend of his, Martin, a meek socialist agitator, who goes to jail for it. This injustice rankles in Esch; it vexes the "solid and legitimate bookkeeping of his soul (*die solide und rechtliche Buchhaltung seiner Seele*)" and, again, "the upright bookkeeping of his soul (*die rechtschaffene Buchhaltung seiner Seele*)."[35] Next, Esch visits a Salvation Army rally, where he is struck by talk of "redemption (*Erlösung*)."[36] From this point on, the novel consists importantly of extended, agonized meditations on Esch's part on how to square the world's accounts, either by some

---

begins by elevating the Muse of Tragedy over the figure of Commerce, but by the end of the novel, having met with no particular success on stage, he will acknowledge commerce as the true form of nobility." Terry Eagleton, *Sweet Violence: The Idea of the Tragic* (Oxford: Blackwell, 2003), 191.

34   Novalis (Friedrich von Hardenberg), "Wilhelm Meisters Lehrjahre," in Stephen Prickett, ed., *European Romanticism: A Reader* (London: Bloomsbury, 2010), 148. "Der unauslöschliche Eindruck eines Bildes—dem Herrn Geheimrat Goethe zum 270. Geburtstag," *AISTHESIS: Texte zur Ästhetik, Philosophie und Kunstkritik sowie vermischte Bemerkungen*, https://bersarin.wordpress.com/2019/08/28/der-unausloeschliche-eindruck-eines-bildes-dem-herrn-geheimrat-goethe-zum-270-geburtstag/.

35   Broch, *Die Schlafwandler*, 199, 266.

36   Ibid., 219.

form of self-inflicted martyrdom (conforming to "a logic of sacrifice" and thus including marriage) or by the punishment of the guilty (part of a more nearly rational settling of accounts). The tangled plot could lead one to conclude, along with Esch, that accounts have indeed been settled—Esch gets married—but the novel actually ends thus: "He realized that it was purely coincidental if the addition of the columns tallied [. . .]."[37]

Two remarks. First, Esch's insight is at least as old as 500 CE. In the *Bereshit Rabbah* (49:20), one reads: "If it is a world you want, then strict justice is impossible. And if it is strict justice you want, then a world is impossible."[38] We·shall soon be hearing about Thomas Mann's manner of "correcting" the world's injustice.

Second, considering the authority that Broch imputes to Goethe, seeing him as "in the truth" of his epoch, it is unlikely that he would consider Goethe's fictive praise of bookkeeping as acidic mockery. Mathematics and bookkeeping—in a more recent critical vocabulary termed "discursive practices"—are robust supports to modern knowledge, although they are *not enough*: they leave out the mystical remainder of heightened experience.

During his stay in Princeton, Thomas Mann wrote an entire novel about Goethe—*Lotte in Weimar* (aka *The Beloved Returns*) —into which, as Kahler observed, Mann secreted details of his own personality, noting "the relationship between your own [Mann's] nature and Goethe's, on the hiding places and underground corridors that you have so cunningly found for highly personal statements."[39] The most striking of these statements appears immediately after the fictional Goethe has asserted his unpopularity: "Das aber ists, daß ich zum Repräsentanten geboren und garnicht zum Märtyrer" ("But the thing is, that I was born to be exemplary [lit. "a representative"] and no way a martyr").[40] And here is Mann, writing to the Dean of the Faculty of the

---

37   "Aber er erkannte, daß es bloßer Zufall war, wenn die Addition der Kolonnen stimmte [. . .]." Ibid., 380. This discussion of bookkeeping in *Die Schlafwandler* is drawn from my "Bookkeeping in the Modernist Novel," in *Modernism*, ed. Astradur Eysteinsson and Vivian Liska (Amsterdam: John Benjamins, 2007), 371–72.

38   Cited in Vivian Liska, " 'Before the Law stands a doorkeeper. To this doorkeeper comes a man . . .': Kafka, Narrative, and the Law," (New Brunswick, NJ: Rutgers University Press, 2013), 5.

39   EF 29. "die Spiegelung Ihres eigenen in dem Goetheschen Wesen, über die Verstecke und unterirdischen Gänge, die Sie darin für höchst persönliche Aussprachen listenreich gefunden haben" (BR.K 24).

40   LW 327. This crucial proposition is merely omitted in the English translation, *The Beloved Returns* (!).

Humanities at the University of Bonn after he had rescinded Mann's honorary degree: "From the beginning of my intellectual life I had felt myself in happiest accord with the temper of my nation and at home in its intellectual traditions. I am better suited to represent those traditions than to become a martyr for them."[41] "Goethe's" brusque intensifier "garnicht (no way!)" marks the tonal difference in contexts.

Moreover, on this topic of the Mann-Goethe affinity, we might recall from our preface that the chief British prosecutor at the Nuremberg trials, Sir Hartley Shawcross, confirmed the intimacy—if not indeed the identity—of these two geniuses of personal *Bildung*: in an astonishing historical contretemps, Shawcross attributed a jeremiad against the Germans, which Mann had invented for his fictional Goethe, to Goethe himself. Here is Mann's commentary on the consternation which this substitution provoked: "It is true, the quoted words do not appear literally in Goethe's writings or conversations; but they were conceived and formulated strictly in his spirit and although he never spoke them, he might well have done so."[42] "But I could warrant," he then added, in *The Story of a Novel: The Genesis of Doctor Faustus*, "that if Goethe had not really said the words the prosecutor attributed to him, he might very well have said them. In a higher sense, therefore, Sir Hartley had quoted correctly."[43]

The watchwords of Mann's Goethe in *Lotte in Weimar* are, once again, those of Einstein and Broch: totality, wholeness, the unity of competing parts. Goethe's trenchant monologue continues:

> But the thing is, I was born far more apt for reconciliation than for tragedy. Reconciliation, balance—are they not all my striving? To affirm, to acknowledge, to make fruitful: to give both sides balance, harmony. Only the combination of all forces makes up

[41] https://www.pro-europa.eu/europe/mann-thomas-god-help-our-darkened-and-desecrated-country/2/. "Seit ich ins geistige Leben eintrat, habe ich mich in glücklichem Einvernehmen mit den seelischen Anlagen meiner Nation, in ihren geistigen Traditionen sicher geborgen gefühlt. Ich bin weit eher zum Repräsentanten geboren als zum Märtyrer" (GW XII: 787).

[42] Mann, *Tagebücher 1946–1948*, 869; cited in LW *Kommentar*, 170–71. I discuss this incident in my *The Mind in Exile: Thomas Mann in Princeton* (Princeton, NJ: Princeton University Press, 2022).

[43] Thomas Mann, *The Story of a Novel—The Genesis of Doctor Faustus*, tr. Richard and Clara Winston (New York: Knopf, 1961), 193–94. "Doch verbürgte ich mich dafür, daß, wenn Goethe nicht wirklich gesagt habe, was der Ankläger ihm in den Mund gelegt, er es doch sehr wohl hätte sagen können, und in einem höheren Sinne habe Sir Hartley also doch *richtig* zitiert." *Die Entstehung des Doktor Faustus: Roman eines Romans* (Frankfurt am Main: Fischer Taschenbuch Verlag, 1993), 131.

the world; each is important, each worth developing, each talent reaches perfection only through itself. Individuality and society, consciousness and naïveté, romanticism, and practical sense— both, the other side as well, always and equally complete. To absorb, to integrate, *to be the whole,* to shame the partisans of every principle by fulfilling it—and the other side too [. . .]. Humanity as universal, ubiquitous [. . .].[44]

Is this Goethe? Is this Mann? "*Both,* the other side as well, always and equally complete." The essayist Algis Valiunas writes aptly of Mann's *Weltbild:*

Mann's mind is alert to every weakness in every line of thought, and accordingly unwilling to reduce profound moral complication to hapless formulae. Art is required to render truth adequately: For Mann, a story, often a very long story, outdoes the treatise or disquisition or broadside every time. He is a novelist of ideas, but in his work poetry has it over philosophy. Philosophical argument or theological contention is unfailingly partial, in both senses of that word: The whole eludes it. In Mann's hands moral instruction is of a piece with the account of the whole, and in this account the mystery of life remains mysterious.[45]

Mann's elective affinity with Goethe is of an almost inexhaustible breadth. It dates from the very beginning in the character likeness of their parents: paternal rigor in the conduct of life ("des Lebens ernstes Führen") and maternal lightheartedness and artistic sensibility. In a most engaging essay, Frederick Lubich notes another shared feature of

---

[44] LW 331; translation modified; emphasis added. "Das aber ists, daß ich zum Repräsentanten geboren und garnicht zum Märtyrer; für die Versöhnung weit eher, als für die Tragödie. Ist nicht Versöhnung und Ausgleich all mein Betreiben und meine Sache Bejahen, Geltenlassen und Fruchtbarmachen des Einen wie des Anderen, Gleichgewicht, Zusammenklang? Nur alle Kräfte zusammen machen die Welt, und wichtig ist jede, jede entwickelnswert, und jede Anlage vollendet sich nur durch sich selbst. Individualität und Gesellschaft, Bewußtheit und Naivität, Romantik und Tüchtigkeit,—beides, das andere immer auch und gleich vollkommen,—aufnehmen, einbeziehen, das Ganze sein, die Partisanen jedes Prinzips beschämen, indem man es vollendet—und das andere auch [. . .] Humanität als universelle Ubiquität [. . .]" (LWG 327–28).

[45] Algis Valiunas, "Thomas Mann's Civilized Uncertainty," *Humanities* 41, no.3 (Summer 2020), https://www.neh.gov/article/thomas-manns-civilized-uncertainty.

young Goethe and young Mann: their *Bildung* as the scions of two flourishing cities—Frankfurt and Lübeck—rich in culture and rich in trade. Both cities—free cities, the first "imperial," the second Hanseatic—offered Goethe and Mann, as the sons of upper-class (*großbürgerlich*) families, "an urban horizon, which they would further expand throughout their lives into a cosmopolitan *Weltbild*."[46] Still, in both cases, a comfortable socialization was hardly assured. We have the impressive analogy of the marginal artist figures portrayed in their early works—Goethe's *The Sufferings of Young Werther* and Mann's *Tonio Kröger*—nurtured by their own schizoid turmoil. Both outcasts are denied the "bliss of ordinariness." Despite their agonizing, asocial protagonists, these youthful works were received enthusiastically (Goethe composed his short novel in 1774 at the age of 24; Mann composed the novella under extreme tension at the age of 25). In his lecture on *Werther* at Princeton University in 1939, Mann describes this tension: "In order to portray a human creature, forfeit to death, too good or too weak for life, a literary artist need only portray himself [. . .] . Goethe did not kill himself, because he had to write *Werther*" (B 124). One can refer this conclusion to Mann's own state of mind on the verge of writing *Tonio Kröger* and thereafter see his achievement, like Goethe's, as liberating him "for new dimensions of creativity."[47] One new dimension, the so-called *Bildungsroman* (novel of education, of self-realization), was again laid out for Mann by Goethe, as Mann was to confess. Here is Frederick Lubich:

> With his novels *Wilhelm Meisters Lehrjahre* (Wilhelm Meister's Apprenticeship) and *Wilhelm Meisters Wanderjahre* (Wilhelm Meister's Journeyman Years), Goethe created the classic German *Bildungsroman* and thus contributed a seminal literary genre to world literature. Wilhelm Meister's experience of social and personal self-realization became the great pedagogical and cultural program of the German *Bildungsbürgertum* in the nineteenth century [the social class pegging its rise to its degree of cultivation]. Thomas Mann continued this national agenda when he turned to a literary project, which, after more than a decade of gestation, emerged as the representative masterwork of its period: *Der Zauberberg* (*The Magic Mountain*). Originally conceived as a

---

46 Frederick Lubich, "Goethe and Thomas Mann: Elective Affinities between German Classicism and Modernity," *Germanic Notes and Reviews* 43, no. 1 (Spring 2012): 21.

47 Esther Leser, *Thomas Mann's Short Fiction: An Intellectual Biography* (Madison, NJ: Fairleigh Dickinson University Press, 1989), 128.

literary parody of Richard Wagner's opera *Tannhäuser*, Thomas Mann reconceptualized his novel in the spirit of Goethe's *Wilhelm Meister*. According to Thomas Mann, Hans Castorp, the novel's young hero, "walked in the footsteps of Wilhelm Meister (*ist in die Fußstapfen von Wilhelm Meister getreten*)." Castorp's gradual ascent from the practical world of a young Hamburg engineer into the upperclass regions of European culture and the esoteric realms of ancient wisdom is an exemplary *éducation sentimentale et intellectuelle*, which has arguably no parallel in literary modernity.[48]

Lubich discusses in detail what he calls "Mann's Political Reorientation through Goethe," marking the key stations of the conversion with which we are familiar—from "unpolitical," arch-conservative to engaged democratic humanist—via Mann's references to Goethe. Mann's 1921 essay "Goethe and Tolstoy" concludes: "In *Wilhelm Meister's Apprenticeship*, the idea of adventurous, personal self-development changes more and more clearly into that of education, thence, in *Wilhelm Meister's Journeyman Years* [...], to flow completely into the social, indeed political."[49] It is now not just Hans Castorp of *The Magic Mountain* who walks in the footsteps of Wilhelm Meister but Mann himself. In 1932, the year of the 100th anniversary of Goethe's death, Thomas Mann published his programmatic essay "Goethe als Repräsentant des bürgerlichen Zeitalters" (Goethe as Representative of the Bourgeois Age). On the subject of the nation and cosmopolitanism, Goethe is once again Mann's Virgil: "Instead of limiting oneself to one's self, the German needs to absorb the world in order to have an effect on the world [...]. And so, I enjoy looking at foreign nations and advise everyone to do the same. Now, national literature has little resonance: the time of the epoch of world literature has come, and everyone must act so as to accelerate this epoch."[50] Mann's exile, his own "Wanderjahre," began in 1933 and brought him to Princeton, as we know, in 1938, where he all but completed his Goethe novel *Lotte in Weimar*. I have written at some length about this

[48]   Lubich, "Goethe and Thomas Mann," 23.
[49]   "[...] immer deutlicher wandelt sich in den 'Lehrjahren' die Idee der persönlich-abenteuernden Selbstausbildung in die der Erziehung, um in den 'Wanderjahren' [...] völlig ins Soziale, ja Politische zu münden" (GW IX: 150).
[50]   "Anstatt sich in sich selbst zu beschränken, muß der Deutsche die Welt in sich aufnehmen, um auf die Welt zu wirken. [...] Ich sehe mich daher gern bei fremden Nationen um und rate jedem, es auch seinerseits zu tun. Nationalliteratur will jetzt nicht viel sagen, die Epoche der *Weltliteratur* ist an der Zeit" (GW IX: 326).

work in *The Mind in Exile: Thomas Mann in Princeton.* Lubich is right: "In this novelistic retelling of the late re-encounter between the Geheimrat Goethe and Charlotte Kestner, the model for Werther's unrequited love, Thomas Mann's own imitations of Goethe's life and literature reach their idolic and ironic culmination."[51]

Goethe has been associated with many geometrical figures, par excellence: "the eternal screw"—or, bowdlerized, "the spiral." The rhythm of development he celebrated—polarity and intensification (*Polarität und Steigerung*)—is captured in the geometrical figure. In this chapter, I have referred Goethe to an external figure, in which he continues to exercise his authority as the virtual center of a circle. His authority lies in his exemplary self-realization (*Bildung*), which, at a privileged historical moment, assimilated the cognitive capital (*Wissensgut*) of his time. At the same time, this self-realization is readable—declarable—in Goethe's Wilhelm Meister novels and *Faust*— works that establish these "totalizations" in turn as goods for the *Bildung* of the reader. The products of a life of adventurous sensory stimulation and contemplation (*Anschauung*), together with the results of a "two-eyed" science of mensurative logic (*Verstand*) and metaphysical intuition (*Vernunft*), are here brought to a second life:[52]

What is destructible
Is but a parable;
What fails ineluctably,
The undeclarable,
Here it was seen,
Here it was action.[53]

Goethe is representative of an entire culture, a man the measure of his age, suggesting a wholeness of self and world as an ideal, sunk below the horizon of real life and yet a glimmer for exiles in a dark time. Writing in praise of Erich Kahler, George Steiner sums up Goethe's significance for the entire Kahler Circle:

[51]   Lubich, "Goethe and Thomas Mann," 24.
[52]   One reads: "In Goethe's sense, *Verstand* 'deals with what has become formed and congealed, in order to put it to use,' while *Vernunft* 'is concerned with what is evolving and living,' with becoming rather than being." *Goethe on Science: An Anthology of Goethe's Scientific Writings*, ed. Jeremy Naydler (Edinburgh: Floris Books, 1996), cited in Lee-Anne Broadhead and Sean Howard, "Confronting the Contradictions Between Western and Indigenous Science: A Critical Perspective on Two-Eyed Seeing," *AlterNative* 17, no. 1 (2021): 117.
[53]   *Goethe's Faust*, tr. Walter Kaufmann (New York: Random House, 1961), 503.

To read Kahler's books, to hear him teach, is to be in immediate reach of that lineage of humanistic hope which extends from Erasmus to Goethe. Underlying the manifold of Goethe's work, we experience the conviction—profoundly rational yet animate beyond reason—that certain harmonic structures initiate and energize the seeming chaos of sensible and historical life. Both the arts and the sciences are, to Goethe, complementary aspects of a unity which the philosopher, the religious leader and the poet perceive, are wholly mastered by, in moments of illumination.[54]

For the exiles of the Circle, foremost Kahler and Broch, intimations, via Goethe, of a higher harmony—the "mystic rest"—course through the lifeblood of humanistic civilization, inspiring it. They fled the full secularism of barbarism—the politics of rage, the "systematic organization of hatreds"—and erected a Goetheanum in its stead.[55]

[54]   George Steiner, "A Note in Tribute to Erich Kahler," *Salmagundi*, no. 10/11 (Fall 1969–Winter 1970): 193–94.
[55]   The phrase in quotes is by Henry Adams. Cited in Brenda Wineapple, "A Posthumous Life," a review of David S. Brown, *The Last American Aristocrat: The Brilliant Life and Improbable Education of Henry Adams* (New York: Scribner, 2021). *The New York Review of Books,* April 8, 2021, https://www.nybooks.com/articles/2021/04/08/henry-adams-posthumous-life/. We are certainly not done with a politics of rage, witness Pankraj Mishra, *The Age of Anger: A History of the Present* (New York: Farrar, Straus and Giroux, 2017).

Five Mann and Einstein

In 1938, with Arturo Toscanini, [they were] the three most prominent European antifascists in America.

—*Hans Rudolf Vaget*

In his engaging biography of Albert Einstein (1879–1955), Jürgen Neffe writes:

> The former inveterate traveler barely left [. . .] [Princeton], his small town. Still, in the course of twenty years [ca. 1935–55], he appears to have led an eventful life there as well. There were visits from and to the great men of his era, from Niels Bohr and Wilhelm Reich, Nehru and Ben Gurion to Thomas Mann, who lived just a few blocks away from him for several years.[1]

Knowing of their propinquity, and relying on the plural in Neffe's mention of visits "from and to [. . .] Thomas Mann," one might readily imagine their many meetings and conversations. Indeed, as Alexander Leitch wrote in *A Princeton Companion*, "He and Albert Einstein, who had been friends in Germany, met frequently in each other's homes."[2] This claim is repeated in Hermann Kurzke's biography: "In Mann's diary there is [. . .] talk [. . .] always of high respect and friendship." In a letter written by Mann in 1925, continues Kurzke, we read that "being with Einstein" while they were having their portraits painted by Max Liebermann had been "gripping [. . .] thanks to his [Einstein's] gentleness [*Sanftmut*], childlike nature [*Kindlichkeit*], and

---

[1]   Jürgen Neffe, *Einstein—A Biography*, tr. Shelley Frisch (Baltimore, MD: Johns Hopkins University Press, 2005), 375.

[2]   Leitch, *A Princeton Companion* (Princeton: Princeton University Press, 1978), 313.

modesty [*Bescheidenheit*]![3] During Mann's time at Princeton they were neighbors and visited one another often."[4] This claim reappears, even raised to a higher power, in Richard Winston's introduction to his translation of Mann's letters: "From 1938–1940 [Einstein] [. . .] was Mann's near neighbor in Princeton, New Jersey, and the two became *close* friends" (L198; emphasis added). Such allusions to an intimate friendship based on frequent visits between two extraordinary minds are elating— but are they true? What is the evidence for them? It is morally and aesthetically pleasing to think of this intimacy as a fact, especially in light of Mann's own statement, decades later, in his encomium on Einstein's death: "Our acquaintanceship goes back in time, and during the years that I spent in Princeton it became a friendship."[5] Or does the pithy description of their bond by Mann's devoted editor, Peter de Mendelssohn, bespeak as much cordiality between them as can be proved—"In Princeton they were good neighbors"—and not, as Julius Kaplan has it, "neighbors and good friends"?[6] Even good neighborliness needs its quantum of fence.[7]

Their acquaintance is certainly a fact and begins decades earlier. They may have met as early as March 1922—well before 1925, the year their portrait was painted—on the occasion of a "Goethe Week" in Frankfurt, a celebration of Goethe with lectures. In a diary entry for October 28, 1921, Mann wrote of his "Correspondence with H. Simon in Frankfurt about a planned Goethe week with [Gerhart] Hauptmann, [Adolph von] Harnack, Einstein, and me."[8] That celebration took place in March 1922, the year that Einstein received the 1921 Nobel Prize for Physics, which had been reserved for the presentation ceremony on December 10, 1922. At the Goethe celebration in Frankfurt, on March 1, 1922, Mann did indeed deliver a lecture on "Goethe and

3   Extract from a letter from Thomas Mann to Ida Herz, ca. October 31, 1925, in *Die Briefe Thomas Manns: Regesten und Register, Die Briefe von 1889 bis 1933*, ed. Hans Bürgin & Hans-Otto Mayer (Frankfurt am Main: S. Fischer Verlag, 1976), II: (25)/193.

4   Hermann Kurzke, *Thomas Mann, Life as a Work of Art: A Biography*, tr. Leslie Willson (Princeton, NJ: Princeton University Press, 2002), 519.

5   Thomas Mann, "Die Bekanntschaft mit ihm war alt und wurde während der Jahre, die ich in Princeton verbrachte, zur Freundschaft." Thomas Mann, "Zum Tode von Albert Einstein" (GW X: 549). Einstein died on April 18, 1955.

6   Julius Kaplan, from an interview with Thomas, Katia, and Erika Mann, *Boston Evening Transcript* (March 8, 1939), in *Frage und Antwort, Interviews mit Thomas Mann, 1909–1955*, ed. Volkmar Hansen and Gert Heine (Hamburg: Albrecht Knaus, 1983), 240.

7   "Es bestand ein freundnachbarliches Verhältnis" (T3 701).

8   D 120. "Korrespondenz mit H. Simon-Frankfurt über eine geplante Goethe-Woche mit Hauptmann, Harnack, Einstein und mir." *Tagebücher 1918–1921*, 551–52.

Tolstoy;"[9] but there is no record of Einstein having spoken, although, on the occasion of other public lectures (as we have just learned) Einstein would cite Goethe, whom he admired.[10] From 1918 to 1932, Einstein lived in the Bavarian Quarter of Berlin, offering Mann a fine opportunity to visit his acquaintance, whose work interested him very much, especially in connection with *The Magic Mountain* and its frequent meditations on time. But according to Konrad Wachsmann, Einstein's confidant—and the architect of the one house that Einstein had built for himself—"Mann was a guest of Einstein's on only one occasion. The meeting was probably made at the request of Thomas Mann and arranged by Professor Pringsheim," a physicist and brother of Katia Mann. Elsa Einstein, Einstein's divorced cousin and later his wife, recalls that it was rather Franz Kafka (!) who visited Einstein several times during this period.[11]

In spring 1933, Einstein wrote Mann a congratulatory letter, to which Mann replied, on May 15, calling it "the greatest honor that has come my way, not only in these evil months, but perhaps in my entire life." But one must doubt the harmony of the effect on Einstein produced by Mann's pathos—his insistence on his *ur*-German "nature," "which has been formed by elements of the Goethean tradition of representation, so that I cannot feel I was destined for martyrdom."[12]

---

9   W. H. Bruford, *The German Tradition of Self-Cultivation: "Bildung" from Humboldt to Thomas Mann* (Cambridge, UK: Cambridge University Press, 1975), 243.

10   Gerald Holton, "Einstein and the Cultural Roots of Modern Science," *Daedalus, Science in Culture* issue, 127, no. 1 (Winter 1998): 1–44.

11   Michael Grüning, *Ein Haus für Albert Einstein* (Berlin: Verlag der Nation, 1990), 248–49. In a private communication, Michael D. Gordin, historian of science and Einstein scholar, notes that Wachsmann does not tell us *when* Elsa Einstein reported this information. "She died in the mid-thirties [December 20, 1936], and this does not sound like the kind of thing Elsa would have said [. . .] . I doubt she would have recalled Kafka from a decade earlier." From Walter Hinderer's unpublished account of the memoirs of Johanna Fantova, Einstein's last consort, which turn on Einstein's daily conversations, we learn that Fantova was the wife of Otto Fanta, whose parents' salon was, for a time, Kafka's watering hole. Grüning, as we have heard, reports that Elsa Einstein had told him that Kafka visited them "several times" on the Haberlandstraße. While that now seems unlikely, she can have confused Kafka's real presence there with the possibility that she discussed Kafka with Fantova and conjured his presence. So, in a certain sense, Kafka would have been present on the Haberlandstraße. A second parallel that links Mann and Einstein, though they were not otherwise—or barely—linked, is J. Edgar Hoover's desire to "get" both of them! And he failed.

12   L 198. "Es war das Ehrenvollste, was mir nicht nur in diesen schlimmen Monaten, sondern vielleicht in meinem Leben überhaupt widerfahren ist [. . .] [meiner Natur], die mehr durch goethisch-repräsentative Überlieferungselelemnte bestimmt ist, als daß sie sich eigentlich und bestimmungsgemäß zum Märtyrertum geschaffen fühlte." *Briefe 1889–1935*, ed. Erika Mann (Frankfurt am Main: S. Fischer Verlag, 1961), I: 331–32.

As two of the most highly visible European antifascists, Mann and Einstein met for the first time in America on June 20, 1935, the day that they received honorary doctoral degrees from Harvard.[13] Mann noted in his diary: "Yesterday, the twentieth, the academic ceremonies, starting with music. [. . .] On the platform under a canopy. Six thousand people. Awarding of the honorary degrees with tremendous acclamation for Einstein and me. Pictures taken of us in academic regalia."[14] They sit together on a bench, though far apart, Mann conversing with Henry Wallace, Roosevelt's secretary of agriculture, and Einstein with James Conant, the president of Harvard—and a casual anti-Semite.[15] Mann was later to write that he had heard that the choice of Einstein and himself—"quite particularly" in his case—as recipients of honorary degrees from Harvard had involved a show of interest by President Roosevelt. It could even appear that this attractive rumor was confirmed when, three days after the award of the honorary degree, the Manns were flown to Washington to dine the next evening with the president *en*

---

13   "The June 20, 1935, *Boston Evening Transcript* carried a front-page article titled 'Einstein and Thomas Mann Hailed at Harvard Exercises: Two German Exiles "Steal" Commencement.' Shown next to the article was a group photo with Einstein and [Harvard president James] Conant center stage front row." Arnold Reisman, "Harvard: Albert Einstein's Disappointment," January 20, 2007, https://historynewsnetwork.org/article/32682.

14   (D 242). "Gestern den 20. akadem. Festtag, Morgenmusik [. . .]; Tribüne des Festzeltes, 6000 Menschen, Promotionsfeier, gewaltige Akklamationen für Einstein und mich. Photogr. Aufnahmen im akademischen Ornat." Thomas Mann, *Tagebücher 1935–1936*, ed. Peter de Mendelssohn (Frankfurt am Main: S. Fischer Verlag, 1978), 122.

15   In a judicious discussion of James Conant's imputed anti-Semitism, Wayne Urban and Marybeth Smith conclude, "There is little doubt that Conant was anti-Semitic, although direct evidence of clearly anti-Semitic statements by him is difficult to find. When considering his actions, however, Conant's anti-Semitism emerges clearly, although he was not as open or virulent as many of his colleagues" (Wayne J. Urban and Marybeth Smith, "Much Ado about Something? James Bryant Conant, Harvard University, and Nazi Germany in the 1930s," *Paedagogica Historica* 51, no. 1 [2015]: 161). Here is one example of his "less virulent" statements: "Conant made clear his position on separating the issue of academic integrity from the issue of treatment of Jews when he declined an award from the *American Hebrew Magazine* for Harvard's refusal of the [Hanfstaengl] scholarship from the Nazis: he remarked that in taking his 'stand against the forces which have threatened liberty both in this country and abroad, I have been actuated solely by my conviction of the importance of academic freedom, entirely irrespective of considerations of race or religion' [cited in William M. Tuttle, 'James B. Conant, Pressure Groups, and the National Defense, 1933–1945' (PhD diss., University of Wisconsin, 1967), 68]." Urban and Smith, "Much Ado," 154.

famille. Unfortunately for this "proof," the invitation to the White House did not arise spontaneously with the president but was arranged by their mutual friend Willem Hendrik van Loon. Hans Rudolf Vaget considers this fact decisive in *destroying* the hypothetical connection between Roosevelt's role (such as it was) in the award of Mann's and Einstein's honorary degrees and the Manns' appearance, four days later, at the Roosevelts' dinner table. "Based on what Thomas Mann states [in his diary]," Vaget writes, "most accounts would have us understand, *erroneously,* that the invitation to the White House was initiated by President Roosevelt, as, so to speak, the crowning of his proposal to have Mann receive an honorary doctorate" (emphasis added). Here, Vaget is correcting the scholar Angelika Abel, for one, who writes that "the choice [of Mann to receive a Harvard doctorate] came about not without President Roosevelt's having taken an interest in it"—a sentence that asserts as fact the literal content of the rumor—and then adds the misleading claim that it was Roosevelt "who then subsequently invited the Manns to Washington, to the White House."[16] On the other hand, with respect to Mann's honorary degree, Vaget nonetheless suggests that there might be some truth to the mention of Roosevelt's involvement: "That Franklin Roosevelt could have made a remark about Thomas Mann's being honored at his old university—one that could be interpreted as his 'taking an interest'—is no doubt understandable but should not mean that Roosevelt proposed him or recommended him" (VA 87). And so, it would be very interesting to know what sort of remark Roosevelt might have made about the selection of Einstein and Mann for honorary degrees.

The common source of the claim that Roosevelt's support was crucial is a seemingly reputable website listing Einstein's various honors, prizes, and awards. There, one reads that "Thomas Mann later stated in a letter to his publisher that his and Einstein's honorary doctorate 'had not been possible without any interference [sic] of President Roosevelt.'"[17] Mann did send the letter in question to Gottfried Bermann Fischer on July 10, 1935 (as it happens, while on board the Cunard White Star liner *Berengaria* sailing to Cherbourg). The report on the Einstein website, however, invoking the "impossibility" of the awards were it not for Roosevelt's involvement, is far too emphatic. Mann merely wrote, "Ich hörte, daß unsere Wahl, besonders auch meine, nicht ohne Anteilnahme

---

16   VA 511. Vaget is citing Angelika Abel, *Thomas Mann im Exil: Zum zeitgeschichtlichen Hintergrund der Emigration* (Munich: Wilhelm Fink, 2003), 85.
17   http://www.einstein-website.de/z_information/honours.html.

des Präsidenten Roosevelt zustande gekommen ist (I heard that our selection, and especially mine, came about not without President Roosevelt's having taken an interest in it)."[18]

We can only speculate about the motive and degree of Roosevelt's interest. Roosevelt was a graduate of Harvard College and would certainly have been in the loop about the scandal attending the very public presence of Ernst ("Putzi") Hanfstaengl, Hitler's intimate and piano player, at the previous year's Harvard commencement—that is, in June 1934. Hanfstaengl had come to attend his twenty-fifth class reunion and then spent a good deal of time teaching dubious marching songs to the university band. There was worse: according to John Sedgwick, a relative of Hanfstaengl, "Hitler's leading international propagandist [. . .] was cheered by several admiring classmates when he gave the Nazi salute. He was also recommended for an honorary degree by the *Harvard Crimson* and invited to university president James Bryant Conant's house for tea."[19]

Interestingly, in his time at Harvard College, Roosevelt had been managing editor of the *Harvard Crimson*. One might wonder what he thought of his legacy in 1934 at the outset of the Nazi imperium. Other commentators have concluded that Hanfstaengl's scandalous performance was the reason that "invitations to Einstein and Mann (arguably the two most prominent émigrés from Nazi Germany at the time) were issued in an attempt to restore the university's reputation in time for its 1936 tercentennial" (TB 95).

It is furthermore of interest that Roosevelt *knew* Hanfstaengl from early days, after both had graduated from Harvard (Roosevelt in 1903 and Hanfstaengl in 1909). Sedgwick adds, "After graduation, he [Hanfstaengl] ran his father's New York art gallery and occasionally dropped by the Harvard Club and played the piano there at breakfast for a young New York State senator, Franklin Delano Roosevelt. It was a contact that would prove useful later." These visits would have occurred in the period 1910–12 (when Roosevelt was already a New York State senator; by 1913, at the age of 31, he would become assistant secretary of the Navy). And so, it is unlikely that this proud young man would take the younger Hanfstaengl very seriously, but he might well have been amused by his "aristocratic"—some say, "clownish"—ways. Now, decades later, Roosevelt would know that Hanfstaengl had become a

---

[18]   *Thomas Mann, Briefwechsel mit seinem Verleger Gottfried Bermann Fischer, 1932–1955*, ed. Peter de Mendelssohn (Frankfurt am Main: S. Fischer Verlag, 1973), 107.

[19]   John Sedgwick, "The Harvard Nazi," *Boston* [a magazine], May 15, 2006, https://www.bostonmagazine.com/2006/05/15/the-harvard-nazi/.

trusted intimate of Hitler—and played the piano *for him*. This development can have mutated the earlier easier acquaintance into serious dislike.

Following dinner with the Roosevelts in 1935, Mann jots down what might be construed as Roosevelt's antifascist sentiments: "Scant respect for degenerating democracy and undisciplined overthrow of governments."[20] Would these phrases imply respect for robust democracy and contempt for such a thing as Hitler's power grab? That would be a "strong" if not indeed an "interested" reading, since a letter written about this time qualifies the sort of revolution Roosevelt abhors as basically "French," a people always about overthrowing their government. And with his contempt for a "degenerating democracy," Roosevelt appears to have been thinking quite particularly of the American Congress (!). And so—if we nonetheless still entertain the strong reading of Roosevelt's table talk— he can have had more than a merely private interest in urging Conant to make amends for his toleration of Hanfstaengl, in the form of a gesture to the victims of the *degenerate* revolutionary Hitler and his intimates.

It is ironic that years later, having fled Hitler's Germany for England in 1939 and thereafter been interned in Canada, Hanfstaengl would write to Roosevelt to beg his support. He succeeded. Hanfstaengl had evidently seen the light and might now be useful to the Allied cause. In fact, he was enlisted to "work for President Roosevelt's 'S-Project,' revealing information on approximately 400 Nazi leaders. He provided 68 pages of information on Hitler alone" that proved valuable to an officially produced psychological portrait of Hitler.[21] On the other hand, Sedgwick considers the work he did for Roosevelt to be useless: "He managed to get a letter to his old Harvard Club friend FDR, offering to provide analysis of the Nazi regime in exchange for his freedom. The president bit, and though he wasn't freed, Putzi was eventually quartered at Bush Hill, a rural estate outside Washington. He monitored Nazi radio broadcasts and wrote the president advisory memos but offered no useful tips." Putzi, Sedgwick concludes, died an unregenerate Nazi, preoccupied with Hitler, in lasting awe of his Führer. Nonetheless, if Hanfstaengl turned out to be the indirect reason for Harvard's awarding honorary doctorates to Einstein and Thomas Mann, which they accepted with pleasure, one can be reconciled to the scandal of his having existed.

Before returning to the matter of the alleged frequent visits between Einstein and Mann in the years they lived in Princeton, there is another,

---

[20]   D 244. "Geringschätzung der degenerierenden Demokratie und der wilden Regierungsstürzerei [. . .] ." *Tagebücher 1935–1936*, 131.

[21]   https://en.wikipedia.org/wiki/Ernst_Hanfstaengl, last modified August 10, 2021, at 15:46 UTC.

more notable, if obscure, instance of their association: they were co-contributors to a "Message to the People of 6939," which was inserted in the 5,000-year Time Capsule planted on September 23, 1938—a week before Mann's definitive arrival in Princeton—to a depth of fifty feet at the site of the 1939 New York's World's Fair.

Einstein's message reads:

Our time is rich in inventive minds, the inventions of which could facilitate our lives considerably. We are crossing the seas by power and utilize power also in order to relieve humanity from all tiring muscular work. We have learned to fly, and we are able to send messages and news without any difficulty over the entire world through electric waves.

However, the production and distribution of commodities is entirely unorganized, so that everybody must live in fear of being eliminated from the economic cycle, in this way suffering for the want of everything. Furthermore, people living in different countries kill each other at irregular time intervals, so that also for this reason anyone who thinks about the future must live in fear and terror. This is due to the fact that the intelligence and character of the masses are uncomfortably lower than the intelligence and character of the few who produce something valuable for the community.

I trust that posterity will read these statements with a feeling of proud and justified superiority.[22]

---

[22]   "Einstein Hopeful for Better World," *The New York Times*, September 16, 1938, 22.
"In unserer Zeit gibt es viele erfindungsreiche Köpfe, deren Erfindungen unser Leben in hohem Masse erleichtern könnten. Wir durchqueren die Meere mit Maschinenkraft und benutzen die letztere auch, um die Menschen von aller anstrengenden Muskelarbeit zu befreien. Wir haben fliegen gelernt und senden uns bequem alle Nachrichten über die ganze Erde durch elektrische Wellen.
"Aber die Produktion und Verteilung der Güter ist völlig unorganisiert, so daß jeder in der Angst leben muß, aus dem Kreislauf der Wirtschaft ausgeschaltet zu werden und an allem Mangel zu leiden. Außerdem töten einander die Menschen, die in verschiedenen Ländern wohnen, in unregelmäßigen Zeitabschnitten, so daß auch aus diesem Grunde alle in Furcht und Schrecken leben, welche sich irgendwie über die Zukunft Gedanken machen. Alles hängt damit zusammen, daß die Intelligenz und Charakter-Bildung der Massen unvergleichlich tiefer steht als die entsprechenden Eigenschaften der wenigen, die für die Gesamtheit Wertvolles hervorbringen.
"Hoffentlich liest das spätere Geschlecht diese Konstatierungen mit dem Gefühl stolzer und berechtigter Überlegenheit. A. Einstein."

Thomas Mann's letter reads:

We know now that the idea of the future as a "better world" was a fallacy of the doctrine of progress. The hopes we center on you, citizens of the future, are in no way exaggerated. In broad outline, you will actually resemble us very much as we resemble those who lived 1,000 or 5,000 years ago. Among you, too, the spirit will fare badly—it should never fare too well on this earth, otherwise men would need it no longer. That optimistic conception of the future is a projection into time of an endeavor which does not belong to the temporal world, the endeavor on the part of man to approximate to his idea of himself, the humanization of man. What we, in this year of our Lord 1938, understand by the term "culture"—a notion held in small esteem today by certain nations of the Western world—is simply this endeavor. What we call the spirit is identical with it, too. Brothers of the future, united with us in the spirit and in this endeavor, we send our greetings.[23]

One feels the tension—perhaps it is dialectical—between the massive evidence of the brutality of men in the increasing fascist seizure of power, and the hope for the most exalted cultivation of mankind expressed, in Mann's text, in a rhetoric of surpassing sublimity.

* * *

If Mann and Einstein visited one another in Princeton, one would have to think of the event as occurring at Mann's or Erich Kahler's home, where Mann dined from time to time: Einstein's living room and sockless lifestyle would not have attracted the patrician Mann, who cannot be imagined having dinner there. Even after dining privately at the White House with the Roosevelts, he had found the meal "very

---

23 "Einstein Hopeful for Better World," *The New York Times,* September 16, 1938, 22. Thomas Mann, "Die Zukunft als 'bessere Welt' war wohl ein Mißverständnis des Fortschrittsglaubens. Wir setzen keine übertriebenen Hoffnungen in Euch, Erdenbürger der Zukunft. Im wesentlichen, schlecht und recht, werdet Ihr uns gleichen, wie wir denen gleichen von vor tausend und fünftausend Jahren. Auch unter Euch wird der Geist es schlecht haben—er soll es wohl nie zu gut haben auf Erden, sonst würde er überflüssig. Jene optimistische Auffassung der Zukunft ist die Projektion einer Bemühung ins Zeitliche, die nicht dem Zeitlichen angehört: der Bemühung um die Annäherung des Menschen an seine Idee, um die Vermenschlichung des Menschen. Was wir vom Jahre 1938 post Christum unter dem zu unserer Zeit von einigen Nationen des Westens geringgeschätzten Begriff 'Kultur' verstehen, deckt sich mit dieser Bemühung. Was wir 'Geist' nennen, ist gleichfalls identisch mit ihr. Im Geiste und in der Bemühung grüßen wir euch, Brüder der Zukunft." "[Für die Time-Capsule]," GW X: 920.

bad" ("als Dinner sehr schlecht") (!).[24] In fact, Mann's diaries of three years in Princeton mention only one meeting with Einstein in any detail—Einstein's highly formal visit to the Manns on January 20, 1939: "Einstein visited, bringing his citation for the medal; I then wrote my reply."[25] We have an explanation of this event:

> On the occasion of its eightieth anniversary, the American journal *Jewish Forum* established the Einstein Medal, an award to be given annually to someone chosen by Einstein himself for his outstanding humanitarian service [. . .]. The organizers planned a banquet in honor of Thomas Mann, but he did not wish it. Accordingly, the medal was presented to him by Einstein at a small private ceremony at Thomas Mann's house in Princeton on January 28, 1939.
>
> (D 381)

I shall draw up a reasonably full account of their meetings in Princeton in the hope of appraising the character of their relationship of three decades—in a word, of calibrating the degree of their intimacy. The strongest claim, as we have heard, rests on Mann's invocation of friendship in his brief eulogy to Einstein on his death in 1955, when Mann himself was frail and ill. There is also material of a more general sort to frame the detail of their encounters—differently. First is Einstein's alleged need for solitude, leading to his famous admission, in *The World As I See It*: "I have never belonged to my country, my home, my friends, or even my immediate family, with my whole heart." The passage reads in full:

> My passionate sense of social justice and social responsibility has always contrasted oddly with my pronounced freedom from the need for direct contact with other human beings and human communities. I gang my own gait and have never belonged to my country, my home, my friends, or even my immediate family, with my whole heart; in the face of all these ties I have never lost an obstinate sense of detachment, of the need for solitude—a feeling which increases with the years. One is sharply conscious, yet without regret, of the limits to the possibility of mutual understanding and sympathy with one's fellow creatures. Such a

---

24   Letter to René Schickele, July 25, 1935 (L 235). *Briefe 1889–1935*, I: 396.
25   D 317. "Besuch von Einstein, der seine Medaillen-Rede brachte, worauf ich die meine schrieb" (T3 350).

person no doubt loses something in the way of geniality and lightheartedness; on the other hand, he is largely independent of the opinions, habits, and judgments of his fellows and avoids the temptation to take his stand on such insecure foundations.[26]

This stance is confirmed by Philipp Frank, Einstein's biographer and successor to the chair of theoretical physics at the German Charles-Ferdinand University of Prague: "[Einstein] was averse to entering into very intimate personal relations with other people, a trait that has always left [him] a lonely person among his students, his colleagues, colonies, his friends, and his family."[27]

This description of a state of mind fits well with Einstein's description of Princeton society:

Princeton is a wonderful little spot, a quaint and ceremonious village of puny demagogues on stilts. [. . .] Here the people who compose what is called "society" enjoy even less freedom than their counterparts in Europe. Yet they seem unaware of this restriction, since their way of life tends to inhibit personality development from childhood.[28]

[26] "Mit meinem leidenschaftlichen Sinn für soziale Gerechtigkeit und soziale Verpflichtung stand stets in einem eigentümlichen Gegensatz ein ausgesprochener Mangel an unmittelbarem Anschlußbedürfnis an Menschen und menschliche Gemeinschaften. Ich bin ein richtiger "Einspänner," der dem Staat, der Heimat, dem Freundeskreis, ja, selbst der engeren Familie nie mit ganzem Herzen angehört hat, sondern all diesen Bindungen gegenüber ein nie sich legendes Gefühl der Fremdheit und des Bedürfnisses nach Einsamkeit empfunden hat, ein Gefühl, das sich mit dem Lebensalter noch steigert. Man empfindet scharf, aber ohne Bedauern die Grenze der Verständigung und Konsonanz mit anderen Menschen. Wohl verliert ein solcher Mensch einen Teil der Harmlosigkeit und des Unbekümmertseins, aber er ist dafür von den Meinungen, Gewohnheiten und Urteilen der Mitmenschen weitgehend unabhängig und kommt nicht in die Versuchung, sein Gleichgewicht auf solch unsolide Grundlage zu stellen." *Mein Weltbild,* 13–14. Some Einstein scholars are skeptical of such statements. In a personal communication (July 27, 2018), Michael Gordin notes that "first, Einstein was very often at the center of groups of people: in his science, in his public political activism. Second, there's the rhetorical function of these texts, and I think people discount how much Einstein wanted to 'project' this kind of image."
[27] Philipp Frank, *Einstein, His Life and Times* (New York: Alfred A. Knopf, 1953), 89.
[28] Albert Einstein, in a letter to Queen Elisabeth of Belgium. Peter Michelmore, *Einstein: Profile of the Man* (New York: Dodd, Mead & Company, 1962), 196–97. "Princeton ist ein wunderbares Plätzchen, eine spaßige und zeremonielle

It is not that Einstein never made friends or kept them: *primus inter pares* was Michele Besso, whom Einstein knew intimately from early days at the Bern patent office. Besso is the only person who might be acknowledged as a collaborator on the special theory of relativity of 1905. In 1949, Einstein wrote to him, "The best that remains to us are a few genuine friends, whose head and heart are in the right places and who understand one another, as we do."[29] After Besso's death, Einstein wrote a letter to his family, with the famous and wonderful idea: "Now he has again preceded me a little in parting from this strange world. This has no importance. For people like us who believe in physics, the separation between past, present and future has only the importance of an admittedly tenacious illusion."[30] This thought bears the imprint of Einstein's conversations with the mathematician Kurt Gödel.

But what of Einstein's Princeton "friend," Thomas Mann? Alas, we learn from an intimate acquaintance of Einstein, the architect Konrad Wachsmann, that Einstein could barely endure the impression that Mann made—first of all, "in a silk shirt," anathema to Albert, and, moreover, Mann's habitual mode of address, that of an "oppressive schoolmaster," who, given half the chance, would explain to Einstein the theory of relativity. There is a famous photo of the two together, with Mann pointing his index finger at Einstein's chest and a third person (Rabbi Stephen Wise) holding back Mann's hand at the wrist—rather pointed evidence![31] The picture was taken on the evening of May 10, 1938, when, with Einstein and Stephan Wise, Mann watched "pacifist-antifascist propaganda films (*pazifistisch-antfascistischen Propaganda-Films*)," presumably on the invitation of the writer and activist Hendrik van Loon, whose activity as a mediator between Mann and Roosevelt we have noted (T3 221).

Siedlung von kleinen Halbgöttern auf Stelzen. [. . .] Die Leute, die hier das bilden, was man die Gesellschaft nennt, erlauben sich weniger Freiheit als ihre europäischen Zwillinge. Übrigens empfinden sie, wie mir scheint, keinerlei Einschränkungen, weil ihre gewöhnliche Lebensweise schon von Kindheit an zur Unterdrückung der Individualität geführt hat." Cited in Boris Kuznecov, *Einstein: Leben—Tod—Unsterblickheit* (Basel: Birkhäuser, 1977), 190.

29   "Das Beste, was bleibt sind ein paar aufrechte Freunde, die Kopf und Herz am rechten Fleck haben und einander verstehen, so wie es bei uns beiden ist." http://www.einstein-website.de/z_biography/princeton.html.

30   "Nun ist er mir auch mit dem Abschied von dieser sonderbaren Welt ein wenig vorausgegangen. Dies bedeutet nichts. Für uns gläubige Physiker hat die Scheidung zwischen Vergangenheit, Gegenwart und Zukunft nur die Bedeutung einer wenn auch hartnäckigen Illusion." *Albert Einstein/Michele Besso. Correspondance 1903–1955*, ed. and tr. Pierre Speziali (Paris: Herman, 1972), 538.

31   professor-albert-einstein-rabbi-stephen-wise-and-thomas-mann-noted-picture-id517298314.

Meetings between Mann and Einstein were otherwise few and far between. Months later, in a diary entry for October 2, 1938, Mann mentions a telephone call with Einstein; and here, for the first and last time in the diaries, he quotes some of the actual words of Einstein, who declared that "never before in his life was he so unhappy" ("noch nie in seinem Leben so unglücklich war") (T3 303).[32] It cannot have been Mann's obligation to palliate Einstein's grief, but there is little evidence that their association was a source of much comfort to Einstein. They heightened their mutual distress by telephoning in crisis situations. On October 8, Mann noted "the ghastly news of the deportation of German emigrants" (that is to say, refugees) "from Prague to Germany," and phoned it to Einstein.[33] There is no mention of a meeting until weeks later, on October 22, with the phrase "visit from Einstein and Dr. Kayser"—the latter being Einstein's son-in-law and the point being that he presented Mann with an essay on the *Joseph* novels (T 312, 742).[34] On November 17, Mann mentions a casual conversation with Einstein, which took place after a lunch hosted by H. T. Lowe-Porter, Mann's translator, and her husband. On the way home on a wintry day— together with Einstein in a car, very likely—Mann spoke to him about the fate of three Jewish émigrés, all of whom had touched *his* life intimately: Viktor Zuckerkandl, once an editor at Mann's publisher Bermann Fischer, who was now enjoying a moderately happy finale as a professor of music at St. John's College in Annapolis; Siegfried Marck, who had published essays on Mann; and the eminent playwright and translator Ludwig Fulda, who, having once fled Germany, grew homesick, returned to Nazi Germany, and . . . committed suicide. Fulda's son had written to Mann two days before asking him to help his father in his hour of need (T3 321). What goes unsaid is Mann's likely insensitivity to Einstein's feelings about Fulda. Fulda was the leading author of the notorious "Manifesto of the Ninety-Three" ("Aufruf an die Kulturwelt"), proclaimed in support of Germany's war aims and its behaviors in Belgium, decried among Germany's enemies as atrocities

---

[32]   The following year, September 13, 1940, Mann noted in his diary that he had received a letter from Einstein on *Lotte in Weimar* but adds no comment (T4 148).

[33]   "[die] schauerlichen Nachrichten von der Auslieferung der deutschen Emigranten in Prag an Deutschland" (T3 307).

[34]   Interestingly, this same Dr. Rudolf Kayser published an interpretive essay, "Über Thomas Manns Joseph-Roman," in *The German Quarterly* 12, no. 2 (March 1939): 99–105. It is possible that his father-in-law Einstein glanced at *some* of it. Einstein did read Kayser's earlier work—*Spinoza—Bildnis eines geistigen Helden* (Vienna: Phaidon, 1932)—and in fact contributed an introduction to the American translation, published in 1946: *Spinoza: Portrait of a Spiritual Hero*, tr. Amy Allen and Maxim Newmark (New York: The Philosophical Library, 1946).

and yet endorsed by ninety-three German scientists, scholars, and artists. Einstein very pointedly did not sign, and instead signed an ineffectual counter-manifesto.

Significantly, too, on the day before dining at the Lowe-Porters, Mann noted that "Dr. Zuckerkandl" had written glowingly of Mann's essay *This Peace* (*Dieser Friede*, GW XII: 829–45); and that a cablegram from Bermann Fischer himself, Mann's publisher, announced that he would print Mann's essays. Mann does not record anything that Einstein might have said in what appears to have been a "conversation" about persons of little apparent interest to Einstein. This notation might be compared (unfavorably) with the entry three days later, after Mann's lunch with Erich Kahler at Kahler's place: "[We talked . . .] a lot about the fate of Switzerland, which is now getting the first of its threats. Of course, Switzerland is a relic of liberal times. The coming atomization [. . .] and Europe's—to which then the swollen Reich falls prey." This is a topic on which Kahler would have had a lot to say.[35]

The day before, Mann and Einstein had been together for an ulterior purpose: they were having portraits made by an eminent Berlin photographer, Lotte Jakobi, now an émigré. On the question of a plan to exhibit them in New York, Einstein declined. On February 7 of the following year, 1939, we find an obscure mention of movie stills being taken of Mann for a "portraitist [. . .] with Einstein." In all these entries, Einstein, regrettably, does not come alive. Why, on February 21, did Mann choose *to write a letter* to Einstein, who lived just up the street from him? Einstein had excused himself from hearing Mann's lecture on Freud. Mann now took the opportunity to thank Einstein for having sent his regrets and invite him to join the ultimately forty guests who, on the evening of February 28, came to the Manns' from Princeton and New York to hear the recitator Ludwig Hardt declaim works by Heine and Goethe. (In the letter, Mann did not—perhaps prudently—mention texts by Kafka, whose work Hardt also recited.) This is the sole letter that Mann wrote to Einstein during the nearly three years of his stay in Princeton. Evidently realizing that the letter would be too little or too late, together with Katia, he "visited" Einstein the next day (not something Mann would ever have done by himself) so as to repeat the invitation. Significantly, as Mann reports in a letter to Agnes Meyer, although the evening of recitations as a whole turned out to be a flop—the performance judged to be "overdramatized and alienating (*befremdend*)"—Einstein

---

[35]   "Mit Kahler viel über das Schicksal der Schweiz, gegen die die ersten Drohungen fallen. Natürlich ist sie ein Relikt aus liberalistischen Zeiten. Die kommende Atomisierung und Europas,—der dann auch das geschwollene Reich verfällt" (T 323). For further discussion, see chapter 2 *supra*.

was the only guest who liked it.[36] It would be wonderful to know which text Einstein enjoyed the most, and whether hearing Kafka read aloud would bring him closer to his alleged acquaintance from Berlin days. Meanwhile, one implication is that Mann's and Einstein's tastes were situated as far apart as Lübeck and Ulm.

Some months later, on April 20, 1939, Mann did visit Einstein, to judge from Mann's diary, for the second and last time, "with K.[atia] to present [Einstein] with roses, after the fact of Einstein's birthday (*Mit K. bei Einstein, Rosen abgegeben, nachträglich zum Geburtstag*") on March 14 (T3 396). Mann had been en route to Chicago that day, preparing to lecture. Both recorded visits seem somewhat hesitant or awkward in conception. Interestingly, Einstein made an exceedingly rare visit to Mann that very afternoon, coming to Stockton Street to speak with Mann about Mann's brilliant, daring essay "A Brother," which treated the unnamed object of this figurative relationship—Hitler—as a kind of distorted genius.[37]

I will note that Einstein—the real thing, if we are to continue to speak of genius—being well aware of the existence of Robert Musil's masterpiece, the massive, forever unfinished *The Man without Qualities* (1930–43), written and staged in a not-yet-Hitlerian Vienna, can have well appreciated Musil on the topic of the contemporary use and abuse of the term "genius" and known that Musil had anticipated Mann. True, an authority no less than Hermann Broch would cast doubt, some months later, on the degree of Einstein's knowledge of the book, promising "to take pains to supply him with a [correct] orientation."[38] And so the jury is out. Still, Musil continues: "Goethe was relying on Kant"—and the mention of Goethe would have captivated Einstein, who loved him— "when he [Goethe] defined the geniative (*das Genialische*) with the words 'to have many objects present and easily relate the most remote ones to each other: this free of egotism and self-complacency.'"[39]

36   Mann to Agnes E. Meyer (n.d.), cited in Inge and Walter Jens, *Frau Thomas Mann: Das Leben der Katharina Pringsheim* (Hamburg: Rowohlt, 2003), 322.
37   "A Brother," in *Order of the Day: Political Essays and Speeches of Two Decades* (New York: Knopf, 1942), 153–61.
38   [. . .] ihm, diese Orientierung zu liefern [. . .]." Hermann Broch, Letter to Rudolf Olden, June 22, 1939, in *Hermann Broch, Kommentierte Werkausgabe, Briefe 2 (1938–1945)*, ed. Paul Michael Lützeler (Frankfurt am Main: Suhrkamp, 1981), 91.
39   "Chapter 48: A mentality directed toward the significant, and the beginning of a conversation on the subject," in Robert Musil, *The Man without Qualities: From the Posthumous Papers*, tr. Burton Pike (New York: Knopf, 1995), II: 1341. "Goethe lehnte sich später wohl an ihn [Kant] an, als er sogar das Genialische mit den Worten 'viele Gegenstände gegenwärtig haben und die entferntesten leicht aufeinander beziehen. Dies frei von Selbstischkeit und Selbstgefälligkeit' beschrieb. *Der Mann ohne Eigenschaften: Aus dem Nachlass* [chapter 48: "Eine auf das Bedeutende gerichtete Gesinnung und beginnendes Gespräch darüber"] (Hamburg: Rowohlt, 1952), 1133.

This intellectual paradigm accords with Einstein's personality and, moreover, fits perfectly Mann's opening argument justifying "the painful relationship" he has perceived between himself and his miscreant "brother"—Hitler! ("Bruder Hitler," GW XII: 849, 852). Musil continues: "But that's a view [of genius] that was very much designed for the achievements of reason, and it leads to the rather gymnastic conception of genius we have succumbed to."[40] At which point we are returned to Musil's earlier citation of "a racehorse of genius (*ein geniales Rennpferd*)" discussed in the sporting news.[41] Mann, if not Einstein, did decidedly read these words in *Der Mann ohne Eigenschaften*: Musil was, moreover, a solid acquaintance, whom Mann had known from 1919 on. Einstein would soon be provably aware of the grim conditions under which Musil was attempting to finish his life's work, and even undertook personally to better them.[42]

Einstein, who did not lack empathy, might also have sympathized with Mann's concern that his essay on "Brother Hitler," which was circulating on the continent and being read in the wrong places, could bring him grief. On the Ile de France that summer Mann *would* indeed worry about its effect: "Our presence in Switzerland might be disturbed, since the 'Schwarze Corps' [the official newspaper of the SS] and other Nazi papers are reprinting the 'Hitler' piece."[43]

The following month, on May 19, 1939, Mann spoke in the Princeton University Chapel, together with Einstein, "for the theologians," at which Mann presented an abbreviated form of the ["Problem of] Freedom" lecture. In a disagreeable comment, he found Einstein's lecture "unintelligible"—indeed, "very much so";[44] the next day, he merely noted Einstein's presence during their visit to "Cheney State," a

---

40 Ibid. "Aber das ist eine Auffassung, die es sehr auf die Verstandesleistung abgesehen hat und zu der etwas turnerhaften Vorstellung vom Genialen führt, der wir erlegen sind."

41 "Chapter 13: A Racehorse of Genius Crystallizes the Recognition of Being a Man without Qualities," in Musil, *The Man without Qualities: A Sort of Introduction*," tr. Sophie Wilkins (New York: Knopf, 1995), I:41. *Der Mann ohne Eigenschaften: Eine Art Einführung* [13: "Ein geniales Rennpferd reift die Erkenntnis, ein Mann ohne Eigenschaften zu sein"] (Hamburg: Rowohlt, 1952), 44.

42 See Mann's short essay "Robert Musil, Der Mann ohne Eigenschaften" (GW XI: 782–85).

43 Emphasis added. "Außerdem könnte unsere Anwesenheit in der Schweiz stören, namentlich da das "Schwarze Corps" u.a. Naziblätter 'den Bruder' wiedergegeben" (T3 420).

44 Noted as well in Donald Prater, *Thomas Mann—A Life* (Oxford: Oxford University Press, 1995), 296. " [. . .] abgeholt *zum Vortragsabend bei den Theologen*. [. . .] Sehr unverständlicher Vortrag Einsteins. Danach meine ½ stündige Lecture, die sich wiederum gut ausnahm" (T3 409, 801).

Black college in Cheyney, Pennsylvania.[45] Einstein, together with, very likely, his stepdaughter Margot, the Panofskys, and the Swarszenkis, assembled outside the building and thereafter joined Mann and the officers of the college for lunch.[46] Five months later, on October 14, 1939, Mann joined "the Einsteins" and the director Otto Preminger on the stage of the McCarter Theatre following a performance of Clare Booth Luce's anti-Nazi play *Margin for Error*, which Mann happened to judge "formidably stupid *(formidabel dumm)*" (T3 488). It was the occasion of the photograph, which we have mentioned, of Mann in schoolmasterish pose, presumably teaching Einstein a lesson.

On November 9, 1939, they were both present—"with many others"— at a concert of chamber music in honor of Abraham Flexner. Several weeks later, on December 1, Einstein (in italics!) visited the Manns, again, along with several others—including a certain "Princeton Professor X with his wife"—for tea (Mann was simply not scrupulously attentive to every one of the thousands of the mostly highly distinguished personalities he met during these years). Three days later, he did dine again with Einstein (almost certainly not at the Manns'), along with Erich Kahler and the "Lowes" (H. T. Lowe-Porter, his translator, and her husband, Elias Lowe, the paleographer). Their paths did not cross again until well into the following year, when both were in attendance, on March 21, 1940, at a lecture by a certain Professor Rappard of Geneva.

It is noteworthy that Mann did receive a *unique* solo visit from Einstein on the evening of May 31, after dinner, but only in answer to Mann's request for Einstein's help in rescuing Peter Pringsheim, the capable physicist and brother of Katia Mann, who had fled to Belgium but had gone missing after the Nazi invasion. (After Einstein had "taken steps" in a "very friendly" manner, it proved possible to bring Pringsheim to safety in the United States.). Along with the Hebraist polymath Abraham Yahuda, Einstein visited Mann briefly on June 1 "for further planning of an 'action' addressed to President Roosevelt" (T4 95). There is no further indication of any contact between them until six months later, at the end of January 1941, when together with Kahler and Einstein's sister Maria (Maja)—who was, more likely, his stepdaughter Margot— they dined together, presumably at the Manns'. Mann records no impression of their visit. A week before Mann's final departure for California, he and Einstein were present among a large company at the home of Mann's acquaintance (and Einstein's and Kahler's friend) the

---

[45]   "Cheney State," at the time of Mann's visit a Black college, is today a Black university named Cheney University of Pennsylvania.

[46]   Georg Swarszenski was an eminent museum director, and his wife, Marie, the subject of a famous painting by Max Beckmann.

mathematician Hermann Weyl, a professor at the Institute for Advanced Study. As the conversation turned to Schopenhauer, Mann promised to send Einstein an abridgment of his celebrated essay on Schopenhauer, which introduced his edited volume, *The Living Thoughts of Schopenhauer* (T4 232). This evening event was surely conceived as an opportunity for Mann's several Princeton acquaintances to wish him well in California. Some months later, from Pacific Palisades, Mann mailed a phonograph record to Princeton containing reciprocal greetings "for Einstein and Princeton." On a brief return visit to Princeton, on November 18, 1941, Mann telephoned to Einstein from the Nassau Inn, even today a Princeton institution and a likely temporary bedroom for guests of the university; and on a second return to Princeton a year later, in December 1942, Mann saw Einstein at "a soiree at the Lowes." That is the last time they saw one another during the next thirteen years of their lives (Einstein died on April 18, 1955, and Mann on August 12, 1955). I have risked losing you, amiable reader, with these late, perhaps flaccid notations; but my gambit is all for the sake of completeness: they are the sum total of the brief, untelling mentions in Mann's diaries, which indicate little more than Mann's treasuring, as important, the *idea* of an intimacy with Einstein.

To sum up this evidence: during the three years of Mann's stay in Princeton, Einstein was very rarely at Mann's house and, with one exception, *never alone*, always in the company of other guests; and Mann was at Einstein's house only twice, on both occasions accompanied by members of his family. Einstein's behavior toward Mann in this respect is consistent with his general behavior in Princeton: "He rarely made calls without an entourage of Margot [his step-daughter] and, usually, his secretary Helene Dukas."[47] And so, there is nothing here to corroborate the biographical commonplace that Mann and Einstein visited one another "frequently." It is true Mann's diaries tend generally to be very reticent about his conversations with his acquaintances; Kahler is the one exception: "The greatest study of Mann," in these diaries—as the wit Janet Flanner observed—"is Mann."[48] Aside from Einstein's confession, following the Nazi invasion of Prague, that he had never before in his life been so unhappy, there is nothing in the diaries to convey the intellectual or emotional outcome of any single encounter with Mann's "close friend" Einstein.

---

[47] I cite a comment made to me by Michael Gordin, author of *Einstein in Bohemia* (Princeton, NJ: Princeton University Press, 2020).

[48] Janet Flanner, "Profiles: Goethe in Hollywood I," *The New Yorker* December 13, 1941, 32. With apologies to Alexander Pope's *Essay on Man* (Epistle II) of 1734: "The proper study of mankind is man." https://www.gutenberg.org/files/2428/2428-h/2428-h.htm.

Konrad Wachsmann reports an even harsher message. Asked in an interview with Michael Grüning, "How did these two important intellectuals (*bedeutende Köpfe*) get along?" Wachsmann replies, "Einstein never said anything about this." Grüning: "That sounds rather guarded. Was there any animosity between them?" "I think that is the right word," Wachsmann says, and then goes on to describe Einstein's famous antipathy to men "in silk shirts," concluding, "They probably did not like each other." "But," the interviewer presses on, "later, in Princeton, Einstein and Mann were practically neighbors and visited one another. Somehow they must have liked one another?" Wachsmann sticks to his last: "I wouldn't say that. I think, actually, that their being in the same neighborhood only intensified what you call their 'animosity.' I clearly remember my last meeting with Einstein. I led our conversation onto the topic of Thomas Mann. [. . .] Einstein liked [Mann's children] Klaus and Erika well enough, but he could not make any headway with their father (*mit dem Vater der beiden kam er nicht zurecht*). Certainly, Einstein's remarks did leave me rather speechless. For example, 'Thomas Mann is an oppressive schoolmaster. He always needs someone to set straight (*zum Belehren*). Apparently, for him there are very few things he can't explain. I always waited, tense with curiosity (*Ich habe immer neugierig und gespannt darauf gewartet*) that he would expound the theory of relativity to me. [. . .] This fellow belongs to those not so rare types that begin to age with thirty.'"[49] This would be one way of identifying the aspect of his character that Mann himself describes from a conversation with Agnes Meyer, who was planning to write his biography, namely, his "'coldness'—his lack of organic spontaneity in his relations with his fellow men and women" (T3 391). Mann's reaction to the birth of his first grandchild, for one thing, could confirm this view, if elliptically: "Becoming a grandfather (*Großvaterschaft*) comes late and makes little impression on me."[50]

Mann wrote a few letters to Einstein following his move to California, but always in the name of a third party or a cause asking for his cooperation. A letter written on November 27, 1945, addresses his erstwhile acquaintance with the most formal salutation thinkable, "Sehr verehrter Herr Professor Einstein!," and concludes with "Ihr sehr ergebener Thomas Mann (Your very devoted Thomas Mann)." With Mann in California, their association could certainly not grow any more intimate. On the few occasions in the following years when Mann

---

49   Grüning, *Ein Haus für Albert Einstein*, 151–52.
50   "Die Großvaterschaft kommt spät und macht mir geringen Eindruck" (T4 124).

returned to Princeton, he did manage to see his acquaintance, but always in the company of others. The fact confirms Wachsmann's sardonic report that Einstein could scarcely bear being alone with Thomas Mann.

The drift of all this data is that the personalities of Mann and Einstein were *not* compatible. If they are to be reckoned friends, it is solely in their sharing with intense conviction the political and liberal-humanist ideals of the Circle. They were "good neighbors" morally and—in a necessarily limited sense—intellectually, but their relation was nothing like Mann's friendship with Kahler, who, living in Princeton, with Mann's encouragement, also just ten minutes away on foot, was—leaving aside occasional visits from Borgese and Broch—Mann's only Princeton friend of a comparable intellectual intensity.[51] When Mann finally moved from Princeton to California, as Erich Frey writes, he "came with his Munich writing-desk and manuscripts, built himself a [rather lavish] house, and resumed, as he put it, 'his worthy and to some extent representative existence in a firmly-delineated, personal frame of life (*Lebensrahmen*).'"[52] Were Einstein asked if he had had a similar prospect in mind on settling into his small frame house at 112 Mercer Street, I think he would have scratched his mighty head—in contrived perplexity.

* * *

On my showing these pages to Paul Michael Lützeler, the eminent scholar of German exile literature—most particularly, the life and work of Hermann Broch—Paul wrote back:

> I have one anecdote to tell you about the Thomas Mann–Albert Einstein relationship. Trude Geiringer emigrated with her husband—a factory owner from Austria—to the United States in 1938 after the Nazi annexation of Austria. She was a well-known

---

[51]   The publisher Charles Scribner "graduated from Princeton University in 1943 in classics, but often found scientists more stimulating than novelists. Once, while at Princeton, he was offered the choice of lunch with Albert Einstein or Thomas Mann and chose the latter—a decision he soon regretted, finding the novelist 'pretentious and deadly boring.'" Mann would have been pleased by the choice and dismissive of the judgment, since he found undergraduates, on at least one occasion, "curious fellows (*kuriose Burschen*) "(T3 404). The anecdote is narrated in Robert P. Crease, "The Last of Its Breed," *Physicsworld*, January 3, 2008, https://physicsworld.com/a/the-last-of-its-breed/.

[52]   Cited in Erich Frey, "Thomas Mann's Exile Years in America," *Modern Language Studies* 6, no. 1 (Spring 1976): 84.

photographer of prominent Viennese authors, including Franz
Werfel and Hermann Broch. [. . .] It must have been in 1939 or
1940 that she went to Princeton to take photographs of Albert
Einstein in the morning and then to do the same with Thomas
Mann in the afternoon. The morning session with Einstein went
very well, and she mentioned to him that she was invited to the
Manns to take photos there as well. That was not a problem. But
when she arrived at the house of Thomas Mann, she was naive
enough to mention that she had taken photos of Albert Einstein
that morning. Mann was so upset that she had not concentrated
all day on preparing herself for the visit to him that he asked her
to leave: no photos could be taken. He simply could not bear the
idea that one (as a photographer) could apply herself to *two* such
prominent figures on the same day.[53]

Something of the distinctive atmospheres surrounded these two
geniuses is conveyed by a second anecdote, recorded by the historian
Jamie Sayen, who grew up next door to Einstein on Mercer Street.

Thomas Mann lived in Princeton from 1938 to 1941 but, except for
a shared hatred of the Nazis, the two famous refugees had little in
common. [. . .] The patrician Mann [. . .] lived in an imposing red-
brick fortress on Library Place, just a block away from Einstein's
first Princeton home. An undergraduate of the time describes the
reception that a group of Christmas carolers received from the
two men in December 1938. At Mercer Street, "[Einstein] came
out in shirt sleeves [and no socks]. His housekeeper came out and
put a coat over his shoulders. He stood listening until we were
done, then shook each of our hands. [. . .] [T]hat same night we
sang outside the rented abode of Thomas Mann, a grand place
with high French doors facing the street. Through cracks in the
curtains, we could see elegant guests moving about. No one came
out, though some peeked out. The contrast impressed me."[54]

---

53   Personal communication, October 18, 2018.
54   Letter, G. B. Calkins, Princeton University, Class of 1939, to Jaime Sayen, July 11,
     1977, in Jamie Sayen, *Einstein in America* (New York: Crown, 1985), 126–27.

Six Did Einstein Read Kafka's *Castle* on Mann's Recommendation?

An engaging anecdote about Mann and Einstein has been circulating for years; it recently appeared in a study of Kafka's cinema-like narration in his novel *The Castle*.[1] At one point in Princeton, it is said, Mann, who was already very busy, sought out Einstein in order to give him a copy of this very novel—*The Castle*—to read. Almost immediately afterwards, Einstein returned the novel to Mann—unread—saying, "I couldn't read it for its perversity; the human mind isn't complicated enough."[2] The story and the question it poses open up an entire field of inquiry, which I hope will be interesting to explore.

First off, why would Mann have asked Einstein to read *The Castle*? The idea is not in itself implausible. During his years in Princeton, Mann greatly admired Kafka's work, although that admiration did not come about at once. On August 1, 1921, when both were contemporaries, Mann noted in his diary that he had met the recitator Ludwig Hardt, "who read me the prose of a man from Prague, Kafka, strange and curious enough. Otherwise quite boring."[3] A few weeks later, Mann's view changed, importantly. "[I] have developed considerable interest in the writings of Franz Kafka."[4] And "when asked in 1930 to identify an

---

1   *Mediamorphosis: Kafka and the Moving Image*, ed. Shai Biderman and Ido Lewit (New York: Wallflower Press, 2016), 1.

2   Cited from R.W. Stallman, "A Hunger Artist," in Angel Flores and Homer Swander, *Franz Kafka Today* (Madison: University of Wisconsin Press, 1958), 61. The story has been variously recirculated.

3   Cited in Todd Kontje, *Imperial Fictions: German Literature before and beyond the Nation-State* (Ann Arbor: University of Michigan Press, 2018), 178. "Zum Thee L. Hardt, der mir Prosa eines Pragers, Kafka, vorlas, merkwürdig genug. Sonst ziemlich langweilig." *Thomas Mann Tagebücher 1918–1921*, ed. Peter de Mendelssohn (Frankfurt am Main: S. Fischer Verlag, 1979), 542.

4   D 120. "Sehr interessiert war ich von den Schriften Franz Kafka's, die der Recitator Hardt mir empfahl." Ibid., 547.

unjustly forgotten author, Mann singled out Franz Kafka, 'the German-Bohemian, whose works I love greatly,' and noted that his friend Hermann Hesse had once dubbed 'this lonely man the secret king of German prose.'"[5] In a diary entry for April 4, 1935, Mann wrote of "continuing my reading of Kafka's 'Metamorphosis.' I must say that K.'s literary remains are the most genius-level (*genialste*) German prose in decades. What is there in German that would not be philistinism in comparison."[6] In his various advertisements for Kafka's "masterpieces" that followed, Mann praised Kafka's humorous religiosity, his fascinating strangeness, and the "Korrektheit" of his prose.[7] Finally, during his years at Princeton, where he was alleged to have given Einstein *The Castle* to read and where he would compose an admiring introduction to the American translation of *The Castle*, Mann wrote to the urbane publisher of New Directions, James Laughlin, that the work of "this Bohemian Jew" (*sic*) belongs among "the most fascinating phenomena in the field of artistic prose."[8]

There are a number of data points to support Mann's admiration for Kafka. One involves Kafka's greatest friend and booster, Max Brod. In 1938, when Brod had many of Kafka's manuscripts in tow, he feared for his life and his possessions in Nazi-occupied Prague. Mann spent a good deal of time and effort attempting to rescue them. "At the end of 1938 and the beginning of 1939, he [Mann] emphatically but vainly advocated for Max Brod at several American and English universities

5   Kontje, *Imperial Fictions*, 178. "Ich nenne [. . .] Franz Kafka, den Deutsch-Böhmen, dessen Werke ich außerordentlich liebe. [. . .] Hermann Hesse [. . .] hat diesen Einsamen einmal den heimlichen König deutscher Prosa genannt." Thomas Mann, "Die Vernachlässigten" (E3 176) [GW XIII: 424].

6   "Ich setzte die Lektüre von Kafkas 'Verwandlung' fort. Ich möchte sagen, daß K.'s Hinterlassenschaft die genialste deutsche Prosa seit Jahrzehnten ist. Was gibt es denn auf deutsch, was daneben nicht Spießerei wäre?" *Thomas Mann Tagebücher 1935–1936*, ed. Peter de Mendelssohn (Frankfurt am Main: S. Fischer Verlag, 1978), 72 (E5 345–46). "Only in 1952, as he read Gustav Janouch's notoriously unreliable *Conversations with Kafka*, did Mann distance himself from Kafka, calling him a 'pious Jew, very alien after all.'" Kontje, *Imperial Fictions*, 178. "Las in Gesprächen mit Kafka. Frommer Jude, doch sehr fremd." *Thomas Mann Tagebücher 1951–1952*, ed. Inge Jens (Frankfurt am Main: S. Fischer Verlag, 1993), 162.

7   See the materials assembled in Jutta Linder, "'Was für ein grundsonderbares Gewächs . . . !' Thomas Mann liest Kafka," in *Versprachlichung von Welt/ Il mondo in parole*, *Festschrift zum 60. Geburtstag von Maria Lieber*, ed. Simona Brunetti, et al. (Tübingen: Stauffenberg, 2016), 432.

8   Cited in Jutta Linder, "'Religiöser Humanist': Thomas Mann über Kafka," in *Thomas Mann Jahrbuch*, ed. Katrin Bedenig and Hans Wißkirchen, vol. 31 (2018), 25.

and libraries: Brod wanted to leave Kafka's estate to these institutions and asked only for money for the exit visa from Czechoslovakia, then threatened by the Nazis, and an appointment as curator of the collection" (E5 346). Mann and Brod were turned down by them all. With a suitcase full of Kafka's manuscripts, Brod managed to immigrate to Palestine, where, from 1940 on, he began his new life as the dramaturge of the Habima Theater in Tel Aviv. In his autobiography *Streitbares Leben* (A life of disputes), Brod wrote:

> When staying in Prague meant torment and death, Thomas Mann took an interest in my case without my having asked. An act of *noblesse*. By means of Mann's intervention, things came together so skillfully that a professorship awaited me at an American college. I preferred to follow the genius of my life and go to Palestine. Thomas Mann fully understood my decision and did not mind that I had thwarted his well-meant efforts.[9]

Brod appears to have forgotten the true state of affairs in a well-meaning effort to dignify the behavior of both parties. In fact, "Mann's attempt to help was instigated by a letter he had received from Brod himself, in which Brod states that he had been 'encouraged' to ask Mann for help by Klaus Mann, whom he knew from Prague, and by Dr. Robert Klopstock, Kafka's friend and deathbed physician." Furthermore, Brod was already in Palestine—viz., Tel Aviv--when, through Mann's intervention, he was indeed offered a teaching post at the Hebrew Union College in Cincinnati.[10] It is little known, however, that Brod was still ready to reconsider the appointment, if—as he wrote to Einstein, in June 1940—it could still be reactivated, which meant that he wasn't

---

[9] "Aus der von TM mit viel Mühe und Zeitaufwand betriebenen Hilfsaktion für Max Brod wurde nichts. Brod entschloß sich 1939, statt nach den Vereinigten Staaten nach Palästina zu emigrieren, wo er ab 1940 Dramaturg des Habimah Theaters in Tel Aviv war und 1968 starb. In seiner Autobiographie 'Streitbares Leben' (1960) schreibt er: '—als [. . .] ein Verbleiben in Prag Qualen und den Tod bedeutete, hat sich Thomas Mann meiner angenommen, ohne daß ich ihn darum hätte ersuchen müssen. Eine Tat von Noblesse. Durch Manns Intervention war alles so geschickt gefügt, daß eine Professorenstelle für mich an einem amerikanischen College wartete. Ich zog es vor, dem Genius meines Lebens zu folgen und nach Palästina zu gehen. Thomas Mann hatte volles Verständnis für mich, nahm es mir nicht übel, daß ich seine wohlgemeinten Bemühungen durchkreuzte.' [Max Brod, *Streitbares Leben: Autobiographie* (Munich: Kindler, 1960), 396–97]." Peter de Mendelssohn, "Notes" (T3 783). I have corrected de Mendelssohn's citation from *Streitbares Leben* by referring to the text.

[10] Hannah Arnold, "Brod's Case," *Times Literary Supplement*, October 15, 2014, 15.

averse to leaving Palestine after he had arrived. It is not surprising that
Brod would turn to Einstein for help, since their acquaintanceship dates
at the latest from "an evening in 1912 when Einstein was teaching in
Prague: Brod and the physicist played a violin sonata together."[11] There
is no record of a response from Einstein in the matter of Brod's returning
to Cincinnati.[12] In the meantime, Kafka's manuscripts stayed with Brod
in Israel until "some were returned to Kafka's nieces who, by chance,
deposited them in the Bodleian Library in Oxford."[13] Today, a
considerable number of manuscripts that had remained with Brod's
virtual stepdaughter have been secured by Israel's National Library,
digitized, and made accessible on the Web.[14]

So much for Brod's miraculous rescue of Kafka's manuscripts. Brod,
of course, was animated by an almost worshipful admiration of Kafka's
work, and he greatly admired Mann's work as well. On the occasion of
Mann's fiftieth birthday, Brod wrote:

> May he permit me on his joyous day of celebration to commemorate
> one of my saddest days, and to associate his life with a dead man,
> Franz Kafka. I always saw Thomas Mann through the infinitely
> loving, lovingly thoughtful medium of my friend, who treasured
> few of today's authors with such dedication as Thomas Mann. He
> read each of his works with excitement. For him it was a matter of
> life at stake. There was more than one connecting line between
> them: I believe that something very fine and something ornate
> and something noble and something mischievously clever in
> Kafka enjoyed the fine, ornate, noble, mischievous turns in the
> constructed world of Thomas Mann. "Be still! we want to look
> into a soul!"—Kafka, once read to me a novella by Mann ["Ein
> Glück"], which began with these words, with such delight,
> unforgettably. Of the two who today so gladly congratulate the
> jubilee, only I am on hand.[15]

[11]   Benjamin Balint, *Kafka's Last Trial: The Case of a Literary Legacy* (New York:
       Norton, 2018), 21.
[12]   Brod to Einstein, June 28, 1940, AEA 34-064. I owe this finding to the investigative
       work of my colleague Michael D. Gordin, the author of *Einstein in Bohemia*
       (Princeton, NJ: Princeton University Press, 2020).
[13]   Arnold, "Brod's Case."
[14]   https://www.nli.org.il/en/discover/literature-and-poetry/authors/franz-
       kafka.
[15]   "Er gestatte mir, zu seinem frohen Tage eines meiner traurigster zu gedenken,
       sein Leben mit einem Toten, mit Franz Kafka, zu verknüpfen. Immer sah ich
       Thomas Mann durch das unendlich liebevolle, in Liebe bedachtsame Medium
       meines Freundes, der wenig der heutigen Autoren mit solcher Hingabe schätzte,
       wie Thomas Mann. Jedes seiner Werke las er mit Spannung. Es wurde für ihn zu

Kafka's admiration for Mann is documented, although in all his extant writings, he rarely mentions Mann by name—he writes about him briefly while still a university student in his correspondence with Brod and once, thereafter, many years later, in 1915, in his travel diaries. But these notations are fascinating. He followed Mann's work in *Die Rundschau* as soon as it appeared: he read *Tonio Kröger* once in 1903, then read it again and found "profitable (*nutzbringend*)" its central theme—pertinent to the whole of Mann—this "being-in-love with opposites" ("Verliebtsein in das Gegensätzliche"). But he made a subtle distinction: the opposition between the sensitive artist and the healthy bourgeois as such struck him as not original and moreover as intimidating: "Thank God, I no longer have to believe in it (*Gott sei Dank, daß ich nicht mehr an diesen Gegensatz glauben muß*)." Kafka emphasizes the force of the attachment—the infatuation—in Mann's case, informing this play of opposites.[16]

A year later, Kafka read Mann's story "Ein Glück" (Happiness), calling it "a masterpiece"; and, being especially taken with its "exposition," he wrote to Brod, as we have heard, "Still! Wir wollen in eine Seele schauen" (Brod misremembered the citation by a bit).[17] Kafka's passion for Mann was again alive years later when, in October 1917, he confessed to Brod, "Mann is one among those whose writings I hunger for."[18]

---

einer wahren Lebensangelegenheit. Es gab mehr als eine Verbindunglinie. Ich glaube, etwas sehr Feines und etwas Geziertes und etwas Edles und etwas diebisch Schlaues in Kafka erfreute sich an feinen, gezierten, edlen, schlauen Wendungen in Th. Manns Gestaltungswelt. 'Still! wir wollen einen Blick in eine Seele tun' [*sic*]—eine Novelle Manns, die mit diesen Worten begann, las mir einst Kafka so entzückt, unvergeßlich vor.—Von zweien, die dem Jubilar heute gern gratulieren, bin nur ich zur Stelle." Max Brod, in *Thomas Mann im Urteil seiner Zeit: Dokumente 1891–1955*, ed. Klaus Schröter (Hamburg: Christian Wegner, 1969), 127.

16   *Franz Kafka, Briefe 1900–1912*, ed. Hans-Gerd Koch (Frankfurt am Main: S. Fischer Verlag, 1999), 42. It is interesting here to cite the aperçu of Klaus Harpprecht, one of a great many in his scintillating biography of Thomas Mann (in 2253 pages): "The contrast between art and life, which he [Mann] had stylized into an existential conflict in his youth, had leveled off in the course of the years [. . .]. His anticipation is evident in his abandoning the world of 'Tonio Kröger' for *Death in Venice*." *Thomas Mann—Eine Biographie* (Reinbek bei Hamburg: Rowohlt, 1995), 1073.

17   Thomas Mann, *Die Erzählungen*, vol. 1 (Frankfurt am Main: S. Fischer Verlag, 1979), 265; Max Brod, *Über Franz Kafka* (Frankfurt am Main: S. Fischer Verlag, 1966), 295. Cited in Peter-André Alt, *Franz Kafka, Der ewige Sohn: Eine Biographie* (Münich: C.H. Beck, 2005), 141.

18   "Mann gehört zu denen, nach deren Geschriebenem ich hungere." Franz Kafka, *Briefe 1902–1924*, ed. Max Brod and Klaus Wagenbach (Frankfurt am Main: S. Fischer Verlag, 1975) (originally 1958), 182. Cited in Alt, *Franz Kafka*.

In a letter to his friend Oskar Pollak, dated January 27, 1904, when Kafka was not yet twenty-one, he drafted his famously admirable poetics:

> I think one ought to read only those books at all that bite and sting. If the book we are reading does not wake us up with a blow of the fist on the skull, then why are we reading that book? So that it makes us happy? My God, we would be happy too if we had no books. And such books as make us happy we could in a pinch write ourselves. No, we need the books that affect us like a misfortune, that cause us a lot of pain, like the death of someone whom we loved better than ourselves, as if we were cast out in forests cut off from all human beings, like a suicide; a book must be the axe for the frozen sea in us.[19]

This aphorism, especially with its grandly concluding imagery of ice, might plausibly allude à rebours to Mann's *Tonio Kröger*, a work that we know Kafka especially admired, for consider Tonio's alternative poetics, in his excited speech to his friend Lisaweta:

> Now for the "Word." It isn't so much a matter of the "redeeming power" as it is of putting your emotions on ice and serving them up chilled! Honestly, don't you think there's a good deal of cool cheek in the prompt and superficial way a writer can get rid of his feelings by turning them into literature? If your heart is too full, if you are overpowered with the emotions of some sweet or exalted moment—nothing simpler! Go to the literary man, he will put it

---

[19]   Translation in *Kafka's Selected Stories*, a Norton Critical Edition, ed. and tr. Stanley Corngold (New York: Norton, 2007), 193. Oskar Pollak (1883–1915) was a fellow student of Kafka's at the Old Town Gymnasium (advanced high school); their friendship continued throughout their university years. Pollak studied Baroque art in Rome but at the outbreak of the First World War volunteered to fight for Austria, achieved officer's rank, and was killed in action on June 11, 1915. The letter to Oskar Pollak of January 27, 1904, reads: "Ich glaube, man sollte überhaupt nur solche Bücher lesen, die einen beißen oder stechen. Wenn das Buch, das wir lesen, uns nicht mit einem Faustschlag auf den Schädel weckt, wozu lesen wir dann das Buch? Damit es uns glücklich macht, wie Du schreibst? Mein Gott, glücklich wären wir eben auch, wenn wir keine Bücher hätten, und solche Bücher, die uns glücklich machen, könnten wir zur Not selber schreiben. Wir brauchen aber die Bücher, die auf uns wirken wie ein Unglück, das uns sehr schmerzt, wie der Tod eines, den wir lieber hatten als uns, wie wenn wir in Wälder verstoßen würden, von allen Menschen weg, wie ein Selbstmord, ein Buch muß die Axt sein für das gefrorene Meer in uns." *Franz Kafka, Briefe 1900–1912*, ed. Hans-Gerd Koch (Frankfurt am Main: Fischer, 1999), 36.

all straight for you instanter. He will analyze and formulate your affair, label it and express it and discuss it and polish it off and make you indifferent to it for time and eternity—and not charge you a farthing. You will go home quite relieved, cooled off, enlightened; and wonder what it was all about and why you were so mightily moved. And will you seriously enter the lists in behalf of this vain and frigid charlatan? What is uttered, so runs this credo, is finished and done with. If the whole world could be expressed, it would be saved, finished and done [. . .]. Well and good. But I am not a nihilist—.[20]

Kafka's axe obviously strengthens Tonio's implied *criticism* of a superficial, merely therapeutic theory of literature. Moreover, Tonio employs the same image code (of frigid ice) en route to conjuring *per contrarium* the vital effect he is aiming at. In the matter of Kafka's attentiveness to Mann's story, we might also note the resonance of the "naming" theme in Kafka's *Description of a Struggle* (1904–9), a text replete with references to *Tonio Kröger*.

Meanwhile, there is a wonderful symmetry to this play of allusions. If Kafka's reminiscence of *Tonio Kröger* is a marker of his devotion to Mann's work, we have Mann's extended salute to Kafka's *Castle* via an allusion to his own *Tonio Kröger*, though we may wish to greet this trope with incredulity. "It can be said," wrote Mann, "that the 'aspirational effort' (*das strebende Bemühen*) expressed by a work like *The Castle*—the tragicomic pathos that underlies it—enhances and transposes into the religious sphere Tonio Kröger's pains of artistic loneliness vis-à-vis simple, human feeling, his bad bourgeois conscience, and his love of the 'blond and ordinary.'"[21] Furthermore, the judgment could arise that

---

[20] Thomas Mann, "Tonio Kröger," 16–17. (https://literaturesave2.files.wordpress.com/2009/12/thomas-mann-tonio-kroger.pdf. "Was aber das 'Wort' betrifft, so handelt es sich da vielleicht weniger um eine Erlösung als um ein Kaltstellen und Aufs-Eis-Legen der Empfindung? Im Ernst, es hat eine eisige und empörend anmaßliche Bewandtnis mit dieser prompten und oberflächlichen Erledigung des Gefühls durch die literarische Sprache. Ist Ihnen das Herz zu voll, fühlen Sie sich von einem süßen oder erhabenen Ereignis allzusehr ergriffen: nichts ist einfacher! Sie gehen zum Literaten [. . .] Er wird Ihnen Ihre Angelegenheit analysieren und formulieren, bei Namen nennen, aussprechen und zum Reden bringen. [. . .] Sie aber werden erleichtert, gekühlt und geklärt nach Hause gehen [. . .] Und für diesen kalten Charlatan wollen Sie ehrlich eintreten?" *Tonio Kröger/ Mario und der Zauberer* (Frankfurt am Main: Fischer Taschenbuch, 1996), 37.

[21] My translation. The version that appears at the beginning of Franz Kafka, *The Castle*, tr. Willa and Edwin Muir, with an introduction by Thomas Mann (New York: Alfred A. Knopf, 1941), is unreliable. "Man kann sagen, daß das 'strebende Bemühen,' das eine Dichtung wie 'Das Schloß' zum Ausdruck bringt, das tragikomische Pathos, das ihr zugrundeliegt, eine Transponierung und

Kafka's famous story *The Metamorphosis*, with its haunting image of hungering, alludes to a scandalous short story by Mann that Kafka might very well have read—or surely did hear about. At the close of *The Metamorphosis*, Kafka describes the verminous bug Gregor Samsa's way of experiencing music as his *use* of music. On hearing his sister's violin playing, Gregor heads directly for his sister's shapely neck, which he intends to kiss while remaining on aggressive alert for intrusive strangers as she plays her violin entirely for him. When Gregor was a man, and he had money, he was a music-philistine; without money, he is a music-lover, or more precisely, the decadent lover of a musician. It is at this point that we can detect a wild parody of the final scene of Mann's story "The Blood of the Walsungs" (1905, 1921), which tells of incestuous lovemaking between brother and sister after they have been enthralled by the music of Wagner's "The Valkyries."[22]

On the question of whether, at the root of their mutual admiration, there is any likeness of Mann and Kafka in their standpoint as writers, in their view of poetic practice and the poetic character, opinions diverge—sharply. For the Mann scholar Todd Kontje, "Despite their admiration for each other's works, it is difficult to imagine two authors more different in their creative process, attitude toward the reading public, and sense of self-importance than Thomas Mann (1875–1955) and Franz Kafka (1883–1924)."[23] On the other hand, Hermann Kurzke

---

Erhöhung der künstlerischen Einsamkeitsschmerzen Tonio Krögers um das schlichte, menschliche Gefühl seines schlechten bürgerlichen Gewissens und seiner Liebe zu den 'blonden und gewöhnlichen' ins Religiöse ist" (GW X: 773).

[22]   The passage is taken from my "Introduction," in *Franz Kafka for the Twenty-First Century*, ed. Stanley Corngold and Ruth V. Gross (Rochester, NY: Camden House, 2011), 5–6. "Mann's story was composed in 1905 and due for publication that year in *the Neue Rundschau*. It was already typeset when Mann suddenly withdrew it, finally realizing that its anti-Semitic tenor would give grievous offense to his wife and her Jewish family. He eventually published it privately in 1921. How then can Kafka have known of it? As early as 1906 Mann sent copies of the story to Arthur Schnitzler and Jakob Wassermann, among others. The story then circulated in *samizdat*, and news of the scandal was bruited about in Vienna and thereafter, it might well be supposed, in Prague. Kafka was a devoted reader of the *Neue Rundschau* and of the works of Schnitzler and Wassermann and would have perked up at any mention of writings coming from their desk. (Wassermann was one of the several authors whom Kafka declares he was 'thinking of' apropos of his breakthrough story 'The Judgment.')" Ibid., 21n16.

[23]   Kontje, 179. The Mann-scholar Tobias Boes stresses their *thematic* difference. "Mann's [. . .] writings from the 1940s [. . .] document his growing conviction that the younger writer's [Kafka's] embrace of metaphysical ambiguity, not his own culturally overdetermined realism, would come to define modernist literature." "Thomas Mann, Joseph Conrad, Franz Kafka," in *The Cambridge*

and Stephan Stachorski, the editors of *Thomas Mann Essays*, defend a consanguinity of outlook: "How closely Kafka's artistry . . . approached that of Mann's is shown by a passage from Mann's working notes to [his essay] *Goethe and Tolstoy* (1921), in which the problem of the justification of the artist by his art is formulated in a manner almost identical to Mann's essay on Kafka's *The Castle*, 'In Honor of the Poet'" (E5 346). The passage from Mann's notes reads: "And so, self-denial consists simply in work, in working like the devil: work is crucial in itself and for one's own salvation."[24] Nonetheless, Peter-André Alt, a formidable Kafka scholar, stresses the disparity in their "mode of production": Unlike Mann, Kafka begins his manuscripts without a precise plan—hence, in a manner exactly opposite to Mann's "meticulous labor economy"—namely, as "a spontaneous form of work shunning the economic self-limitation of the creative act that ritually sets the time when writing is to begin and then break off."[25] On the other hand, once again, Alt sees Kafka sharing with Mann a Schopenhauerian irony that plays off the tension between uncontainable "aorgic" life and the self-conscious individual;[26] and given the opportunity to support a text by Max Brod declaring aestheticism reprehensible, Kafka finds instead a "wonderful nourishment" in a supplement to Mann's *Reflections of a Nonpolitical Man* advancing just such a pure aestheticism.[27] Complex structures invariably share features: how many and with what weight will depend on the thesis-hunger of the investigator. There is this one haunting detail: During his trip to Weimar in 1912, Kafka imitated Mann's signature on a writing pad . . . but then crossed it out![28] Perhaps this gesture of affinity and then of repudiation says it all.

History of Modernism, ed. Vincent Sherry (Cambridge, UK: Cambridge University Press, 2016), 621. Boes's essay develops a rich comparison and contrast of the themes of *The Magic Mountain* and *The Castle*.

24 "Selbstverleugnung besteht also einfach in der Arbeit, im Sichs sauer werden lassen. Denn die Arbeit an sich selbst und um des eigenen Seelenheils willen ist von nöten" (E2 316).

25 Alt, 319.

26 Ibid., 327. The "aorgic" is Friedrich Hölderlin's neologism for the mutually conditioning dialectical term opposed to the "organic," the former suggesting "something" universal and undifferentiated, sometimes "Nature"— an opposition said to forecast Nietzsche's opposition between the Dionysian and the Apollinian.

27 Ibid., 469.

28 Bernd Hamacher, "'Wieviel Brüderlichkeit bedeutet Zeitgenossenschaft ohne weiteres!' Franz Kafka und Thomas Mann—Versuch eines 'Kulturtransfers,'" in *Textverkehr: Kafka und die Tradition*, ed. Claudia Liebrand and Franziska Schößler (Würzburg: Königshausen & Neumann, 2004), 364.

144 Weimar in Princeton

To return to our primary thesis on the mooted affinity between Kafka and Mann: If we were to state a conclusion on the basis of the little information we have so far set down, Kafka's decisive answer to Mann's "being-in-love with opposites" would be his own "revulsion at antitheses (*Widerwille gegen Antithesen*)."[29] But here too—beseeching the reader's patience—there is another hand. On closer scrutiny, there is little in Mann's recurrent staging of the conflict of opposites bound to inspire Kafka's revulsion: Mann's affection opens up a field of play in which, with a sort of logical *agapē* love, he empowers the diminished opposite to keep the balance. "If in 'Tonio Kröger,'" Mann declared, in a speech to the students at Princeton, "spirit and art on one side stood opposed to life, then in *Fiorenza*, the spirit that has become ascetic, absolute to the degree of nothingness, turns itself against art which is understood as the sublimated enjoyment of life."[30] So tense an equilibrium between ostensible opposites is, of course, the very hallmark of Kafka's art. His stories identify, differentiate between, and then "bundle together" opposing positions within different cultural enterprises and in this way level the risk of defeat to one or the other party to the conflict. *The Trial* contains a literal example of this bundling together of the disputants: court and supplicant, once distinct, merge when, as the prison chaplain declares, "The judgment isn't simply delivered at some point; the proceedings gradually merge into the judgment."[31] This is to say that the verdict of the court is a judgment on the way in which the accused conducts his defense: the accused delivers his own verdict. Both parties, court and victim, share responsibility for the killing.[32]

The tension between the impulses Morality and Life, which Mann takes from Nietzsche, becomes one more opportunity for him to deconstruct their opposition and then combine, playfully, the one figure with the other, as in, par excellence, the Princeton novella *The Transposed*

---

29 Franz Kafka, *Tagebücher in der Fassung der Handschrift*, ed. Michael Müller (Frankfurt am Main: S. Fischer Verlag, 1990), 259. See "Kafka and Sex," in Stanley Corngold and Benno Wagner, *The Ghosts in the Machine* (Evanston, IL: Northwestern University Press, 2010), 136.

30 Thomas Mann, "On Myself: From Childhood Play to *Death in Venice*" (B 47).

31 Franz Kafka, *The Trial*, tr. Breon Mitchell (New York: Schocken, 1998), 213. "Das Urteil kommt nicht mit einemmal, das Verfahren geht allmählich ins Urteil über" (P 289).

32 This paragraph, beginning with the words "His stories identify, differentiate between, and then bundle together opposing positions," is taken from my essay "The Organization Man, Franz Kafka, Risk Insurance, and the Occasional Hell of Office Life," in *Kafka: Organization, Law, Writing*, ed. Jana Costas, Christian Huber, Günther Ortmann, and Marianne Schuller (Weilerswist: Velbrück Wissenschaft, 2019), 21.

Heads. (I discuss this work at length in my *The Mind in Exile: Thomas Mann in Princeton*). Another word for such play in Mann's lexicon is the third term—Irony. Some sophisticated critics of Mann would have us believe that Mann's world is one without steadfast beliefs. This charge extends beyond "the fictional world of Thomas Mann, [which] is a play with contradictions and polarities—a play that, to be sure, through the distanced humor of the narrator—Mann's celebrated 'irony'—is tempered in a charitable-philanthropic and pseudo-bourgeois manner but will never lead to a final overcoming." And so the conceptual oppositions in Mann's *fiction* remain "in play," so as perpetually to postone a resolution.[33] In the far graver context of Mann's real life in 1938, such suspended oppositions persist. He will support civilized democracy against the raw brutality of war, and at the same time subliminally urge the United States to go to war against the Germans. This is his current stance, after he has played the opposite hand earlier in his ferocious, national-conservative defense of the German war party in World War I. But to further explore this question, to which the answer in either case would have to be "Yes (or 'No') ... *but* ... ," would, once again, take us too far afield for now, when we mean to be considering the relation between Mann and *Einstein*!

What is certain is that of Kafka's works, Mann particularly admired *The Castle* and wrote a laudatory introduction to it, at considerable length, which appeared in translation in its first American edition. He took great pains with it, and even approached the task in his precious morning hours, normally reserved, as in Goethe's phrase, for the main business of the day ("sein Hauptgeschäft"--writing fiction.[34] It is now plausible to think—as we return to our anecdote—that Mann would have encouraged Einstein to read Kafka's last novel and hoped he would be moved by it and have something incisive to say about it. But, as we have heard, according to the anecdote, Einstein promptly returned the novel to Mann, saying that the human mind was not constituted to cope with such mischief.

I am not alone as one who has often wondered about the truth of this story, which enriches the haunting but meager history of Einstein's relation to Kafka, which began with a mere handshake, it is surmised, at the conclusion of a lecture in 1911 at the Haus Fanta in Prague. It was allegedly followed up, as we've noted, by Kafka's alleged visits to

---

[33] Herbert Lehnert and Eva Wessel, "Vorwort," *Nihilismus der Menschenfreundlichkeit: Thomas Manns "Wandlung" und sein Essay "Goethe und Tolstoi"* (Frankfurt am Main: Vittorio Klostermann, 1991), 7.

[34] Linder, "'Was für ein grundsonderbares Gewächs ... !,'" 429–30.

Einstein in Berlin.[35] At no point, however, does either of these savants refer to any of these meetings or indeed to one another or to any of the other's works.[36]

So, is there any truth to our anecdote? If we consult Konrad Wachsmann, Einstein's architect and conversationalist, we will think Einstein's reaction plausible, since Kafka's *Castle* would *not* have suited his taste in casual reading—at all. Einstein much preferred philosophy to fiction, but he did like novels with exciting outcomes. He read Dostoyevsky's *The Brothers Karamazov* with passionate enthusiasm, declaring, in an interview, "If you ask in whom I am most interested at present, I must answer Dostoyevsky—Dostoyevsky gives me more than any scientist, more than Gauss." He went on:

> It is the moral impression, the feeling of elevation, that takes hold of me when a work of art is presented. And I was thinking of these ethical factors when I gave preference to Dostoyevsky's works. There is no need for me to carry out a literary analysis, nor to enter on a search for psychological subtleties, for all investigations of this kind fail to penetrate the heart of a work such as *The Brothers Karamazoff* [sic]. This can be grasped only by means of feelings that find satisfaction in passing through trying and difficult circumstances, and that become intensified to exaltation when the author offers the reader ethical satisfaction. Yes, that is the right expression, "ethical satisfaction"! I can find no other word for it.

Furthermore, we learn from Einstein's conversation with the mathematician J. W. W. Sullivan and the Irish writer James Murphy that Einstein pronounced Dostoyevsky "a great religious writer":

---

[35]   Philipp Frank, *Einstein: His Life and Times* (New York: Knopf, 1947) affirms the meeting of Einstein and Kafka in Prague, but there is indeed radio silence about what they might have said to each other. Frank supplies the context: "At this time in Prague there was already a Jewish group who wanted to develop an independent intellectual life among the Jews. They disliked seeing the Jews taking sides in the struggle between Germans and Czech nationalists. [. . .] They were Zionists, but at that period they paid little attention to practical politics and concerned themselves mainly with art, literature, and philosophy. Einstein was introduced to this group, met Franz Kafka, and became particularly friendly with Hugo Bergmann and Max Brod" (84).

[36]   Yet, once again, *on the other hand*, it can be safely concluded that Kafka's work is saturated with an awareness of *Nietzsche's* thought—for one—although at no point did Kafka commit the name "Nietzsche" to writing. The Kafka scholar Franz Kuna has published a chapter titled "Rage for Verification: Kafka and Einstein" with suggestions for further reflection in *On Kafka: Semi-Centenary Perspectives* (New York: Barnes and Noble, 1976), 83.

But that was only in the sense, he [Einstein] said, that Dostoyevsky was concerned with presenting a picture of "the mystery of spiritual existence [. . .] clearly and without comment"; Dostoyevsky was not interested in interpreting specific religious problems. Science, preoccupied with the work of nature, Einstein continued, had no power over the depths of spiritual existence—over "the valuation of life and all nobler expressions" of humanity. Built on the foundations of spiritual existence, ethical norms could not be reduced to scientific formulas; they could be felt only through the kind of aesthetic creation Dostoyevsky bequeathed.[37]

The Brothers Karamazov approaches its end with Smerdyakov's confession of the murder of Fyodor Karamazov, but his confession is not believed. Dmitri, Fyodor's son, is convicted of this parricide, but Dmitri can still find "exaltation" in the verdict: through suffering he will become a "new man." But that may not be the ending that Einstein delighted in. It is more likely to be the moment of love and goodness shared between Alyosha and Ilyusha's friends at Ilyusha's funeral. The very last sentence of *The Brothers Karamazov* reads, "'And always so, all our lives hand in hand! Hurrah for Karamazov!' Kolya cried once more rapturously, and once more the boys took up his exclamation: 'Hurrah for Karamazov!'" By contrast, as we return to our primary author, Kafka's unfinished novel *The Castle* ends thus: "It was Gerstäcker's mother. She gave K. her trembling hand and had him sit down next to her, she spoke with difficulty, it was difficult to understand her, but what she said . . . ."[38]

On grounds of personality, as well, Einstein might have been skeptical of a recommendation coming from Mann. The brutal fact, according to Wachsmann, is, once more, that "he never felt any affinity with Thomas Mann. [. . .] In his eyes, Mann was 'an oppressive schoolmaster, always in need of someone to instruct.'"[39] One might

---

[37] The first interview is recorded in a biography published by the Polish philosopher Alexander Moszkowski. This information and the following account of Einstein's admiration for *The Brothers Karamazov* and the "ethical satisfaction" it afforded him is provided by Alexander Vucinich, *Einstein and Soviet Ideology* (Stanford, CA: Stanford University Press, 2001), 181–82.

[38] Franz Kafka, *The Castle*, tr. Mark Harman (New York: Schocken, 1998), 316. "Es war Gerstäckers Mutter. Sie reichte K. die zitternde Hand und ließ ihn neben sich niedersetzen, mühselig sprach sie, man hatte Mühe sie zu verstehn, aber was sie sagte" [no period]. *Das Schloß*, ed. Malcolm Pasley (Frankfurt am Main: S. Fischer Verlag, 1982), 495.

[39] Michael Grüning, *Ein Haus für Albert Einstein* (Berlin: Verlag der Nation, 1990), 152.

wonder whether Mann, who, on October 10, 1939, was reading "Die Karamasows," would also have suggested that Einstein read the book (T3 369). But in the matter of Kafka: was Kafka's writing really a forever-unknown quantity to Einstein, so that he could have been so astonished by *The Castle* ca. 1939? Had he never looked at it before?

Michael Grüning posed this very question to Wachsmann: "In a work by Philipp Frank, I noticed that during his stay in Prague, Einstein was acquainted not only with Max Brod but with Franz Kafka. Do you know if he *read* Kafka?"[40] Wachsmann replied: "Absolutely. But I think that Einstein was more interested in the man Kafka, who died too young, than his novels—I borrowed a copy of 'Das Schloß' (The Castle) *from his library* but could understand very little of it."[41]

Ergo, it now appears implausible that Einstein can have returned *The Castle* to Thomas Mann with the air of having scrutinized a bit a work *utterly strange to him* and only then decided it was not worth the effort. The anecdote would seem to be contrived, though charming in its intent to favor Kafka.

And yet, if we will look even closer at the matter, there is actually nothing in Wachsmann's sketchy remark to *disprove* absolutely the truth of the anecdote, which speaks, again, of Kafka's great complexity and a work unknown to Einstein. For it was not Einstein who originally gave Wachsmann *The Castle* to read: Wachsmann merely borrowed the book. True, he took the book from Einstein's *personal* library; and so here, once again, we have to conclude that Einstein would have been at least acquainted with Kafka's novel decades before he arrived in Princeton. And yet again, not quite, for Michael Grüning quotes Wachsmann:

You said that Einstein was sent a lot of books gratis by authors and publishers. And so, his Berlin library—the biggest part of which could be sent to Princeton—does not give an accurate picture of his literary interests.

[Wachsmann replies:] You're right, there. Moreover, not only was Einstein sent a lot of books, he also gave a lot of them away. From a bibliographical standpoint, the library in the Haberlandstraße

---

40   Emphasis added. Frank, *Einstein*, 84.
41   Emphasis added. The notation continues: "Einstein told me that he was impressed by Kafka's knowledge of Judaism (das Judentum) [. . .]. I knew from Elsa Einstein that during his time in Berlin, Kafka sometimes came to [our apartment] on Haberlandstraße and that she was frightened by his rather odd way of being." Ibid., 248–49. The content of this "recollection" needs to be taken with a grain of salt. It can have been concocted after Kafka became famous. There is no trace of such visits in Kafka's extant papers.

apartment was not in fact a library that would allow you to draw any conclusions as to their owner. One could apply such a scheme only to the books in the Tower Room. When the conversation turned to books, Einstein told everyone, quite frankly—to the horror of his wife—that the library really consisted only of books that had been sent to him gratis. [. . .] The Einsteins did not really have a library in the classical sense of the word.[42]

And so, the anecdote hovers in the mist between truth and untruth. It is pleasant to imagine it, and we can still leave the matter with a reliable "new acquist of true experience" (Milton, *Samson Agonistes*): Einstein preferred Dostoyevsky to Kafka, and Kafka's *The Castle* defies rational understanding. But the matter of whether Mann did or did not lend Einstein a book is not, finally, our going concern, which is the alleged intimacy between Einstein and Mann in Princeton. Even had they exchanged this book, this fact does not speak strongly in favor of extensive social interaction. Of course, Mann was privy to Einstein's *theoretical* achievements. He was fascinated by reflections on time, and in *The Magic Mountain* and *Joseph and His Brothers* was not shy of contributing to this mystery. In a diary entry for March 3, 1920, he had seen himself as a thinker ahead of Einstein:

This afternoon and evening [I] read various interesting and stimulating things: [. . .] an epistemological critique of Einstein's theory (which, incidentally, has been analyzed by Flammarion and largely rejected by him); it deals again with the problem of time, one that today assumes a real urgency, and one that I anticipated in my conception of *The Magic Mountain*, just as I had anticipated the political antitheses leading up to the war. My satisfaction at my seismographic sensitivity in more than one respect in those days is diminished, even nullified, by sorrow in the recognition, constantly, absolutely confirmed, that this novel [*The Magic Mountain*] as well as *The Confidence Man* [*The Confessions of Felix Krull*] should have been finished in 1914.[43]

---

[42]   Grüning, *Ein Haus*, 248–49.

[43]   "Las nachmittags und abends allerlei Interessantes und Erregendes. [. . .] Eine erkenntnistheoretische Kritik der Einstein'schen Theorie (die übrigens auch von Flammarion kritisiert und weitgehend abgelehnt wird), worin das Problem der Zeit wieder die Rolle spielt, deren heutige Urgenz ich bei der Conception des Zbg, wie die politischen Antithesen des Krieges, anticipierte. Die Genugtuung über meine seismographische Empfindlichkeit von damals in mehr als einer Beziehung wird beeinträchtigt und aufgehoben durch die immer und in jeder Hinsicht sich bestätigende Einsicht davon und den Kummer darüber, daß der Roman, wie auch der Hochst., anno 14 hätte fertig sein müssen." *Tagebücher 1918–1921*, 390–91.

This passage gives some credence to Wachsmann's report that Einstein half-seriously suspected that Mann, given half a chance, would seize the opportunity to explain the theory of relativity to him.[44]

The accomplished ecologist Jamie Sayen, who grew up on Mercer Street in the house next door to Einstein's, concludes: "Thomas Mann lived in Princeton from 1938 to 1941 but, except for a shared hatred of the Nazis, the two famous refugees had little in common."[45] Granting their disparity of temperament and manner of self-presentation, Sayen's judgment is nevertheless too blunt: there is more to their shared *Weltbild* than this "hatred," though the emotion was not unknown to them. There is, foremost, their "moral" socialism: "*Like that of Thomas Mann,* Einstein's socialism is be understood [far less as involving a 'radical transformation of the conditions of production'] than as a moral-political statement"—conceived, very simply, as the "sole humane alternative."[46] Erich Kahler and Hermann Broch, too, were deeply involved in this conception. Since I have discussed the content of Mann's socialism at length in *The Mind in Exile*, it will be best to leave it now and proceed to a conclusion.

---

[44]   Neffe, *Einstein—A Biography,* 303.

[45]   Jamie Sayen, *Einstein in America* (New York: Crown, 1985), 126.

[46]   Emphasis added. Werner Mittenzwei, in Grüning: *Ein Haus,* 547.

Toward a Conclusion

Kahler-Kreis *(Kahler Circle) refers to the circle, lasting from 1939 to the early 1970s, of intellectual friends of Erich Kahler.*

—*Anonymous*

I hope to have accomplished what I proposed to do in the Introduction: By conjuring the mind and presence of Thomas Mann in Princeton and his circle of friends in the years 1938–41, I would bring alive "the intellectual atmosphere of an extraordinary place and constellation" (Heinrich Detering).[1] For "with the coming of the Einsteins, Weyls, and Manns, Princeton began to become a little capital of German culture in exile"—thus Eugene Paul Wigner, the Hungarian-American theoretical physicist, "Einstein's younger friend."[2] Thomas Mann's interactions with his fellow exiles—chiefly, Hermann Broch, Giuseppe Antonio Borgese, Albert Einstein, and, above all, Erich Kahler—constitute the first phase of a Princeton "Kahler Circle"—a hitherto unacknowledged prelude to the "Weimar on the Pacific," the latter famously involving such artists and thinkers, along with Thomas Mann, as Theodor Adorno, Bertolt Brecht, Alfred Döblin, Lion Feuchtwanger, Max Horkheimer, Erich Wolfgang Korngold, and Arnold Schoenberg.

In the less celebrated Princeton group, Mann, Broch, and Kahler, in frequent conversation, produced a remarkable corpus of written work—great chunks of Mann's *Lotte in Weimar,* the novella *The Transposed Heads,* and the fourth volume of the grand tetralogy *Joseph and His Brothers*; Broch's *The Death of Virgil*; and Kahler's vast universal history, *Man the Measure.* This tally does not include the countless

---

[1] Heinrich Detering, in a letter to the Princeton University Press. Detering is the Professor of Modern German Literature and the Study of Comparative Literature at the University of Göttingen.

[2] Eugene Paul Wigner, "I was Einstein's Younger Friend," in Michael Grüning, *Ein Haus für Albert Einstein—Erinnerungen, Briefe, Dokumente* (Berlin: Verlag der Nation, 1990), 529.

speeches, lectures, and articles that flowed from this circle. These exiles wrote out of the inner compulsion to serve the best of human qualities— the better angels of our nature—under lethal political threat, egregiously in Europe and not inconspicuously in America, which is not to downplay the economic—the merely survival—factor in play, especially in the case of Kahler and Broch, who were reduced to near-penury after the Nazi confiscation of their assets in Europe. Princeton meant safety, but it also meant exilic moods of desperation and lostness.

On his arrival in New York in 1938, Thomas Mann famously remarked, "Where I am, there is Germany. I carry my German culture in me."[3] This might also have been said by Erich Kahler and Hermann Broch and other members of this Circle. In their joint cultural memory, certain writers held pride of place—foremost Goethe and Kafka— constituting a good deal of the tissue that bound these exiles together. It was no one less than Thomas Mann's son-in-law, W. H. Auden, a peripheral member of the Circle, who wrote famously about Kafka in 1941: "Had one to name the artist who comes nearest to bearing the same kind of relation to our age that Dante, Shakespeare, and Goethe bore to theirs, Kafka is the first one would think of."[4] Here he speaks for each of his elders.

In scrutinizing the Circle, some high-minded commonplaces about their relationships do not hold up. For one, Mann and Einstein were not close friends. A solid confidant of Einstein's alleged that Mann's pedantry and patrician airs inspired Einstein's "animosity"—an emotion heightened by the very fact of their living in the same neighborhood.[5] On the other hand, Mann's indisputable qualities should not obscure the fact—it is exhilarating to know!—that he took great pains to advance the troubled careers of his friends—Erich Kahler, Hermann Broch, and even Max Brod, Kafka's great patron and booster. Against his better aesthetic judgment, Mann supported Broch's *The Death of Virgil*, writing a forceful letter to the Guggenheim Foundation for funds that Broch badly needed. On friendship and nurture within the Circle: without Erich Kahler's hospitality, and the affection of Antoinette von Kahler, it is doubtful that *The Death of Virgil* would ever have been finished. Einstein did not care

---

3   Cited in Tobias Boes, *Thomas Mann's War: Literature, Politics, and the World Republic of Letters* (Ithaca, NY: Cornell University Press, 2019), 3.

4   Cited conveniently in Alan Stone, a review of Saul Friedländer, *Franz Kafka, The Poet of Shame and Guilt*, https://momentmag.com/book-review-franz-kafka-the-poet-of-shame-and-guilt/.

5   From Michael Grüning's report of his conversation with the architect Professor Konrad Wachsmann, who designed Einstein's summer house in Caputh near Potsdam. Grüning, *Ein Haus*, 152.

for everything that Broch wrote, but he encouraged his ambitious projects and, better still, gave him run of his house one summer when Broch was once again homeless.

Here, patient reader, I must end. I have already set down what I know. I should like the Kahler Circle, in its nascent days and thereafter, to constitute an object worthy of the same interest as "Weimar on the Pacific." There will, I hope, be more to read and learn about this illustrious band—The Kahler Circle—as compiled by other hands. We would see the work and memoirs of scholars and writers whose names we have glimpsed only in passing, authors of paeans to Erich Kahler alongside expectable praise by Thomas Mann, Giuseppe Antonio Borgese, Hermann Broch, and Albert Einstein—namely, John Berryman, Rudolf Kassner, Victor Lange, Frank Jewett Mather Jr., Ben Shahn, and many others.[6] Friendly shadows rise to mind: the faces of Martin Buber, Ernst Kantorowicz, Wolfgang Pauli, Roger Sessions. . . . All played their part. I welcome my completers across the years.

---

[6]   *Erich Kahler,* ed. and partly tr. Eleanor Wolff and Herbert Steiner (New York; Eleanor Wolff, 1951).

Appendix I A Chronicle, with Commentary

Here is the promised chronicle of Mann's meetings with Erich Kahler, in the hope—as I wrote—that it will convey something of their tempo and characteristic flavor, which a single, generalizing picture cannot. I omit mention of the several lunches and dinners during Mann's last fall and winter in Princeton where nothing of their conversation is known. But even the knowledge of these absent mentions should heighten the sense of how very often they were together and how deeply they valued their friendship.

On May 15, 1939, after dinner at home with the writer Annette Kolb—an important old friend—Mann "read next to the fire in the library the twenty-five new pages of chapter 7 [of *Lotte in Weimar*]. The tragicomic side of politics in the scene with John [Goethe's secretary]." Kahler and his wife were present at the reading, and Kahler appears to be the source of the following remark, "Preserving the mythic, universal element despite the ironic, critical approach." Mann continues this thought, elliptically: "A more audacious counterpart to the *Joseph*. Discussion."[1] (The aperçu attributed to Kahler will be at the center of Kahler's several essays on Mann and his novels.) Several days thereafter, on leaving for a summer's travel—chiefly to rest and write on the seashore in Holland and thereafter to visit Zurich and London—Mann took pains to record in his diaries, after another evening's dinner and conversation with Kahler "about politics and America," that he had said goodbye to his friend for the summer and "cautioned" him "to be on the qui vive," i.e., to look alive and stay in touch (T3 416).

---

[1] "Nachher in der Bibliothek bei Kaminfeuer. Vorlesung neuer 25 Seiten des VII. Kapitels. Das humoristisch Quälende des Politischen in der John-Szene. *Kahler*, der mit seiner Frau zur Vorlesung kam: 'Erhaltung des Mythos bei ironisch-kritischer Realisierung.' Gewagteres Gegenstück zum Joseph. Diskurs" (T3 407).

Mann returned to Princeton on September 23, 1939. Plainly hungry for Kahler's company, he invited him to stay at Stockton Street for the entire weekend. They dined together and spent the rest of the evening discussing the politics of the day: "The fatuousness of Italy. Russia is decisive—thanks to Hitler's idiocy. A thorough revenge for the Munich insult"—the Munich Pact, which ceded the Sudetenland to Germany.[2] Mann and Kahler breakfasted the next morning, with no hint of Kahler's trespassing on Mann's privacy for his crucial morning's work; and after lunch, they continued their conversation on "the misfortune of the German people, which will no longer know what to make of itself." In the evening, after dinner, Mann read aloud to Kahler his revised chapter 7 of *Lotte*—Goethe's interior monologue—"which expanded until late into 'world-political' and 'world-problematical' matters."[3]

Some weeks later, after a typically "excellent" dinner, Mann read from *Lotte* again to Erich and Antoinette von Kahler, who responded enthusiastically. Mann consistently read his new work aloud to Kahler, as, once again—for example, on November 28, with Broch present— Mann read what he had so far written of a "political essay," *This War* (*Dieser Krieg*) (T3 493). On December 9, 1939, their topic was again "the political: the course of the war, the future of Germany [. . .]" (T3 508). In this respect Kahler was a mentor; Mann admired Kahler for his erudition and was grateful to share in it. It would not be wrong to suggest that *all* of Mann's current political opinions were informed by—and vetted—in conversation with Kahler. Again, on December 18, they were together— this time at dinner at the Kahlers in the presence of Antoinette and a so-called housekeeper, Alice (Lily) Loewy, who many years later, just before Kahler's death, was to become his second wife. (Lili cultivated Kahler's memory for decades after his death. Her memoir of her life with her husband in Princeton appears as Appendix II to this volume.) Again, Mann and Kahler read together the "pamphlet"—equally, "the political text" on which Mann had worked that morning, namely, *This War*, with Mann commenting afterwards: "Applause for its moral dimension, discussion about the facts." We know that Mann would

---

[2]   In this diary entry, Mann's distinguished friend is addressed as "E. v. Kahler." "Viel über das Politische. Die Läppischkeit Italiens. Rußland entscheidend— dank Hitlers Idiotie. Revanche für die Münchener Beleidigung gründlich" (T3 476).

[3]   "Viel über das Politische und das Unglück des deutschen Volkes, das überhaupt nicht mehr wissen wird, wie über sich denken. [. . .] [Diskussion über den Gegenstand, die sich bis spät ins Welt-politische und -Problematische erweiterte" (T3 476).

ultimately be dissatisfied with this piece. He does become fully alive on his return home on meeting the poodle, "whose joy was great."[4] The Kahlers were with Mann at home on Christmas Eve 1939 for the exchange of Christmas presents.

The first day of the new year was a remarkable one for Mann, since it celebrated his putting pen to paper for the first time his new "Indian" novella "The Transposed Heads." The day dawned in a questioning mood, described in Mann's diary the night before: "The second close of a year in this country. [. . .] With what suspense one regards the year ahead! One's work more and more assumes the character of a pastime. May it be an honorable one."[5] That evening he invited Kahler and his mother to dine with him and thereafter—quite typically—to meet in the library in front of the fire for a literary and political discussion, now on "Stifter; a certain embittered provincial literature in Germany; the coming 'Significant' in literature arising from the unconscious and from a [competent] knowledge of art."[6] In the weeks following, Kahler contributed the important essay mentioned in chapter 2—"Was soll werden?" (What is to become [of us]?)—to Mann's journal *Mass und Wert* (Measure and Value), which incorporated "work" done on it by Mann, who described its contents as "the immanent tragedy of liberal democracy on the example of America. The inescapable alternatives are socialism or fascism."[7]

The Kahlers invited Mann to dinner on February 2, 1940, after which Mann read aloud the opening pages of *The Transposed Heads* and noted how happy he was about the effect. There were "young people" present—Kahler was and would always be great friends with Mann's children: "Young Gret's enthusiasm was especially moving" (T4 19–20). Gret was Mann's daughter-in law, the wife of his sixth child, Michael (called "Bibi").

---

4   "Nachher in K.'s Arbeitszimmer Vorlesung größerer Teile des Pamphlets [,der politischen Schrift']. Beifall für Moralisches, Diskussion über Sachliches. Zu Hause den Pudel, dessen Freude groß war, noch ausgeführt" (T3 511–12).

5   (D 345). "Das zweite Jahresende in diesem Lande. [. . .] Mit welcher Spannung sieht man dem kommenden verhängnisvollen Jahr entgegen! Was man treibt gewinnt mehr und mehr den Charakter des Zeitvertreibs. Möge er ehrenvoll sein." (T3 517).

6   "Über Stifter. Über eine gewisse verbitterte Provinzial-Literatur in Deutschland. Das aus dem Unbewußten und aus Kunstwissen kommende 'Bedeutende' in der Dichtung" (T4 3).

7   "Vorlesung aus [. . .] [Kahlers "Was soll werden?"]: Immanente Tragik der liberalen Demokratie am amerikan. Beispiel gezeigt. Alternative von Sozialismus oder Faschismus, unausweichlich" (T4 10).

On February 29, 1940, Kahler was with Mann, who recorded their grievous "worry about the war," predicting "the financial ruin of the wealthy states, big and small. The capitalist economy is becoming impossible." A desideratum: "the economic and social overthrow of Germany—like Russia—precisely as a way to save their systems. One expects military action in the coming or next month, combined with a change of government in England, perhaps in France. But will Germany ever be forced to do such a thing?"[8]

March 12, 1940. "The *Kahlers* [Erich Kahler and his wife and or mother] for dinner. Radio report: a catastrophic Russia-Finland peace accord [signed] under German pressure, regardless of the offer of Allied aid. A diplomatic victory for Germany, which will be disastrous for the small, neutral countries, especially in the Balkans. A lost battle. America was probably not uninvolved in this outcome. Roosevelt's domestic political successes—whose reelection in the end could mean the entry of America into the war, which is what matters in the end."[9]

On March 22, more of the very same: dinner together with Kahler and then a wide-ranging political discussion—and again on April 11 and again, on May 10. Mann appeared to welcome the company of Kahler especially when there was terrible news of German conquests (T4 48, 57, 72–73).

On May 20, Kahler was again at the Manns for dinner. These were dreadful days for both, on learning of the Nazi penetration deep into France. Mann sought to enliven the evening by reading aloud the tenth chapter of *The Transposed Heads* to Kahler, Katia, and "the children." The sequence centers on the eccentric hermit Kamadamana and was found very funny: a calculated distraction (T4 79).

On the evening of May 22, both Kahler and Broch were together with Mann for a "conversation about anxiety attacks at the universal prevalence of Evil, with no way out and no refuge for the mind. The

---

8   "Sorgenvollstes über den Krieg. Finanzieller Ruin der vermögenden Staaten, großer wie kleiner. Unmöglichwerden der kapitalistischen Wirtschaftsform. Wirtschaftlicher und sozialer Umsturz von Deutschland wie Rußland gewollt, deren Systeme eben durch ihn zu retten. Voraussichtlicher Ausbruch der militärischen Aktionen im kommenden oder übernächsten Monat, verbunden mit Regierungswechsel in England, vielleicht auch Frankreich. Wird aber Deutschland je zu einem solchen zu zwingen sein?" (T4 39–40).

9   "Zum Abendessen *Kahlers*. Radio-Nachricht: katastrophaler Friedensschluß Rußland Finnland unter deutschem Druck, ungeachtet des Angebots alliierter Hilfe. Diplomatischer Sieg Deutschlands, der sich bei den kleinen Neutralen, bes. auf dem Balkan verhängnisvoll auswirken wird. Eine verlorene Schlacht. Amerika wahrscheinlich nicht unbeteiligt an diesem Ausgang. Innerpolitische Erfolge Roosevelts,—dessen Wiederwahl am Ende den Eintritt Amerikas in den Krieg bedeuten könnte, worauf es am Ende abgesehen.—" (T4 44).

true situation still not understood. No one imagines what Hitler would do to the old nations of the West"—and here Mann's note is interrupted.[10] This experience will suggest that Kahler's indwelling, indefatigable Germany-mysticism, an inheritance from his participation in the ideology of the Stefan George Circle, was finally closing down.

On May 27, 1940, Mann and Kahler discussed the imminent danger of the internment of the German emigrants, never mind that they had disavowed their "native" land, which threatened to murder them. Kahler contrived a system by which various parties would stand surety for the threatened "aliens" (T4 84).

On June 3, 1940, Mann recorded a visit from Kahler, along with the Austrian poet and dramatist Richard Beer-Hofmann and his daughter, "whom I received in the library." Beer-Hofmann and Kahler's mother were first cousins, an extraordinarily refined and talented pair. At this moment, 150 Nazi planes bombarded Paris with terrifying siren bombs (T4 89).

June 4, 1940. After dinner, Kahler "read to me from the German version of his lecture at the New School on 'The Intellectual Forerunners of National Socialism.' Familiar, terrible things. At the end, Jünger. An old-world sensibility. Delectable nihilism (*Genüßlicher Nihilismus*)."[11] Mann noted, in the days following, that Kahler's discussion of the fascist precursors in German thought had no or little effect on his American audience, who simply did not twig.

June 12, 1940. "Dinner with Kahler und Broch too. We spoke a lot about the political situation. Optimistic desperation [. . .]. In the evening, *a reading from The Transposed Heads to Katia, Eri[ka], Loewenstein, Kahler, and Broch: a portion of the Temple scene and the hermit's chapter*. Great joy. I had to laugh a lot while reading" (T4 95).

In California, September 4, 1940. Mann again received a letter from Kahler: the mere event of receiving the letter was worth noting (T4 143). Kahler imagines that the march of the Nazi armies might have come to a halt (Germany was intent on bombing England and blasted Liverpool the day before). But with the putative standstill, what would be the result other than "stagnation, disintegration, and a protracted, indescribable misery"? One consolation: "our" journal *Measure and Value*

---

10   "Gespräch über die Anfälle von Angst vor dem Universellwerden des Bösen, ohne Ausweg und Refugium für den Geist. Die wahre Lage noch immer nicht verstanden. Niemand stellt sich vor, was Hitler mit den alten Nationen des Westens täte, wenn—" (T4 80).
11   "Kahler [. . .] las mir aus der deutschen Fassung seines Vortrags über die 'geistigen Wegbereiter des Nationalsozialismus' für die New School vor. Bekanntes, Schreckliches. Zuletzt Jünger. Sensorium der alten Welt. Genüßlicher Nihilismus" (T4 90).

continues to appear—a powerful symbol: "As long as it waves, there is still one fort on the European continent where our cause is upheld."[12] October 13, 1940. On the late afternoon of the very first day of Mann's return from his summer holiday to his Princeton house, Kahler was on hand for tea. Mann wrote, "A feeling of homecoming (*Gefühl der Heimkehr*)[!]" (T4 165). November 30, 1940. Mann has invited Kahler und Broch to dinner. "A lot [said] about England, America, and the reasons for the success of the fascistic world"; and, following Broch, "the necessity of a transcendental grounding of humanity." Mann added a question mark to the latter.[13] In the way of explaining Mann's suspicion of the predicate "transcendental," here are his cogent reflections on the thought of Mortimer Adler:

I sense there is something dangerous about the theories and demands of these people [of the Chicago School, Mortimer Adler par excellence, a Thomist Jew], which are in fact closer to a spiritual fascism than to democracy, for which Adler's malice toward Dewey is the clearest symptom. Very well, authority is fine and necessary for the future and a better world—I am thinking now of [Adler's] one ultimate, absolute authority, which limits the concept rather than reinforces it. But we cannot and should not return to the Middle Ages, and that necessary, ultimate authority can scarcely be located in a transcendental order but has to enter into humanity itself and be based on the feeling for the human, its distinction, difficulty, dignity, and mystery. It would be the first and last task of education, meanwhile, to inject youth with this feeling and with it the lost sense of *civility*.[14]

---

[12] (EF 37). "Stagnation, Zersetzung und ein langes unbeschreibliches Elend. [. . .] Solange sie ['unsre Zeitschrift'] noch flattert, gibts noch ein Fort auf dem europäischen Kontinent, wo unsre Sache gehalten wird" (BR.K 31).

[13] "Viel über England, Amerika, die Gründe für den Erfolg der fascistischen Welt,—die Notwendigkeit transcendentaler Begründung der Humanität (Broch) (?)." (T4 187).

[14] "Aber die Theorien und Forderungen dieser Leute haben auch für mein Gefühl etwas Gefährliches und stehen im Grunde einem spirituellen Fascismus näher als der Demokratie, wofür Adlers Tücke gegen Dewey das deutlichste Symptom ist. Autorität ist schon gut und ist notwendig der Zukunft und einer besseren Welt.—ich meine eine letzte, absolute Autorität, wodurch der Begriff eher eingeschränkt als verstärkt wird. Aber wir können und sollen nicht ins Mittelalter zurück und jene notwendige letzte Autorität kann wohl kaum noch im Transcendenten liegen, sondern muss ins Menschliche selber eingehen und auf dem Gefühl für das Menschliche, des Menschen Auszeichnung, Schwierigkeit, Würde und Geheimnis beruhen. Der Jugend dieses Gefühl und damit den verloren gegangenen Sinn für *Anstand* einzuimpfen wäre allerdings die erste und letzte Aufgabe der Erziehung" (BR.M 246).

December 6, 1940. Mann and Kahler dined together again, after which Mann read aloud the first chapter of *Joseph the Provider*, a theological *jeu d'esprit*.[15] They continued their conversation "on the priority of the English and the French vis-à-vis the Germans, who think they have a hold on the humanities, in the area of the ethnological-mythological-religious historical study of the primitive. Frazer [Sir James Frazer, the author of *The Golden Bough*] [is] foundational."[16] Unbeknownst to Mann and Kahler, their contemporary Wittgenstein (1889–1951) had begun taking Frazer very seriously a few years earlier (ca. 1933) and was thereafter preoccupied with refuting Frazer's epistemological prejudgments. Kahler mentioned Frazer's work on totemism briefly and uncritically (Frazer is "the paramount investigator of totemism") in his *Man the Measure*.[17]

December 9, 1940. Kahler provided Mann with some cheering comments on *The Transposed Heads*, which he had taken to read (T4 190).

On Christmas Eve, 1940. Mann, together with Molly Shenstone— Katia's great friend and Mann's sometime translator—her small boys, and Kahler, shared a supper of foie gras and champagne. After the children left, Mann read to Molly and Kahler two chapters from *Joseph* on archaic medicine and the arrival of "The Gentlemen."[18] "High spirits. (*Heiterkeit*). Whisky and soda and late to bed" (T4 197).

December 27, 1940. On the evening before his departure to Chicago, Mann dined with Kahler, after which they listened to the Beethoven Violin Concerto and Mann read aloud the two chapters of *Joseph* he had just written (T4 199).

January 5, 1941. "The good Kahler" was again at hand for dinner. They discussed this topic, evidently with some satisfaction: "The Italian catastrophe in Libya: three or four generals taken prisoner; a great loss of materiel. The Australian troops stood the test. Italy humbled."[19]

---

15   "Prelude in Higher Echelons," *Joseph and His Brothers*, tr. John E. Woods (New York: Alfred Knopf, 2005), 1041–51. "Vorspiel in oberen Rängen," *Joseph und seine Brüder: Vier Romane in einem Band* (Fischer Klassik Plus), Kindle Edition (Frankfurt am Main: S. Fischer Verlag, 2009), loc. 18378–18559 of 26516.

16   "[Gespräch] über die Priorität der Engländer und Franzosen auf dem Gebiet der ethnologisch-mythologisch-religionsgeschichtlichen Primitiven-Forschung vor den Deutschen, die glauben, die Geisteswissenschaften in Pacht zu haben. Frazer [ist] grundlegend" (T4 189).

17   Kahler, *Man the Measure*, 43.

18   "Of Goodness and Cleverness," *Joseph*, 1077–96. "Von Güte und Klugheit," *Joseph* (Fischer Klassik Plus), 961–88.

19   "Zum Abendessen der gute Kahler. Italienische Katastrophe in Libyen. Gefangennahme von drei oder vier Generalen und vielen Truppen, großer Material-Verlust. Bewährung der australischen Truppen. Kleinlaute italien" (T4 207).

January 24, 1941. Kahler was present for dinner. They spoke at length about Roosevelt, who had sent Mann a handwritten letter of thanks for the telegram that (presumably together with Kahler) he had sent Roosevelt following his inauguration on January 20 to a third term, at which Roosevelt spoke eloquently of renewing in the American people a "sense of dedication to the United States."[20]

January 29, 1941. Einstein and his sister came to dinner along with Kahler, who had just received a dedicated copy of *The Transposed Heads* (T4 217).

February 4, 1941. Mann mentioned Kahler's worries in re his academic lectures. It is a significant mention in the diaries of *another* man's grief (T4 219).

February 23, 1941. "At dinner a conversation from time to time [*presumably with Kahler*] about the history of syphilis, recalling the 'Faust' novella that I have in mind as the last work after *Joseph*."[21]

February 28, 1941. As Mann's departure approached, he and Kahler dined together, and Mann read aloud from *Joseph* (Katia, Golo, and Moni were also present for the reading). As their separation loomed, they were very often together, as during the next week, on March 7, when, again, after dinner, Mann read aloud the great chapter on the interpretation of the pharaoh's dream in *Joseph* (T4 226, 229).[22]

March 12, 1941. Mann reported having dinner at Kahler's and his mother's with Golo and Moni. "Later, in Kahler's room, we drank our last bottle of French champagne and discussed the bewildering effect produced by his lecture on the spiritual precursors of National Socialism. Americans do not grasp it and are dumbfounded. One can imagine an American book on Nietzsche as a philosopher of fascism."[23]

---

[20] Franklin D. Roosevelt, "On each national day of inauguration since 1789, the people have renewed their sense of dedication to the United States." Third Inaugural Address of Franklin D. Roosevelt." https://avalon.law.yale.edu/20th_century/froos3

[21] "Beim Abendessen gelegentlich eines Gesprächs über die Geschichte der Syphilis, Erinnerung an die 'Faust'-Novelle, die mir als letzte Arbeit nach dem Joseph vorschwebt" (T4 224).

[22] "The Courier," "Light and Darkness," "Pharaoh's Dreams," *Joseph*, 1115–42. "Der Eilbote," "Von Licht und Schwärze," "Die Träume des Pharao," *Joseph* (Fischer Klassik Plus), 995–1007.

[23] "Später in [. . .] [dem] Zimmer [von Kahler] unsere letzte Flasche franz. Champagner getrunken. Über die verblüffende Wirkung seines Vortrags über die geistigen Wegbereiter des National-Sozialismus. Amerikaner fassen das nicht und sind wie vor den Kopf geschlagen.—Ein amerik. Buch über Nietzsche als Philosoph des Fascismus. Man kann es sich denken" (T4 233).

March 13, 1941. Mann was invited to spend an evening—"really pleasant"—with the Lowes: Dean and Mrs. Gauss were present, as well as the inalienable Erich Kahler. The conversation turned on communism, fascism, and Catholicism. "I chose the latter, if one had to choose" (*Ich entschied mich für das Dritte,—wenn entschieden sein müsse*" (T4 233–34).

As we might recall, on March 17, 1941, Mann's last night in Princeton, he and Kahler spent it at Princeton's "French Restaurant" (T4 235)— surely, Lahiere's on Witherspoon Street, which continued to serve guests of the university until 2010 (T4 235). On April 1, 1941, in California, Mann would write a letter to Agnes Meyer that speaks of his friendship with Erich Kahler. With his obligatory courtesy to his patroness—a nice phrase for the blatant hypocrisy of the comparison that follows—Mann wrote, "Next to our saying goodbye to you, saying goodbye to our friend Kahler was the saddest, the most wistful (*wehmütigste*)."[24]

---

[24] " Nach dem Abschied von Ihnen war der von unserem Freunde Kahler [. . .] der wehmütigste" (BR.M 260).

Appendix II Lili Kahler Remembers

Mann Urged Kahler to Princeton[1]

Following below is the text of an article that appeared in 1980 in a Princeton newspaper, The Princeton Recollector, *now no longer in existence, in which Alice ("Lili") Kahler recollects the life of her husband Erich Kahler. Her voice soon emerges in this reportage by Tom Edgar.*

The political and cultural upheaval in Germany during the rise of the Nazis forced many German intellectuals and scientists into exile. Erich Kahler, best known for his philosophical interpretations of history, was blacklisted by Hitler and fled to Switzerland after casting his vote against the National Socialists in 1933. It was there that a friendship ripened between Kahler and the great novelist Thomas Mann, who was also forced into exile.

Early in 1938 Mann came to the United States and after an extensive lecture tour became a permanent resident. A few weeks later he received an invitation from Harold Dodds, president of Princeton University, to serve as "Lecturer in Humanities."[2] Later that year Mann persuaded Kahler to move to Princeton.

Mann lived in Princeton for only three years. After several more years in Pacific Palisades, California, he returned to Europe in 1952. Looking back on more than a decade of exile, he spoke with gratitude but concluded, "It is a fact that the longer I remained [in America], the more I became conscious of being a European. Despite the most comfortable living conditions, I felt, especially at my advanced age, ever more urgently, an almost anxious wish to return home to that native earth in which I hope one day to come to rest." He died in

---

[1]   Tom Edgar and Alice Kahler, *The Princeton Recollector*, vol. 6, no. 1 (September 1980), 1, 5, 7. I have silently corrected small details of orthography.

[2]   Mann received the formal invitation on May 24, 1938, and wrote his formal acceptance on May 28, 1938.

Switzerland in 1955. Last April [1980], at the age of ninety-seven, his wife, Katia, died in Kilchberg [near Zurich].

Unlike his friend, Erich Kahler remained in Princeton. He became a visiting member of the Institute for Advanced Study and later professor in the humanities department. He wrote most of his important works in the house he purchased at 1 Evelyn Place, where his wife Alice still resides. [Under a photograph of Alice and Erich Kahler, one reads: "A number of German intellectuals were attracted to Princeton by the Institute for Advanced Study as well as by the University. One friendship that grew out of this scholarly community was that between Alice Kahler and Albert Einstein. Above, Alice Kahler is pictured with her husband, Erich, the writer, philosopher, and historian, who taught at Princeton University."] The following is drawn from a recent interview with Mrs. Kahler, whose insights reveal the special friendship between two remarkable men:

"Only lately I found out that already in 1919, Thomas Mann met my husband, Erich Kahler, at a lecture Kahler gave about his book *Der Beruf der Wissenschaft* (The Profession of Science), a response to Max Weber.[3] The second time they met was in Munich shortly before Hitler came to power. Kahler attended the famous Wagner lecture 'Leiden und Größe Richard Wagners' (Sufferings and Greatness of Richard Wagner) of Thomas Mann, which, in fact, led to the persecution of Mann by Hitler, who came to power one month later.[4]

"But the real friendship started later in Zurich, because both gentlemen were exiled writers and, having met before, the acquaintance was re-established and led to a very close friendship between them. Mann used to read his manuscripts to Kahler, whom he considered a good judge, being not only a good historian, but also very versed in literature.

"Now, when Mann was invited to Princeton through the courtesy of Miss Caroline Newton to give lectures,[5] and heard in 1938 that Kahler's family had finally decided to come to the United States, he wrote my husband a letter from the home on Stockton Street where the Manns resided. It is published in the collected exchange of letters between the two gentlemen called *An Exceptional Friendship:*

---

[3]   Erich Kahler, *Der Beruf der Wissenschaft* (Berlin: Georg Bondi, 1920).

[4]   Thomas Mann, "Sufferings and Greatness of Richard Wagner," in *Essays of Three Decades*, tr. H.T. Lowe-Porter (New York: Knopf, 1971), 307–53.

[5]   Mann's appointment to Princeton was actually arranged mainly by Agnes E. Meyer, although Mann was befriended by Caroline Newton at the time.

I read a few lines of yours, a letter to Lion [editor of *Mass und Wert* (Measure and Value), a famous magazine that Mann published in Switzerland] that he sent to me. The happiest news I gathered from it was your growing resolution to come over here. Do so! What's the sense of staying now? And how fine it would be to live as neighbors. Our house, which belongs to an Englishman, is very comfortable and an improvement over all those of the past. I think it important always to fall upstairs. The people are well-meaning through and through, filled with what seems to me an unshakable affability. You would breathe easier among them, would be touched and happy. The landscape is parklike, well suited to walks, with amazingly beautiful trees which now, in Indian summer, glow in the most magnificent colors. At night, to be sure, we already hear the leaves trickling down like rain, but people say that the clear, serene autumn often continues until nearly Christmas, and the winter is short.

(EF 21)

Institute for Advanced Study Attracted World's Scholars

"Of course, Kahler could not resist such an invitation, and already in November 1938 the Kahler family moved to 310 Nassau Street, which we rented. Only in 1942 we moved to 1 Evelyn Place. In fact, we were thrown out of the first house, because our landlady said with so many books, the house looked much smaller. Also, Kahler declared that since he had just lost two houses in Europe, he would never buy a house again.

"I must admit [*Kahler is presumably speaking*] that I consider myself incredibly lucky that I should start my life as an exile in Princeton, which is such a remarkable place. I do have some grievances with the climate. There I only can mention the famous art historian, [Bernard] Berenson, who said in his autobiography, you only can live in New Jersey if you are rich enough to go in winter to Florida and in summer to Maine.

"Erich Kahler wrote most of his later books in English in the house on Evelyn Place. But there are some very interesting books which, of course, he had written before he came to America. Among these was *Der deutsche Charakter in der Geschichte Europas*, which was published in Zurich in 1937.[6] Thomas Mann had some great praise to say in a very wonderful article about Kahler, which he included in a book *Altes und*

---

6   *Der Deutsche Charakter in der Geschichte Europas* (Zurich: Europa Verlag 1937).

Neues, and I'm very proud that I recently got the notice that this book is being reprinted in Germany after forty years.[7]

"Actually, the book on the German character got a very good review by a Nazi historian, who ended it by saying, 'It is a pity that the author does not subscribe to our ideas.' Later, when Cornell University library acquired the copy which had belonged to the Nazi party, I succeeded in exchanging my copy for that one with the stamp of the Nazi Archives: NSDAP [National Socialist Democratic Arbeiter (or Workers) Party].

"But, listen, Kahler was in more than trouble. In fact, he was on the blacklist without knowing it. And he would have gone to a concentration camp if he had ever returned to his house near Munich. But he was in Austria and saved his life in this manner. He lost his German citizenship and all his fortune. He could only publish his book on the German character later in Zurich.

"With the rise of Hitler, many refugees came from Europe to the United States, including quite a few scholars who settled in Princeton. The only answer I can give for this fact is the great venture by the Institute for Advanced Study, which was established in 1933. Although it did not have a building yet, immediately, to give this institution a big name, Albert Einstein was appointed. Einstein was just thrown out of Germany as a Jew, and he was maybe one of the first ones to come to Princeton. Many others followed, including the great art historian, Erwin Panofsky, to mention one of the prominent ones. The universities in general did not appoint German scholars at this point. There was only one institution, the New School for Social Research in New York, that did. Its director, Alvin Johnson, gave an opportunity to scholars from abroad to start lecturing there. And, in fact, Kahler gave his first lecture series about the history of man at the New School. The outcome of these letters was his now well-known book, *Man the Measure,* of which Einstein said, 'This is the work of a man who has searched passionately for the reasons of the breakdown we are now witnessing. I will not feel I have finished this book before having pondered every line of it.'[8]

"I must admit that I regret very deeply that we did not keep a guest book here at the house on Evelyn Place. Maybe instead of a guest book I have a collection of photographs of some of the people who visited us. But to just mention a few names, although I do not like name-dropping, I would have to single out Professor Wolfgang Pauli, Nobel prize-winner, discoverer of the neutrino. His wife, Franka, is still alive, and I

---

7   Thomas Mann, *Altes und Neues* (Frankfurt am Main: S. Fischer Verlag, 1953).

8   The quote from Einstein is on the cover of *Man the Measure: A New Approach to History* (New York: George Braziller, 1956).

visit her in Zurich. I would have to mention Hermann Wile [Weyl], the great mathematician, and perhaps Martin Buber.

And first of all, of course was, Hermann Broch, the great German author, who is considered with Thomas Mann and Franz Kafka and Musil the most prominent author of Germany in the twentieth century. And he lived in this house for seven years, from 'forty-two to 'forty-nine. He would have stayed longer if his broken hip hadn't prevented him from walking up the stairs. Broch wrote in this house his most famous book, the *Death of Vergil*, and this book, written here, makes this house a real landmark.[9] And the Austrian State, on the twentieth day of death [*sic*] of Hermann Broch, sent a crew to America and made a television film of all the places where Broch lived and wrote, which was not only here, but also New Haven."

Einstein Chastised Kahler for Obtaining Visa without Difficulty

"Thomas Mann did not stay in Princeton very long. Once he made a trip to California and fell in love with Pacific Palisades. Eventually, he decided to move out to California after his appointment in Princeton was over. We could not afford to leave Princeton. But there was one benefit from the separation of these two gentlemen, and it was a correspondence, started then, which did not end until Thomas Mann's death in 1955.

"I think I should mention one important thing about Thomas Mann. In his will he gave permission to publish his diaries twenty years after his death. That was in seventy-five [1975] and most of these diaries have already appeared in Germany. The English versions, particularly those of the Princeton years, are being translated by Clara Winston alone, since her husband, Richard Winston, died, and will be published by Knopf. And these diaries will be very interesting for Princetonians because, keeping a diary every day, there will be many remarks about how he felt about this town.

"Thomas Mann left the United States and went to Switzerland in 1952. This I can only explain by what I would like to call a tragic story from the McCarthy era. In that witch-hunt, Thomas Mann was accused of signing the so-called 'Stockholm Peace Petition,' which was a Russian venture. At the Thomas Mann exhibition at Rutgers University, which commemorated his hundredth birthday, it was interesting to see where his son, Michael, showed, enlarged, this petition. I know Thomas Mann's signature very well; it was obvious that this signature had been

---

9   Hermann Broch, *The Death of Vergil*, tr. Jean Starr Untermeyer (New York: Pantheon, 1945).

falsified. Since he did not want to return to Germany, he went back to Switzerland, where the Manns bought the house in Kilchberg. The tragedy was that he no longer felt safe here.

"My husband's first opportunity to return to Germany after the War came in 1952, when he was invited to give lectures in Cologne and Munich. But his main reason was to see to it whether his home near Munich in Isartal could be returned to him. It had been confiscated in 1933. In fact, he succeeded through the help of a farmer and close neighbor to get the Bavarian State to return the house. Later in 1933, an American offered us ten thousand for the house, not having seen it, which we accepted to pay our debts.

"Erich Kahler had no difficulty with the State Department in leaving the country. He was not, thank God, so prominent that a visa would have been withheld. I remember when he went to visit Professor Einstein and said, 'I have my visa,' Einstein said, 'Shame on you.' Apparently, he considered it an honor to be persecuted by McCarthy.

"When Thomas Mann died in 1955, Erich Kahler was Lord Simon Fellow in Manchester, England. He was called to Munich, where a big celebration of the great prominent author took place, and Kahler gave the main address, 'Thomas Mann: Werk und Gestalt.' Even the Bundespräsident, Dr. Theodore Heuss, attended.

"When Kahler returned to Princeton from Germany, he gave lectures at the Christian Gauss seminar. This series was called 'The Crisis of the Individual,' and the outcome of the lectures was his book *The Tower and the Abyss*, which appeared in several languages.[10] It is a very important book of my husband's.

"Following this he was appointed at Ohio State University as Mershon Fellow to give a course only for professors. At that time, he was really retired, but as it so often happens in this country, when you are retired, you get more assignments. Only after the sixties, he got two lectures series in Princeton, one with the German Department about Thomas Mann and the other with the humanities department about history.

---

[10]   Erich Kahler, *The Tower and the Abyss: An Inquiry into the Transformation of the Individual* (New York: George Braziller, 1957). In his review of this work in the *Times Literary Supplement* (December 8, 1958), 186, T. S. Eliot wrote: "The writing of Erich Kahler, to judge by 'The Tower and the Abyss,' has this in common with that of Prof. [Erich] Heller, that whether one agrees with the author or not, what he writes must provoke fresh thinking on the part of any reader capable of that exertion. [. . .] Few books in this field of thoughts since Ortega y Gasset's 'The Revolt of the Masses' have stirred and disturbed my mind so deeply." In Gerhard Lauer, *Die verspätete Revolution, Erich Kahler: Wissenschaftsgeschichte zwischen konservativer Revolution und Exil* (Berlin: De Gruyter, 1995), 436.

"Later in April and May 1967, he gave the three Faber lectures with the title "The Disintegration of Form in the Arts," which was later published by Braziller, who had also published his *Meaning of History* [1964], and it was a very great success.[11] Finally, in 1969 [at the age of 84], he became a doctor *honoris causa* of Princeton, but he was already a very sick man, and he died in 1970."

[11]   Erich Kahler, *The Disintegration of Form in the Arts* (New York: George Braziller, 1968).

Acknowledgments

My thanks go foremost to Professor Imke Meyer, who commissioned this book and brought her unfailing enthusiasm, efficiency, and good cheer to the agony and ecstasy of its production. Rachel Moore and Haaris Naqvi of Bloomsbury Academic have been exemplary for their capable concern, as has the very likable staff at Production—Merv, Rachel, and Zeba. Martin Jay's extraordinary intellectual interventions were a continual delight. Michael Gordin, the author of *Einstein in Bohemia*, contributed invaluable comments to "Mann and Einstein." Jodi Beder lent her superb skills to the vital task of copyediting: it was elating to be at work with her again. The admirable Christopher Phillips was a gracious friend of the editing process. Thanks go to Stephanie Schwartz of the Historical Society of Princeton for permission to reprint the "Oral History Interview with Alice Kahler," originally published in *The Princeton Recollector* (vol. 6, no. 1, September 1980). This book could not have been accomplished in an age of pandemically shuttered libraries without the extraordinary assistance of HathiTrust Emergency Temporary Access, which, through the grace of the internet, provided digital copies of hard-to-find works of critical scholarship. The goodness of my wife Regine Üllner and my best friend Walter Hinderer, which accompanied the entire athletic ordeal, now in retrospect, and with this book in hand, has made it seem a pleasure.

Bibliography

Boldface notations in brackets indicate abbreviations used in text.

Abel, Angelika. *Thomas Mann im Exil: Zum zeitgeschichtlichen Hintergrund der Emigration*. Munich: Wilhelm Fink, 2003.

Adorno, Theodor. *Minima Moralia: Reflections from Damaged Life*. Translated by E.F.N. Jephcott. London: Verso Books, 1974.

———. *Minima Moralia: Reflexionen aus dem beschädigten Leben*. Frankfurt am Main: Bibliothek Suhrkamp, 1976.

Agar, Herbert, Frank Aydelotte, G. A. Borgese, et al. *The City of Man: A Declaration on World Democracy*. New York: Viking Press, 1941. **[C]**

Alt, Peter-André. *Franz Kafka, der ewige Sohn: Eine Biographie*. Munich: C. H. Beck, 2005.

Arendt, Hannah. "Hermann Broch und der moderne Roman." In *Hermann Broch: Perspektiven der Forschung*. Edited by Manfred Durzak, 25–33. Munich: Wilhelm Fink, 1972.

Arnold, Hannah. "Brod's Case." *Times Literary Supplement*, October 17, 2014, 15.

Auden, W. H. "Epithalamion." http://jbgallag.ddns.net/GPC/Auden/real/auden_0121.html.

Bakewell, Sarah. *At the Existentialist Café: Freedom, Being, and Apricot Cocktails*. New York: The Other Press, 2016.

Bade, James N., ed. Thomas Mann: *"On Myself" and Other Princeton Lectures: An Annotated Edition Based on Mann's Lecture Typescripts*. Frankfurt am Main: Peter Lang, 1996. **[B]**

Bahr, Erhard Bahr. "Exil als 'beschädigtes Leben,' Thomas Mann und sein Roman, *Joseph, der Ernährer*." In *Exilerfahrung und Konstruktionen von Identität 1933– 1945*. Edited by Hans Otto Horch, et al., 245–55. Berlin: De Gruyter, 2013.

Balint, Benjamin. *Kafka's Last Trial: The Case of a Literary Legacy*. New York: Norton, 2018.

Bermejo-Rubio, Fernando. "Does Gregor Samsa Crawl over the Ceiling and Walls? Intra-narrative Fiction in Kafka's 'Die Verwandlung.'" *Monatshefte* 105, no. 2 (2013): 278–314.

Bersarin Permanentlink. "Frühromantik, Goethe, Novalis." In *Ästhetische Theorie, Geburtstage, Literatur*. https://bersarin.wordpress.com/2019/08/28/der-unausloeschliche-eindruck-eines-bildes-dem-herrn-geheimrat-goethe-zum-270-geburtstag/.

Biderman, Shai, and Ido Lewit, eds. *Mediamorphosis: Kafka and the Moving Image*. New York: Wallflower Press, 2016.

Bloom, Allan. *The Closing of the American Mind*. New York: Simon and Schuster, 1987.

Boes, Tobias. "Thomas Mann, Joseph Conrad, Franz Kafka." In *The Cambridge History of Modernism*. Edited by Vincent Sherry, 610–25. Cambridge, UK: Cambridge University Press, 2016.

———. *Thomas Mann's War: Literature, Politics and the World Republic of Letters*. Ithaca: Cornell University Press, 2019. **[TB]**

Breidecker, Volker. "Einige Fragmente einer intellektuellen Kollektivbiographie der kulturwissenschaftlichen Emigration." In *Erwin Panofsky: Beiträge des Symposions Hamburg 1992*. Edited by Bruno Reudenbach, 83–108. Berlin: Akademie Verlag, 1994.

Brinkmann, Richard. "Romanform und Werttheorie bei Hermann Broch." In *Hermann Broch: Perspektiven der Forschung*. Edited by Manfred Durzak, 35–68. Munich: Wilhelm Fink, 1972.

Broch, Hermann. *Briefe an Erich Kahler (1940–1951)*. Edited by Paul Michael Lützeler. Berlin: De Gruyter: 2010.

———. *The Death of Virgil*. Translated by Jean Starr Untermeyer. New York: Random House, 1972 [originally, Pantheon, 1945].

———. *Der Tod des Vergil*. Frankfurt am Main: Suhrkamp Verlag, 1976.

———. *Die Schlafwandler: Eine Romantrilogie*. Frankfurt am Main: Suhrkamp Taschenbuch Verlag, 1994.

———. "Ethical Duty." *The Saturday Review of Literature*, October 19, 1940, 8.

———. *Gesammelte Werke*. 10 vols. Zurich: Rhein-Verlag, 1931–61.

———. *Kommentierte Werkausgabe*. Edited by Paul Michael Lützeler. 17 vols. Frankfurt am Main: Suhrkamp Verlag, 1974–81.

Brod, Max. *Streitbares Leben: Autobiographie*. Munich: Kindler, 1960.

———. *Über Franz Kafka*. Frankfurt am Main: S. Fischer Verlag, 1966.

Brooks, David. "The Glory of Democracy," *The New York Times*, December 14, 2017. https://www.nytimes.com/2017/12/14/opinion/democracy-thomas-mann.html.

Bruford, W[alter] H[orace]. *The German Tradition of Self-Cultivation: "Bildung" from Humboldt to Thomas Mann*. Cambridge: Cambridge University Press, 1975.

Caracheo, Armando. "The Measurement of Time: Mann and Einstein's Thought Experiments." *Configurations: A Journal of Literature, Science, and Technology* 25, no. 1 (2017): 29–55.

Coetzee, John M. *Doubling the Point: Essays and Interviews*. Edited by David Attwell. Cambridge, MA: Harvard University Press, 1992.

Collmann, Timm. *Zeit und Geschichte in Hermann Brochs Roman "Der Tod des Vergil."* Bonn: H. Bouvier, 1967.

Corngold, Stanley. "Bookkeeping in the Modernist Novel." In *Modernism* [Series title: Comparative History of Literatures in European Languages]. Edited by Astradur Eysteinsson and Vivian Liska. Amsterdam: John Benjamins, 2007.

———. *The Mind in Exile: Thomas Mann in Princeton*. Princeton, NJ: Princeton University Press, 2022.

———. "A Near-Eastern Template for the Life of Thomas Mann." *Academia Letters*, Article 568. https://doi.org/10.20935/AL568.

———. "The Organization Man, Franz Kafka, Risk Insurance, and the Occasional Hell of Office Life." In *Kafka: Organization, Law, Writing*. Edited by Jana Costas, Christian Huber, Günther Ortmann, and Marianne Schuller, 19–23. Weilerswist: Velbrück Wissenschaft, 2019.

——. "Thomas Mann im Lichte unserer Erfahrung. Zum amerikanischen Exil." In *Thomas Mann Jahrbuch* 32 (2019): 169–81.

——, and Benno Wagner. *The Ghosts in the Machine*. Evanston, IL: Northwestern University Press, 2010.

——, and Ruth V. Gross, eds. *Franz Kafka for the Twenty-First Century*. Rochester, NY: Camden House, 2011.

Deleuze, Gilles, and Félix Guattari. *A Thousand Plateaus: Capitalism and Schizophrenia*. Translated by Brian Massumi. Minneapolis: University of Minnesota Press, 1987.

Dowden, Stephen D., ed. *Hermann Broch: Literature, Philosophy, Politics. The Yale Broch Symposium 1986*. Columbia, SC: Camden House, 1988.

Durzak, Manfred. "Hermann Brochs Auffassung des Lyrischen." In *Hermann Broch: Perspektiven der Forschung*. Edited by Manfred Durzak, 293–313. Munich: Wilhelm Fink, 1972.

——, ed. *Hermann Broch. Perspektiven der Forschung*. Munich: Wilhelm Fink, 1972.

Eagleton, Terry. *Sweet Violence: The Idea of the Tragic*. Oxford: Blackwell, 2003.

Einstein, Albert. *Mein Weltbild*. Amsterdam: Querido Verlag, 1934.

——. "Message to the People of 6939." In "Zeitkapsel aus dem Jahr 1938." Posted by Till Westermayer. https://blog.till-westermayer.de/index.php/2007/02/08/zeitkapsel-aus-dem-jahr-1938/.

——. "On Individual Liberty," a speech delivered on October 3, 1933 at the Royal Albert Hall in London. http://www.openculture.com/2013/04/albert_einstein_on_individual_liberty_without_which_there_would_be_no_shakespeare_no_goethe_no_newton_.html.

——. *The World as I See It*. New York: Covici Friede, 1934.

"Einstein Hopeful for Better World." *The New York Times*, September 16, 1938. https://www.nytimes.com/1938/09/16/archives/einstein-hopeful-for-better-world-his-message-to-people-of-the-year.html?searchResultPosition=1.

Faith, Carl Clifton. *Rings and Things and a Fine Array of Twentieth Century Associative Algebra*. Providence, RI: American Mathematical Society, 2004.

Flanner, Janet. "Goethe in Hollywood." *New Yorker*, December 13, 1941, 31–42, and December 20, 1941, 22–35.

Frank, Jerome New. *Save America First: How to Make Our Democracy Work*. New York and London: Harper and Brothers, 1938.

Frank, Joseph N. "Erich Kahler and the Quest for a Human Absolute." *Responses to Modernity: Essays in the Politics of Culture*, 120–35. New York: Fordham University Press, 2012.

Frank, Philipp. *Einstein, His Life and Times*. New York: Alfred A. Knopf, 1953.

Fuentes, Carlos. "Carlos Fuentes, The Art of Fiction No. 68." Interviewed by Charles E. Ruas and Alfred MacAdam. *The Paris Review* 82 (Winter 1981). https://www.theparisreview.org/interviews/3195/carlos-fuentes-the-art-of-fiction-no-68-carlos-fuentes.

Galitz, Robert. "'A Family against a Dictatorship': Die Rundfunkstrategien der Familie Mann." In *Thomas Mann in Amerika*. Edited by Ulrich Rauff and Ellen Strittmatter, 40–60. Marbach am Neckar: Deutsche Schillergesellschaft, 2019.

Garton, W.R.S. "Allen Goodrich Shenstone. 27 July 1893–16 February 1980." In *Biographical Memoirs of Fellows of the Royal Society* 27 (November 1981): 517.

Goethe, Johann Wolfgang. *The Essential Goethe*. Edited by Matthew Bell. Princeton, NJ: Princeton University Press, 2016.

——. *Goethe's Faust*. Translated with an introduction by Walter Kaufmann. New York: Random House, 1961.

——. "Maximen und Reflexionen," no. 134. https://freeditorial.com.

——. *Wilhelm Meister's Apprenticeship and Travels*. https://www.gutenberg.org/files/36483/36483-h/36483-h.htm.

——. *Wilhelm Meisters Lehrjahre—Band 1*. https://www.gutenberg.org/ebooks/2335.

Gordin, Michael. *Einstein in Bohemia*. Princeton, NJ: Princeton University Press, 2020.

Gottlieb, Susannah Young-Ah. "'With Conscious Artifice:' Auden's Defense of Marriage," *Diacritics* 35, no. 4 (Winter 2005): 23–41.

Gray, John. "Deconstructing Jackie," a review of *An Event, Perhaps: A Biography of Jacques Derrida* by Peter Salmon. London: Verso, 2020. In "Books," *The New Statesman*, March 17, 2021. https://www.newstatesman.com/an-event-perhaps-biography-jacques-derrida-review

Greenstein, Edward L. "Moses and the Fugitive Hero Pattern." *The Torah*, December 27, 2018, 2.

Greif, Mark. *The Age of the Crisis of Man: Thought and Fiction in America, 1933–1973*. Princeton, NJ: Princeton University Press, 2015.

Grüning, Michael. *Ein Haus für Albert Einstein: Erinnerungen, Briefe, Dokumente*. Berlin: Verlag der Nation, 1990.

Hack, Bertold, and Marietta Kleiss, eds. *Hermann Broch-Daniel Brody, Briefwechsel 1930–1951*. Frankfurt am Main: Buchhändler-Vereinigung, 1971).

Hamacher, Bernd. "'Wieviel Brüderlichkeit bedeutet Zeitgenossenschaft ohne weiteres!' Franz Kafka und Thomas Mann—Versuch eines 'Kulturtransfers.'" In *Textverkehr: Kafka und die Tradition*. Edited by Claudia Liebrand and Franziska Schößler, 361–84. Würzburg: Königshausen & Neumann, 2004.

Hanfstaengl, Ernst. Wikipedia. https://en.wikipedia.org/wiki/Ernst_Hanfstaengl, last modified August 10, 2021, at 15:46 UTC.

Hansen, Volkmar. "'Where I Am, There Is Germany': Thomas Manns Interview vom 21. Februar 1938 in New York." In *Textkonstitution bei mündlicher und bei schriftlicher Überlieferung: Basler Editoren-Kolloquium 19.-22. März 1990, Autor- und Werkbezogene Referate*. Edited by Martin Stern, 176–88. Tübingen: Max Niemeyer Verlag, 1991.

Harlass, Gerald. "Das Kunstmittel des Leitmotivs: Bemerkungen zur motivischen Arbeit bei Thomas Mann und Hermann Broch," *Welt und Wort* 15 (1960), 267–69.

Harpprecht, Klaus. *Thomas Mann: Eine Biographie*. Reinbek bei Hamburg: Rowohlt, 1995. **[H]**

Heilbut, Anthony. *Thomas Mann: Eros and Literature*. New York: Alfred A. Knopf, 1996.

Heller, Erich. "Hitler in a Very Small Town," *The New York Times*, January 25, 1987. https://www.nytimes.com/1987/01/25/books/hitler-in-a-very-small-town.html?searchResultPosition=1.

——. *Thomas Mann: The Ironic German*. London: Secker & Warburg, 1958.

Hendel, Charles. "Goethe's *Faust* and Philosophy." *Philosophy and Phenomenological Research* 10, no. 2 (December 1949): 157–71.

Herd, E. W. "Hermann Broch on Goethe's View of the Artist's Task." *PEGS* 29, no. 1 (1960): 26–51.

"Hetty Goldman: Life." https://www.ias.edu/hetty-goldman-life.

"Hobart Confers Degree on Mann: Makes Him Doctor of Letters After His Commencement Address Assailing Nazis." *The New York Times*, May 30, 1939. https://www.nytimes.com/1939/05/30/archives/hobart-confers-degree-on-mann-makes-him-doctor-of-letters-after-his.html?searchResultPosition=2.

Holton, Gerald. "Einstein and the Cultural Roots of Modern Science." *Daedalus*, Science in Culture issue, 127, no. 1 (Winter 1998): 1–44.

Hunt, Leigh. "Abu ben Adhem." https://www.poetryfoundation.org/poems/44433/abou-ben-adhem.

Jens, Inge, and Walter Jens. *Frau Thomas Mann: Das Leben der Katharina Pringsheim.* Hamburg: Rowohlt, 2003.

Jünger, Ernst. *Auf den Marmorklippen.* Hamburg: Hanseatische Verlagsanstalt, 1939.

Kafka, Franz. *Briefe 1900–1912.* Edited by Hans-Gerd Koch. Frankfurt am Main: S. Fischer Verlag, 1999.

——. *Briefe 1902–1924,* Edited by Max Brod and Klaus Wagenbach. Frankfurt am Main: S. Fischer Verlag, 1975 (originally 1958).

——. *The Castle.* Translated by Mark Harman. New York: Schocken, 1998.

——. *The Castle.* Translated by Willa and Edwin Muir. Introduction by Thomas Mann. New York: Alfred A. Knopf, 1941.

——. *Das Schloß.* Edited by Malcolm Pasley. Frankfurt am Main: S. Fischer Verlag, 1982.

——. *Der Proceß.* Edited by Malcolm Pasley. S. Fischer Verlag, 1990.

——. *Kafka's Selected Stories.* A Norton Critical Edition. Edited and translated by Stanley Corngold. New York: Norton, 2007.

——. *Tagebücher in der Fassung der Handschrift.* Edited by Michael Müller. Frankfurt am Main: S. Fischer Verlag, 1990.

——. *The Trial.* Translated by Breon Mitchell. New York: Schocken, 1998.

Kahler, Erich. *An Exceptional Friendship: The Correspondence of Erich Kahler and Thomas Mann.* Translated by Richard and Clara Winston. Ithaca, NY: Cornell University Press, 1975. **[EF]**

——. *Das Habsburg Geschlecht.* Munich: Verlag der Neue Merkur, 1919.

——. "Das Schicksal der Demokratie [1948]." In *Grundprobleme der Demokratie.* Edited by Ulrich Matz, 35–65. Darmstadt: Wissenschaftliche Buchgesellschaft, 1973.

——. *Der Beruf der Wissenschaft.* Berlin: Georg Bondi, 1920.

——. *Der Deutsche Charakter in der Geschichte Europas.* Zurich: Europa-Verlag, 1937.

——. *Die Philosophie von Hermann Broch.* Tübingen: J.C.E. Mohr, 1962.

——. *Die Verantwortung des Geistes: Gesammelte Aufsätze.* Frankfurt am Main: S. Fischer Verlag, 1952.

——. *The Disintegration of Form in the Arts.* New York: George Braziller, 1968.

——. "Einleitung," *Gedichte [von Hermann Broch].* Edited with an introduction by Erich Kahler, 7–60. In Hermann Broch. *Gesammelte Werke*, vol.1. Zurich: Rhein-Verlag, 1953.

——. *The Germans.* Edited by Robert and Rita Kimber. Princeton, NJ: Princeton University Press, 1974.

——. *Israel unter den Völkern.* Zürich: Humanitas Verlag, 1936.

——. *Man the Measure: A New Approach to History.* New York: George Braziller, 1956.

——. "Theater und Zeitgeist." *Jahrbuch für die Geistige Bewegung 3* (1912). Edited by Friedrich Gundolf and Friedrich Wolters, 92–115.

——. "Was soll werden?" *Mass und Wert 3,* no. 3 (March/April 1940): 300–344.

Kahler-Kreis. Wikipedia. https://en.wikipedia.org/wiki/Kahler-Kreis, last modified January 29, 21, at 18:26 UTC.

Kaplan, Julius. "An Interview with Thomas, Katia, and Erika Mann." *Boston Evening Transcript* (March 8, 1939). In *Frage und Antwort, Interviews mit Thomas Mann, 1909–1955*. Edited by Volkmar Hansen and Gert Heine. Hamburg: Albrecht Knaus, 1983.

Kaufmann, Walter. *Discovering the Mind*, vol. 1: *Goethe, Kant, and Hegel*. New Brunswick, NJ: Transaction, 1991 [originally published in 1980 by McGraw-Hill].

———. *Hegel: A Reinterpretation*. Garden City, NY: Anchor Books, Doubleday, 1966.

Kayser, Rudolf. *Spinoza—Bildnis eines geistigen* Helden. Vienna: Phaidon, 1932.

———. *Spinoza—Portrait of a Spiritual Hero*. Introduction by Albert Einstein. Translated by Amy Allen and Maxim Newmark. New York: The Philosophical Library, 1946.

———. "Über Thomas Manns Joseph-Roman." *The German Quarterly* 12 (March 1939): 99–105.

Kettler, David. "Symbolic Uses of Exile: Erich Kahler at the Ohio State University." In *Exile and Otherness: New Approaches to the Experience of the Nazi Refugees*. Edited by Alexander Stephan, 269–310. Bern: Peter Lang, 2005.

Kiel, Anna. *Erich Kahler: Ein "uomo universale" des zwanzigsten Jahrhunderts—seine Begegnungen mit bedeutenden Zeitgenossen: Vom Georgekreis, Max Weber, bis Hermann Broch und Thomas Mann*. Bern: Peter Lang, 1989.

Klugkist, Thomas. *Sehnsuchtskosmogonie: Thomas Manns "Doktor Faustus" im Umkreis seiner Schopenhauer-, Nietzsche- und Wagner-Rezeption*. Würzburg: Königshausen & Neumann, 2000.

Komar, Kathleen. "'The Death of Vergil': Broch's Reading of Vergil's 'Aeneid.'" *Comparative Literature Studies* 21, no. 3 (Fall 1984): 255–69.

Kontje, Todd. *Thomas Mann's World: Empire, Race, and the Jewish Question*. Ann Arbor: University of Michigan Press, 2011.

Koselleck, Reinhart. *Critique and Crisis, Enlightenment and the Pathogenesis of Modern Society*. Cambridge: The MIT Press, 1988.

Krugman, Paul. "Fall of the American Empire," *The New York Times*, June 18, 2018. https://www.nytimes.com/2018/06/18/opinion/immigration-trump-children-american-empire.html?searchResultPosition=1.

Kuna, Franz, ed. *On Kafka: Semi-Centenary Perspectives*. New York: Barnes and Noble, 1976.

Kurzke, Hermann. *Thomas Mann: Life as a Work of Art*. Translated by Leslie Willson. Princeton, NJ: Princeton University Press, 2002.

Kuznecov, Boris. *Einstein: Leben—Tod—Unsterblickheit*. Basel: Birkhäuser, 1977. 190.

Lahme, Tilmann, Holger Pils, and Kerstin Klein, eds. *Die Briefe der Manns. Ein Familienporträt*. Frankfurt am Main: S. Fischer Verlag, 2016.

Lauer, Gerhard. *Die verspätete Revolution—Erich von Kahler: Wissenschaftsgeschichte zwischen konservativer Revolution und Exil*. Berlin: de Gruyter, 1995.

———. "The Empire's Watermark: Erich Kahler and Exile." In *Exile, Science and Bildung, The Contested Legacies of German Émigré Intellectuals*. Edited by David Kettler and Gerhard Lauer, 63–74. New York: Palgrave Macmillan, 2005.

Lehnert, Herbert, and Eva Wessel. *Nihilismus der Menschenfreundlichkeit: Thomas Manns "Wandlung" und sein Essay "Goethe und Tolstoi."* Thomas-Mann-Studien, vol. 9. Frankfurt am Main: Vittorio Klostermann, 1991.

Leitch, Alexander. "Mann, Thomas." In *A Princeton Companion*. Edited by Alexander Leitch, 312–13. Princeton, NJ: Princeton University Press, 1978.

Lerner, Robert E. *Ernst Kantorowicz—A Life*. Princeton, NJ: Princeton University Press, 2017.

Leser, Esther. *Thomas Mann's Short Fiction: An Intellectual Biography.* Madison, NJ: Fairleigh Dickinson University Press, 1989.

Linder, Jutta. "'Religiöser Humanist': Thomas Mann über Kafka." *Thomas Mann Jahrbuch*. Edited by Katrin Bedenig and Hans Wißkirchen. vol. 31 (2018): 25–32.

———. "'Was für ein grundsonderbares Gewächs . . .!' Thomas Mann liest Kafka." In *Versprachlichung von Welt/ Il mondo in parole, Festschrift zum 60. Geburtstag von Maria Lieber*. Edited by Simona Brunetti, et al. 429–43. Tübingen: Stauffenberg, 2016.

Liska, Vivian. "'Before the Law stands a doorkeeper. To this doorkeeper comes a man . . .': Kafka, Narrative, and the Law." New Brunswick, NJ: Rutgers University Press, 2013.

Lothar, Ernst. *Das Wunder des Überlebens: Erinnerungen und Ergebnisse*. Vienna and Hamburg: Paul Zsolnay Verlag, 1961.

Lubich, Frederick. "Goethe and Thomas Mann: Elective Affinities between German Classicism and Modernity." *Germanic Notes and Reviews* 43, no. 1 (Spring 2012): 21–26.

Lützeler, Paul Michael. *Die Entropie des Menschen. Studien zum Werk Hermann Brochs*. Würzburg: Königshausen & Neumann, 2000.

———. "Einleitung: 'Optimische Verzweiflung': Thomas Mann und Hermann Broch im Exil." In *Freundschaft im Exil: Thomas Mann und Hermann Broch*. Edited by Paul Michael Lützeler, 9–30. Frankfurt am Main: Vittorio Klostermann, 2004.

———. *Hermann Broch: A Biography*. Translated by Janice Furness. London: Quartet Books, 1987.

———. *Hermann Broch: Eine Biographie*. Frankfurt am Main: Suhrkamp Verlag, 1985.

———. "Visionaries in Exile: Broch's Cooperation with G. A. Borgese and Hannah Arendt." In *Hermann Broch: Visionary in Exile. The 2001 Yale Symposium*. Edited by Paul Michael Lützeler, 67–88. Rochester, NY: Camden House, 2003.

———, ed. *Der Tod im Exil. Hermann Broch, Annemarie Meier-Graefe. Briefwechsel 1950/51*. Frankfurt am Main: Suhrkamp Verlag, 2001.

———, ed. *Hannah Arendt-Hermann Broch: Briefwechsel 1946 bis 1951*. Frankfurt am Main: Jüdischer Verlag, 1996.

———, ed. *Hermann Broch und Ruth Norden: Transatlantische Korrespondenz 1934–1938 und 1945–1948*. Edited by Paul Michael Lützeler. Frankfurt am Main: Suhrkamp Verlag, 2005.

———, ed. *Materialien zu Hermann Broch "Der Tod des Vergil."* Frankfurt am Main: Suhrkamp Verlag, 1976.

Mann, Thomas. *The Beloved Returns: Lotte in Weimar*. Translated by H. T. Lowe-Porter. New York: Alfred A. Knopf, 1940. **[LWA]**

———. *Briefe*. Edited by Erika Mann. 3 vols. Frankfurt am Main: S. Fischer Verlag, 1961–65.

———. *Briefwechsel mit seinem Verleger Gottfried Bermann Fischer, 1932–1955*. Edited by Peter de Mendelssohn. Frankfurt am Main: S. Fischer Verlag, 1973.

———. *Das Problem der Freiheit*. Stockholm: Bermann-Fischer Verlag, 1939.

———. *Der Zauberberg*. Berlin and Darmstadt: S. Fischer Verlag, 1956.

———. *Die Briefe Thomas Manns: Regesten und Register*. Edited by Hans Bürgin and Hans-Otto Mayer, with the assistance of Gert Heine and Yvonne Schmidlin. 6 vols. Frankfurt am Main: S. Fischer Verlag, 1976–87.

———. *Die Entstehung des Doktor Faustus: Roman eines Romans*. Frankfurt am Main: Fischer Taschenbuch Verlag, 1993.

———. *Die Erzählungen*. Vol. 1. Frankfurt am Main: S. Fischer Verlag, 1979.

———. *Die vertauschten Köpfe. Eine indische Legende*. Stockholm: Bermann Fischer, 1944.

———. *Essays*. Edited by Hermann Kurzke and Stephan Stachorski. 6 vols. Frankfurt am Main: S. Fischer Verlag, 1993–97. **[E]**

———. *Essays of Three Decades*. Translated by H. T. Lowe-Porter. New York: Alfred A. Knopf, 1971.

———. *Freundschaft im Exil: Thomas Mann und Hermann Broch*. Edited by Paul Michael Lützeler. Frankfurt am Main: Vittorio Klostermann, 2004.

———. *Gesammelte Werke in dreizehn Bänden*. Edited by Peter de Mendelssohn. 13 vols. Frankfurt am Main: S. Fischer Verlag, 1974. **[GW]**

———. *Große kommentierte Frankfurter Ausgabe—Werke, Briefe, Tagebücher*. Edited by Heinrich Detering, Eckhard Heftrich, Hermann Kurzke, Terence J. Reed, Thomas Sprecher, Hans Rudolf Vaget, and Ruprecht Wimmer in collaboration with the Thomas-Mann-Archive of the ETH, Zurich. 17 vols. Frankfurt am Main: S. Fischer Verlag, 2002–. **[GKFA]**

———. *Joseph and His Brothers*. Translated by John E. Woods. Everyman's Library. New York: Alfred A. Knopf, 2005.

———. *Joseph und seine Brüder: Vier Romane in einem Band*. Fischer Klassik Plus, Kindle edition. Frankfurt am Main: S. Fischer Verlag, 2009.

———. *Letters of Heinrich and Thomas Mann, 1900–1949*. Edited by Hans Wysling. Translated by Don Reneau. With additional translations by Richard and Clara Winston. Berkeley: University of California Press, 1998. **[BR.H]**

———. *The Letters of Thomas Mann, 1889–1955*. Selected and translated from the German by Richard and Clara Winston. New York: Alfred A. Knopf, 1970. **[L]**

———. *Listen Germany! Twenty-Five Radio Messages to the German People over BBC*. New York: Alfred A. Knopf, 1943.

———. *Lotte in Weimar, Roman*. Edited by Werner Frizen. GKFA 9.1. Frankfurt am Main: S. Fischer Verlag, 2003. **[LW]**

———. *The Magic Mountain*. Translated by John E. Woods. New York: Alfred A. Knopf, 1995.

———. "The Making of 'The Magic Mountain.'" Translated by H. T. Lowe-Porter. *The Atlantic Monthly* (January 1953): 41–45.

———. *Nietzsches Philosophie im Lichte unserer Erfahrung, Vortrag am XIV. Kongress des Pen-Clubs in Zurich am 3. Juni 1947*. Edited by David Marc Hoffmann. Basel: Schwabe, 2005.

———. "On Myself: From Childhood Play to *Death in Venice*" and "On My Own Work." In *"On Myself" and Other Princeton Lectures: An Annotated Edition Based on Mann's Lecture Typescripts*. Edited by James N. Bade, 23–79. Frankfurt am Main: Peter Lang, 1996.

———. *Reflections of a Nonpolitical Mann*. Translated by Walter D. Morris. Introduction by Mark Lilla. New York: The New York Review of Books, 2021.

———. *The Story of a Novel—The Genesis of Doctor Faustus*. Translated by Richard and Clara Winston. New York: Knopf, 1961.

———. *Tagebücher 1918–21 und 1933–1943*. Edited by Peter de Mendelssohn. *Tagebücher 1944–55*. Edited by Inge Jens. 10 vols. Frankfurt am Main: S. Fischer Verlag, 1977–95. **[T3]** (*Tagebücher 1937–1939*) **[T4]** (*Tagebücher 1940–1943*)

———. "This War." Translated by Eric Sutton. *Order of the Day, Political Essays and Speeches of Two Decades*. Translated by H. T. Lowe-Porter, when not by Eric Sutton and Agnes E. Meyer, 186–227. New York: Alfred A. Knopf, 1942.

———. *Thomas Mann und Agnes E. Meyer: Briefwechsel 1937–1955*. Edited by Hans Rudolf Vaget. Frankfurt am Main: S. Fischer Verlag, 1992. **[BR.M]**

———. *Thomas Mann: Diaries 1918–1939*. Selection and foreword by Hermann Kesten. Translated from the German by Richard and Clara Winston. New York: Harry N. Abrams, 1982. **[D]**

———. *Thomas Mann und Erich von Kahler: Briefwechsel 1931–1955*. Edited by Michael Assmann. 2 vols. Hamburg: Luchterhand Literaturverlag, 1993. **[BR.K]**

———. *Thomas Mann/Heinrich Mann. Briefwechsel 1900–1949*. Erweiterte Neuausgabe. Edited by Hans Wysling. Frankfurt am Main: S. Fischer Verlag, 1984. **[BR.HG]**

———. *Thomas Mann–Stefan Zweig. Briefwechsel, Dokumente und Schnittpunkte*. Edited by Katrin Bedenig and Franz Zeder. Frankfurt am Main: Vittorio Klostermann, 2018.

———. *Thomas Mann's Addresses Delivered at the Library of Congress, 1942–1949*. Washington, DC: Library of Congress, 1963).

———. "Tonio Kröger." (https://literaturesave2.files.wordpress.com/2009/12/thomas-mann-tonio-kroger.pdf.

———. *The Transposed Heads: A Legend of India*. Translated by H. T. Lowe-Porter. New York: Alfred A. Knopf, 1941.

———, ed. *The Living Thoughts of Schopenhauer*. Introduction by Thomas Mann. New York: David McKay, 1939.

Marck, Siegfried. *Der Neohumanismus als politische Philosophie*. Zurich: Verlag der Aufbruch, 1938.

Mehring, Reinhard. "A Humanist Program in Exile: Thomas Mann in Philosophical Correspondence with His Contemporaries." In *Exile, Science and Bildung, The Contested Legacies of German Émigré Intellectuals*. Edited by David Kettler and Gerhard Lauer, 47–62. New York: Palgrave Macmillan, 2005.

Melby, Julie. "Recently in *Ephemera* Category: Antoinette von Kahler's Decorative Ribbons," "Graphic Arts," "Exhibitions, Acquisitions, and other Highlights from the Graphic Arts Collection, Princeton University Library." https://www.princeton.edu/~graphicarts/ephemera/index3.html

Mendelssohn, Peter de. "Vorbemerkungen des Herausgebers." *Thomas Mann: Tagebücher 1933–1934*. Edited by Peter de Mendelssohn, v–xxii. Frankfurt am Main: S. Fischer Verlag, 1977.

Meyers, Jeffrey. "Thomas Mann in America." *Michigan Quarterly*, 51:4 (Fall 2012). http://hdl.handle.net/2027/spo.act2080.0051.419.

Michelmore, Peter. *Einstein: Profile of the Man*. New York: Dodd, Mead & Company, 1962.

Mishra, Pankraj. *The Age of Anger: A History of the Present*. New York: Farrar, Straus and Giroux, 2017.

Mittenzwei, Werner. "Nachwort. Die schönen Tage in Caputh. Hausbau am Abgrund der Zeit." In *Ein Haus für Albert Einstein*. Edited by Michael Grüning, 540–54. Berlin: Verlag der Nation, 1990.

Mumford, Lewis. *My Works and Days: A Personal Chronicle*. New York: Harcourt Brace Jovanovic, 1979.

Musil, Robert. *Der Mann ohne Eigenschaften*. Hamburg: Rowohlt, 1952.

———. *The Man without Qualities*. 2 vols. Translated by Sophie Wilkins and Burton Pike. New York: Alfred A. Knopf, 1996.

Neffe, Jürgen. *Einstein—A Biography.* Translated by Shelley Frisch. Baltimore, MD: Johns Hopkins University Press, 2005.

Nietzsche, Friedrich. *Werke: Kritische Gesamtausgabe* (KGW). Edited by Giorgio Colli und Mazzino Montinari. Berlin: Walter de Gruyter, 1967–.

Pinthus, Kurt, ed. *Menschheitsdämmerung. Symphonie jüngster Dichtung.* Berlin: Rowohlt, 1920.

Prater, Donald. *Thomas Mann: A Life.* New York: Oxford University Press, 1995.

Prickett, Stephen, ed. *European Romanticism: A Reader.* London: Bloomsbury, 2010.

Reed, T(erence) J(ames). *Thomas Mann: The Uses of Tradition.* Oxford: Oxford University Press, 1973.

Reffet, Michel. "Thomas Mann und Franz Werfel. Eine deutsch-österreichische Kulturdialektik im amerikanischen Exil." *Studia austriaca* II. Edited by Fausto Cereignani, 233–61. Milan: Edizioni dell'Arco, 1993.

Reisman, Arnold. "Harvard: Albert Einstein's Disappointment." https://historynewsnetwork.org/article/32682.

Ross, Alex. "The Haunted California Idyll of German Writers in Exile." *The New Yorker* (March 9, 2020). https://www.newyorker.com/magazine/2020/03/09/the-haunted-california-idyll-of-german-writers-in-exile.

Rowe, David, and Robert Schulmann, eds. *Einstein on Politics: His Private Thoughts and Public Stands on Nationalism, Zionism, War, Peace, and the Bomb.* Princeton, NJ: Princeton University Press, 2007.

Sayen, Jamie. *Einstein in America.* New York: Crown, 1985.

Schöll, Julia. *Joseph im Exil: Zur Identitätskonstruktion in Thomas Manns Exil-Tagebüchern und -Briefen sowie im Roman* Joseph und seine Brüder. Würzburg: Königshausen & Neumann, 2004.

Schröter, Klaus, ed. *Thomas Mann im Urteil seiner Zeit: Dokumente 1891–1955.* Hamburg: Christian Wegner, 1969.

Sedgwick, John. "The Harvard Nazi." *Boston* [a magazine] (May 15, 2006). https://www.bostonmagazine.com/2006/05/15/the-harvard-nazi/.

Simmel, Georg. "*Der Begriff und die Tragödie der Kultur.*" *Philosophische Kultur.* Leipzig: Alfred Kröner Verlag, 1919.

Simpson, Eileen. *Poets in Their Youth: A Memoir.* New York: Farrar, Strauss and Giroux, 1990.

Speziali, Pierre, ed. *Albert Einstein/Michele Besso. Correspondance 1903–1955.* Edited and translated by Pierre Speziali. Paris: Herman, 1972.

Stallman, R. W. "A Hunger Artist." In *Franz Kafka Today.* Edited by Angel Flores and Homer Swander, 61–70. Madison, WI: University of Wisconsin Press, 1958.

Steiner, George. "A Note in Tribute to Erich Kahler," *Salmagundi,* no. 10/11 (Fall 1969–Winter 1970): 193–95.

Stern, Fritz. *The Politics of Cultural Despair: A Study in the Rise of the Germanic Ideology.* Berkeley, CA: University of California Press, 1974.

Stone, Alan A. "Book Review: *Franz Kafka, The Poet of Shame and Guilt* [by Saul Friedländer]. In *Arts and Culture,* May–June 2013. https://momentmag.com/book-review-franz-kafka-the-poet-of-shame-and-guilt/.

Tarn, Nathaniel. "Poems: Nathaniel Tarn." *Dialectical Anthropology* 11, no. 2/4 (1986): 309–23.

Taubes, Jacob. "Erich Kahler. Zu seinem 70. Geburtstag." In *Apokalypse und Politik.* Edited by Herbert Kopp-Oberstebrink and Martin Treml, 385–87. Paderborn: Wilhelm Fink/Brill, 2017.

Thompson, Ralph. "A Review of *This Peace by Thomas Mann*." *The New York Times* (November 23, 1938). https://timesmachine.nytimes.com/timesmachine/1938/11/23/98211874.pdf.

Tuttle, William M. "James B. Conant, Pressure Groups, and the National Defense, 1933–1945." PhD dissertation. University of Wisconsin, 1967.

Urban, Wayne J., and Marybeth Smith. "Much Ado about Something? James Bryant Conant, Harvard University, and Nazi Germany in the 1930s." *Paedagogica Historica* 51, no. 1 (2015): 152–65.

Vaget, Hans Rudolf. "'The Best of Worlds': Thomas Mann in Princeton." *Princeton University Library Chronicle* 75, no. 1 (2013): 9–37. **[V]**

——. "Confession and Camouflage: The Diaries of Thomas Mann." *The Journal of English and Germanic Philology* 96, no. 4 (Oct. 1997): 567–90.

——. "Deutsche Einheit und Nationale Identität: Zur Genealogie der gegenwärtigen Deutschland-Debatte am Beispiel von Thomas Mann." *Literaturwissenschaftliches Jahrbuch der Görres-Gesellschaft* 33 (1992): 277–98.

——. "Deutschtum und Judentum: Zu Erich Kahlers Bedeutung für Thomas Mann." *Deutsche Vierteljahrsschrift für Literaturwissenschaft und Geistesgeschichte* (*DVjs*) 86, no. 1 (March 2012): 145–64.

——. "Erich Kahler, Thomas Mann und Deutschland: Eine Miszelle zum *Doktor Faustus*." In *Ethik und Ästhetik: Werke und Werte in der Literatur vom 18. Bis zum 20. Jahrhundert*. Edited by Richard Fisher, 509–18. Frankfurt am Main: Peter Lang, 1995.

——. "Kaisersaschern als geistige Lebensform. Zur Konzeption der deutschen Geschichte in Thomas Manns *Doktor Faustus*." In *Der deutsche Roman und seine historischen und politischen Bedingungen*. Edited by Wolfgang Paulsen, 200–235. Bern: Francke, 1977.

——. *Thomas Mann, der Amerikaner: Leben und Werk im amerikanischen Exil 1938–1952*. Frankfurt am Main: S. Fischer Verlag, 2011. **[VA]**

——. "Thomas Mann und die amerikanische Literatur: Eine Skizze." In *Thomas Mann in Amerika*. Edited by Ulrich Raulff and Ellen Strittmatter, 25–39. Marbach am Neckar: Deutsche Schillergesellschaft.

Valiunas, Algis. "Thomas Mann's Civilized Uncertainty." *Humanities* 41, no. 3 (Summer 2020). https://www.neh.gov/article/thomas-manns-civilized-uncertainty.

Volkomer, Walter E. *The Passionate Liberal: The Political and Legal Ideas of Jerome Frank*. The Hague: Martinus Nijhoff, 1970.

Vucinich, Alexander. *Einstein and Soviet Ideology*. Stanford, CA: Stanford University Press, 2001.

Waldeck, Peter Bruce. *The Split Self from Goethe to Broch*. Lewisburg, PA: Bucknell University Press, 1979.

Wineapple, Brenda. "A Posthumous Life," a review of David S. Brown, *The Last American Aristocrat: The Brilliant Life and Improbable Education of Henry Adams* (New York: Scribner, 2021). *The New York Review of Books*, April 8, 2021, https://www.nybooks.com/articles/2021/04/08/henry-adams-posthumous-life/.

Wolff, Alexander. *Endpapers: A Family Story of Books, War, Escape, and Home*. New York: Atlantic Monthly Press, 2021.

Woolf, Eleanor L. and Herbert Steiner, eds. *Erich Kahler*. Partly translated by Eleanor l. Woolf and Herbert Steiner. New York: Eleanor L. Woolf, 1951.

Yourgrau, Palle. *A World without Time: The Forgotten Legacy of Gödel and Einstein*. New York: Basic Books, 2004.

Index

New Directions in German Studies

Vol. 35

DAVID WELLBERY
LeRoy T. and Margaret Deffenbaugh Carlson University Professor,
University of Chicago

SABINE WILKE
Joff Hanauer Distinguished Professor for Western Civilization and
Professor of German, University of Washington

JOHN ZILCOSKY
Professor of German and Comparative Literature,
University of Toronto

Volumes in the Series: